30 DAY GMAT SUCCESS

How I Scored 780 on the GMAT in 30 Days...
and How You Can Too!

3rd Edition

by Brandon Wu

30 Day Books, Seattle.

30 Day GMAT Success is designed to be used alongside *The Official Guide for GMAT Review*, which the author recommends using to practice the most official questions available.

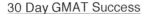

www.30daygmatsuccess.com

The book includes personal experiences as well as information from several sources. It is
published for general reference and is not intended to be a substitute for independent ver-
ification by readers when necessary or appropriate. The manuscript has been prepared
with utmost care and diligence and every effort has been made to ensure the accuracy and
completeness of the information contained. However, we assume no responsibility for
errors, inaccuracies or inconsistencies.

Edited by Laura Pepper

3rd Edition October 2012

ISBN: 978-0-9831701-6-7

1. GMAT Test Preparation 2. Business.

Praise for Editions 1 and 2 of the book

"My score increased from a 690 to a 780!! Brandon Wu's strategy is one of efficient and effective studying ... this book did wonders for me, and I am confident that anyone can achieve an incredible score with Brandon's advice."

- Grete

"Very conversational and down-to-earth. **Cuts through the BS** and is written in a way that is very accessible to the reader."

- Chau

"This books is worth the money just for the Data Sufficiency advice ... Data Sufficiency has to be the most hated section on the GMAT, but after reading through this section in the book and practicing Brandon's strategy I have greatly improved. I'm talking **I have gone from a Data Sufficiency zero to hero."**

- Bob

"...easy-to-read, accessible writing style that has a nice balance of humor and content. The Study Schedule section has been particularly helpful for me and got me organized at the outset. **By dividing my strengths and weaknesses into the four groups, I was able to hone in on the sections I need the most work on** (quant.). So thank you!!"

- Jackie

"The breakdown of groups to focus on is brilliant. The plan is very flexible so it can tailor to each individuals' need. **This book is a great tool to achieve the score you want."**

- John

"…**really helped me to focus and discipline myself to keep studying**. I found *30 Day GMAT Success* to be a great supplement to the GMAC-published Official Guides and **I would definitely recommend it to others.**"

- JM

"… **the method that Brandon outlined for developing a study schedule would never have occurred to me.** …the book is solid and I would totally recommend it to anyone who's thinking of taking the GMAT."

- Fil

"A Systematic and Structured approach to the GMAT.
I personally feel that GMAT is not purely about smarts but a mix of time management, smart preparation anf intelligence. This book acknowledges all three aspects & approaches the preparation in a very structured & simple fashion. **I highly recommend the book to anyone preparing for GMAT."**

- Apoorva

"... a smart book which offers a study plan to strengthen your weaknesses and helps you tackle the test. **I also liked the personal tone of the book, and the practical little tips along the way**."

- Woody

"...an interesting and practical GMAT tool book and motivational book. You will find yourself wanting to keep reading once you start! **I recommend this book to people with a dream to go to business school but without all the time in the world."**

- Daphne

"...a very practical and useful guide for anyone who needs to take the GMAT and get it done with a minimum of fuss**...the best way to QUICKLY study and prepare for the exam so you can pass and get on with your life**."

- Christy

Table of Contents

MY 30 DAY GMAT STORY **11**

INTRODUCTION TO THE 3RD EDITION **14**

THE 5 GMAT SUCCESS PRINCIPLES...**16**

SUCCESS PRINCIPLE 1 - *GET A SCHEDULE AND STICK TO IT!* 16

SUCCESS PRINCIPLE 2 - *AVOID INFORMATION OVERLOAD* 19

SUCCESS PRINCIPLE 3 - *A NOTEBOOK IS YOUR BEST FRIEND!* 21

SUCCESS PRINCIPLE 4 - *"GMAT CORRECT" OVERRIDES COMMON SENSE!*.................... 23

SUCCESS PRINCIPLE 5 - *REMEMBER WHY YOU WANT THIS!* 24

THE GMAT TEST STRUCTURE 25

Analytical Writing Assessment.. 25

Integrated Reasoning.. 26

Quantitative Section.. 27

Verbal Section 28

YOUR SCORE 30

RETAKING THE TEST 31

STUDY SCHEDULE...**35**

WHAT ELSE YOU NEED 35

PHASE I - SELF EVALUATION... 39

DAY 1 (1st Practice Test, Setting Priorities)................................... 39

DAY 2 (Scheduling, Test Review) 47

Macro Schedule (10 day increments) 48

Micro Schedule (daily)... 49

Phase I Study Cycle: The first 10 days in detail.............................. 49

DAY 3 (Group D, Practice Test, Review).. 54

DAY 4 (Group D) 58

DAY 5 (Group C)... 59

DAY 6 (Group B)... 60

DAY 7 (Group A, Rest)... 61

DAY 8 (Group D) 62

DAY 9 (Group C)... 62

DAY 10 (Group A, Group B) 63

PHASE II - BALANCED STUDY WITH TECHNIQUES....................................... 67

DAY 11 (GROUP D) 67

DAY 12 (GROUP D) 69
DAY 13 (GROUP C) 70
DAY 14 (GROUPS A AND B) 70
DAY 15 (INTEGRATED REASONING, ESSAY, REST) 71
DAY 16 (GROUP D) 71
DAY 17 (GROUP D) 72
DAY 18 (GROUP C) 73
DAY 19 (GROUPS A AND B) 74
DAY 20 (INTEGRATED REASONING, ESSAY, REST) 74
PHASE III - FULL SETS, TIME MANAGEMENT, FINAL REVIEW 76
DAY 21 TO DAY 25 (TIME MANAGEMENT, FULL SETS) 76
Day 26 - Day 27 (FINAL REVIEW): 5 DAYS BEFORE THE TEST 80
Day 28 - Day 30 (FINAL REVIEW): 3 DAYS BEFORE THE TEST 81
TEST DAY! 82

GMAT VERBAL 85
TAKING THE VERBAL PORTION 85

SENTENCE CORRECTION 89
UNDERSTANDING GMAT ENGLISH 90
1. Basic Sentence Structure 90
2. Pronouns and Modifiers 97
3. Parallel Structure 102
4. Idioms 103
5. Avoid Redundancy and the Passive Voice 104
Things to Remember 106
SAMPLE QUESTIONS 109

READING COMPREHENSION 119
THE SCOPE OF THE TEXT 119
BREAK IT DOWN 120
THINGS TO REMEMBER... 121
SAMPLE PASSAGES 123

CRITICAL REASONING 151
UNDERSTANDING CRITICAL REASONING QUESTIONS 151
The Question 151
The Short Passage 152
Splitting Up the Argument 153
ASSUMPTION QUESTIONS 160
STRENGTHENING AND WEAKENING QUESTIONS 163
FLAW QUESTIONS 169
INFERENCE QUESTIONS 174
EXPLANATION QUESTIONS 179
EVALUATE QUESTIONS 184

THINGS TO REMEMBER... 189

GMAT MATH.. **193**

THE THREE TECHNIQUES YOU SHOULD KNOW 199

    1. Backsolving.. *199*

    2. Assigning Values... *204*

    3. Drawing the Question *208*

ARITHMETIC **214**

NUMBERS... 214

OPERATIONS 214

LAWS OF OPERATIONS 216

    Commutative Law *216*

    Associative Law *217*

    Distributive Law.. *217*

FRACTIONS 218

    Equivalent Fractions *218*

    Canceling and Reducing *218*

    Addition and Subtraction *219*

    Multiplication *220*

    Division *221*

    Decimal Fractions *222*

NUMBER PROPERTIES **225**

NUMBER LINE AND ABSOLUTE VALUE............................... 225

PROPERTIES OF −1, 0, 1 AND OTHER NUMBERS 226

OPERATIONS AND SIGNED NUMBERS................................ 228

ODD AND EVEN NUMBERS.. 229

FACTORS AND DIVISIBILITY OF PRIMES - THE FACTS 230

CONSECUTIVE NUMBERS 234

STATISTICS.. **235**

AVERAGES 235

STANDARD DEVIATION 237

PROBABILITY 238

RATIOS.. 241

PERCENTAGES 245

WORD PROBLEMS WITH PERCENTS, RATIOS, AND RATES **249**

EXPONENTIATION..**252**

COMBINATIONS AND **254**

PERMUTATIONS...**254**

ALGEBRA **258**

TERMINOLOGY 258
FACTORING EXPRESSIONS 259
WORD PROBLEMS WITH ALGEBRA 260

GEOMETRY **263**
LINES AND ANGLES 263
COORDINATE GEOMETRY 267
TRIANGLES 269
    Area *270*
    Perimeter *272*
    Isoceles and Equilateral Triangles *273*
    Right-angle Triangles *273*
POLYGONS 276
    Quadrilaterals *278*
CIRCLES 280
MULTIPLE FIGURES 284

DATA SUFFICIENCY **291**
BASIC QUESTION STRUCTURE 292
A COUPLE OF SAMPLE QUESTIONS 293
TWO MAIN DATA SUFFICIENCY QUESTION TYPES 297
    Question Type: Concrete Value *297*
    Question Type: Yes/No *299*
CORE TOPICS 303
    Core Topic 1: Linear Equations *303*
    Core Topic 2: Simple Geometry *305*
    Core Topic 3: Mean, Median, and Mode *310*
WHAT ELSE DO I NEED TO KNOW TO DO WELL? 311
    Quick Tip 1: Diagrams Are Your Friend! *312*
    Quick Tip: Abstract Thinking *313*
BONUS QUESTION: THE STUMPER 314
THINGS TO REMEMBER... 319

INTEGRATED REASONING **325**
FAQ ABOUT INTEGRATED REASONING 325
QUESTION TYPE 1 329
GRAPHICS INTERPRETATION 329
QUESTION TYPE 2 335
TWO-PART ANALYSIS 335
QUESTION TYPE 3 342
MULTI-SOURCE REASONING 342
QUESTION TYPE 4 353
TABLE ANALYSIS 353
INTEGRATED REASONING STRATEGY RECAP 363

ANALYTICAL WRITING **369**

    How is the Essay Graded? 370

    The Best Piece of Advice 370

    The Principles 371

    Tips and Tricks 372

FINAL WORD **374**

THE GMAT: NEED TO KNOW LOGISTICS **380**

    Registration 381

My 30 Day GMAT Story

(& why I wrote this book) by Brandon Wu

I had a hard time deciding on a major in university. I have always been fascinated by video games, so I started university majoring in computer science, until I realized I was much more interested in people, culture, and social interactions. After much exploration, I switched subjects in my junior year and graduated with an economics degree.

After university, I became a financial consultant. It was a complete disaster - the company lost two-thirds of my client's money within a month. I soon left after learning more about their shady practices, and decided to give working with video games a try. I joined Electronic Arts (EA) as a tester and got paid just a little more than minimum wage. I was soon promoted to lead a small team of testers and had the pleasure of working on *The Sims* series.

Although I really enjoyed my time at EA, the low salary was putting pressure on me and the stress of the job coupled with a 1.5 hour commute each way was not great for my health. I decided it was time to accelerate my career and increase my opportunities by pursuing a graduate degree. I wanted to stay in the game industry so I applied for a master's program in computer science at Carnegie Mellon University. I was accepted into the program In December 2004.

I took a vacation the following month in January 2005 to visit family and old friends back in Taiwan where I had grown up[1]. Many of my friends asked me what I planned to do next, and I told them that I would be starting a master's program in computer science when I returned to the US.

After answering that question repeatedly, I began to question myself. Hadn't I switched my major in university *away* from computer science? Was this really what I wanted to do or was I following someone else's path? I ended up spending the majority of my vacation reconsidering my

---

[1] If you've never been to Taiwan but love food, you need to schedule your next vacation pronto. The night markets are a foodie's paradise!

future.

One day, as I was walking through the financial district in Taipei, I realized that there were infinite possibilities in the world of business. This triggered an excitement in me that I had been missing for a long time, and this is when I first decided that I wanted to try to get into business school.

It was the beginning of February when I made that decision, and the deadline for the last round of applications for that same year was early March. I didn't want to wait another year before I applied, so I had exactly one month to prepare the application, get recommendation letters, finish all of the essays, and of course, take the GMAT. The earliest deadline for the schools to which I was applying was March 5th, so I registered to take the GMAT exactly one day before the deadline, on March 4th.

Early morning on test day, I headed to the test center. I arrived 30 minutes early, and sat in front of the building to review the notebook I had filled with all the notes I'd written during my studies. It was a beautiful sunny day in San Francisco - there were businessmen walking down the street, vendors selling pretzels and hot dogs, and tourists trying to find their way to Union Square. "What a fine day", I thought, "And I have to sit inside and take this dumb test!"

The computers in the test centers were old, and the monitors flickered during throughout the test. The room was sterile white and I sat in a tiny cubicle surrounded by other test-takers huffing and puffing away. It felt like taking my driving theory test all over again, except with a lot more pressure!

When I finally finished the test, I nervously glanced at the score on the screen. I thought something was wrong... I literally couldn't believe my eyes. 780?! I was hoping for a 700, but I never expected to get a 780!

I want to tell you now that I'm no genius. I consider myself to be quite smart, but I'm definitely no Einstein! So I analyzed what helped me get such a good score so that I could pass this advice on to friends who were also taking the test.

When it came down to it, one of the biggest advantages I had was the limited time I had to prepare for the test. It felt like a huge disadvantage at the time, but I truly think that it helped my score rather

than hindered it.

With limited days to study, I couldn't just study hard; I had to make sure I studied smart. I had to ensure that I used my time efficiently and studied in a structured manner. The short preparation time I had became a motivator rather than an obstacle. The fact that the test date was set before I even started studying put a solid deadline in front of me. As such I was able to craft my plan of attack accordingly instead of aimlessly reading the sea of GMAT information available both online and off.

I decided to write this book to share my unique experience in the hope that it might help a fellow GMAT taker such as yourself who doesn't have the luxury of endless time to study. (And seriously, these days who does?)

A couple of months after the test, I was admitted into the University of Southern California Marshall School of Business with a tuition grant. My work experience was much shorter than the average, but my high GMAT score helped my application. The hard work that I had put in during the month that I had prepared for the GMAT had paid off. I'm not saying it was rainbows and butterflies that month; it was an intense time! But it was absolutely, 100% worth it and I wouldn't have it any other way.

Where Am I Now?

Fast-forward to the present day and I'm doing what I love, everyday.

Getting my MBA was one of the best investments I ever made in myself. It opened doors for me and got me much closer to the kind of life I had always wanted. During the MBA program I secured a job at the Sony headquarters in Tokyo in the strategy division which I enjoyed immensely for three years. The knowledge and skills I gained in business school certainly got me there, and the six-figure salary was a welcome change from what I'd made prior to business school. It was during these years in Japan when I first started writing this manuscript - spending most of my week nights in a coffee shop in Tokyo typing away. It took two years to finish the first draft, and the first edition was finally published in 2010.

After I met my wife in Tokyo (yet another door that was opened for me) we decided to move back to the US. By then I had saved enough money to follow my passion...

You guessed it. I'm back to making video games! I started my own studio (Studio Pepwuper, check us out if you're a gamer!), set my own hours, work with an amazing team, and I can work anywhere in the world without having to worry about a crazy commute each day.

I believe that acing the GMAT and getting into a great MBA program will bring your dream job or life closer too, and that should be at the forefront of your mind during this month. If I can do it, you can too!

Introduction to the 3rd Edition

It's hard to believe that it's been five years since I started working on the very first draft of *30 Day GMAT Success*. The small Starbucks tucked inside Meguro train station in Tokyo was my second home, where I spent many of my week nights typing away. It astonishes me where the book has been since that humble start; best selling spots on Amazon.com, numerous educational magazines and news outlets, and the hands of one of the top business book publishers in the world.[2]

Most importantly, I've been amazed at the response I've received from students who have been able to achieve what they set out to do on the test and more, some far surpassing expectations. One student who emailed me from Germany scored 750 with only two weeks of preparation by adopting my original study plan.

Two years after it was first published, we've gathered feedback from readers all around the world, and taken into account recent changes to the test to craft this latest edition. Here is a list of some of the new improvements you can expect from edition 3:

- New section on Integrated Reasoning, the newest section of the GMAT test.

---

[2] Business Weekly Publications bought the Mandarin rights in Spring 2011

- Improvements to all practice questions and explanations in both the verbal and math sections.

- A streamlined study plan and book structure to further improve the way you study.

- More than 100 new pages of new content and practice questions.

To prevent the book from becoming too thick, we have moved the Mind and Body section from the 2nd edition to the website. You can find it along with other additional resources at:

http://www.30dayGMATsuccess.com/free-resources/

Thanks to all the contributors and editors who helped us keep improving this book. And thank YOU(!) dear reader for your support and feedback that helps us to continue improving the book year after year. I'd really appreciate it if you can take a minute or two and write up an honest review of the book on the site where you purchased the book to keep us going and to help fellow GMAT takers understand more about the book.

Thanks again,

Brandon Wu

September 2012, Seattle, Washington.
brandon@30daybooks.com
30 Day GMAT Success - http://www.30dayGMATsuccess.com/
(First published by 30 Day Books - http://www.30daybooks.com/)

The 5 GMAT Success Principles

"The future belongs to those who believe in the beauty of their dreams".

- Eleanor Roosevelt.

I would like to introduce you to the five success principles I believe you should follow in the coming month. GMAT is not rocket science, even though the current GMAT market would have you believe that it is! Rather than spending months glued to books and thousands of dollars on preparation, I believe that the following principles are 90% of what you need to succeed.

Success Principle 1 - *Get a schedule and stick to it!*

Many people came to me while I was in business school asking for help after hearing my GMAT score and story. I became a GMAT tutor unintentionally. Seriously, it was unintentional, and undesired! I didn't *want* to tutor students in the little free time I had. (As you'll find out soon, b-school is intense. A LOT of fun but still, intense!) But apparently I have a hard time saying no, so I did it.

After tutoring several students, I found that in general they had a pretty good idea of what the GMAT is about, and they had plenty of books, programs, subscriptions etc. containing what they needed to know. Getting their hands on the content and knowing WHAT to study wasn't a problem.

The problem was that they were focusing *only* on what to study, not *how* to study. The hours of work they put in were completely counterproductive.

I soon realized that what most students really need is not piles and piles of study material, but a solid, structured, and effective study plan that tells them exactly **HOW to study for the test**.

And guess what? I already had one. Giving myself only 30 days to study for the test had forced me to put my schedule on paper. Ask my wife or anyone who knows me - this is not what I do. I am not a "schedule" person. I don't like structure, routine, and deadlines. Usually, I procrastinate. But you know what? Don't tell my wife, but writing down and committing to a schedule **really works! It's the most effective way of doing anything thoroughly, and doing anything well.**

This is, in my opinion, what sets the best GMAT test takers apart from the rest. Those *awesomites* scoring above 700 aren't necessarily smarter than anyone else, they don't go to better schools than others, they aren't studying longer or harder. They just know how to study better.

I think you already know what I'm talking about. That person in your class who wasn't that smart at all, but she always did really well on exams and got the top grades? Email or message her on Facebook and ask her. I bet she loves schedules!)

Having a plan is **especially** important for people who are taking the test within a limited time frame. If you are taking the GMAT next month, you don't have time for trial and error. Just like me, you can't afford **not** to have a well-thought out study plan.

I believe everyone can enjoy a high level of success on the GMAT. A good understanding of the most useful techniques, access to quality GMAT sample questions, and most important of all, a proven study plan to maximize the effectiveness of the studying are all you need to achieve your desired score on the GMAT.

30 Day GMAT Success is a study plan created to give everyone a good chance at acing the test. It's the blueprint GMAT test takers have followed in the last 5 years since I took the test, and judged on their emails and scores, it works.

Success Principle 2 - *Avoid Information Overload*

If simply thinking about the GMAT is giving you a headache now, you certainly wouldn't want to live with a 6-month migraine pain!

I found out (accidentally) that it is much better to have your mind stay laser-focused for a shorter period of time than to spread your attention over a long period of time. It is much better to see improvement everyday for a month than to feel frustrated with slow progress over 6 months. Students often find themselves dedicated, even excited, in the first few weeks of studying for the GMAT. However after the initial "honeymoon" period, students begin to feel anxious, exhausted, and frustrated, especially with the realization that they still have to study and suffer for another 5-6 months.

I am not going to lie to you and say that studying for the GMAT is fun. You will get tired from it, and you will want to spend your time somewhere other than sitting at the desk looking at Sentence Correction or Word Problems. With a prolonged study time, you can never really relax when you go out, and you can never really focus when you study. Worse even, by the time you finish studying at the end of the 6th month, you might forget what you learned in the first two months!

This is why I believe (and others are starting to discover) that it is much better to study for a shorter period of time. If you dedicate yourself to a one-month study plan, you can be much more focused, knowing that after this month you'll be able to go back to having a normal social life. And because all you do in this one month is study for the GMAT, your mind is less distracted and is constantly in the "GMAT mode", instead of switching between "GMAT" and all the other things that are happening in your life. When you enter the test center, you will retain the knowledge and information you gained within the month much better.

However, simply shortening your study time from 6 months to 1 month is not going to help either. With a shorter time frame, you need to avoid the pitfall of "information overload". You want your brain to remember the most important strategies and nothing more. Learning too many techniques actually reduces your chance of success because it is confusing and lacks focus. It is extremely important to keep things simple.

And this is exactly how *30 Day GMAT Success* was created, by first giving you a study plan that lasts only 30 days to keep you sharp and focused, and secondly giving you only the most important techniques and strategies for the GMAT that worked for me. My brain could NEVER hold all the information from thick, 600-page books, and I don't expect students to be able to do that either. By keeping the book compact and focused, we can avoid information overflow and concentrate on the important part - to help you achieve your desired GMAT score next month.

Success Principle 3 - *A Notebook is Your Best Friend!*

Forget about iPhones, laptops, or online software, I believe that a simple notebook is the most important tool outside of studying materials. There is a reason that after countless technology revolutions and web 1.0, 2.0, 3.0...etc, the notebook is still the most trusted tool when it comes to learning. Studies have proven that writing things down helps you to remember them better. Visualization - seeing things on paper - is the best way for you to process the new information you are absorbing.

In addition, using a notebook helps you simulate the test conditions. Remember that during the test, you will be transferring information from the computer screen down to your whiteboard. You will not be able to mark up reading passage or draw on geometry figures. It's a good idea to always do your practice scratch work in your notebook, or on a separate piece of paper to get used to having to transfer the information in an organized way without making mistakes.

Besides improving your studies and simulating the test environment, the notebook serves another important purpose - to help you review and strengthen your weaknesses on the day of the test. Your notebook should be the only thing you bring to the test center on the test date. Do not bring all your study materials as they will only make you feel panicked and unsettle your state of mind. Just bring your notebook and let it do its magic. You need to know how to use this tool properly to maximize the value it brings to you. Here are a few points;

1. *Write down only the things you found difficult to understand or to remember.* Remember that "information overflow" is the enemy (see Princi-

ple 2), and that the last thing you want is to turn your notebook into another reference book. Keep it simple and effective.

2. *Write clearly and write BIG.* You need to be able to see your notes clearly to make it work. Visualization works best when the "visual" is clear and not clustered together. Don't worry about wasting paper or not have enough space to write. If you follow rule number 1, you'll be left with plenty of room for the important stuff.

3. *Label each page with the section of the test the page is related to.* If you write down notes on Sentence Correction, put a big "Sentence Correction" or "SC" at the top corner of the page so you know what the notes on a specific page is for. This helps you organize the information in your head and makes it easier to find particular notes.

4. *Take the notebook with you as much as possible during this one month of studying.* You want to be in the "GMAT mode" all the time, and having access to your notebook will remind you what you need to continue working on. It also makes sitting in the subway or waiting in line much more pleasant. You have one month to study for the GMAT, don't waste a minute!

5. *Make notes on your existing notes.* Don't be afraid to cross out existing notes or write over them. You will learn new things everyday and you might find better ways of doing certain types of questions. Personalize your notebook and make it uniquely yours!

You should keep it with you at all times when you are studying. It will be your best friend on test day!

Success Principle 4 - *"GMAT Correct" Overrides Common Sense!*

It is very important for you to understand the concept of "GMAT Correct". A correct answer on the GMAT could look very wrong for people unfamiliar with the test. For example, compare the following two sentences taken from the Sentence Correction section.

"Charlie and the Chocolate Factory has been bought and read by millions of readers since it was first published in 1964. "

vs.

"Millions of readers have enjoyed Charlie and the Chocolate Factory since it was first published in 1964."

Which one is "GMAT Correct"? At first glimpse, the first sentence might sound more professional, more eloquent. If you read it out loud, it also sounds quite natural, (this is particularly true for British English speakers for whom the passive tense is considered correct). However, the second sentence is actually the correct sentence in terms of GMAT correct. "Has been" in the first sentence is in the passive voice and should be avoided in place of an active verb. This is one of the many sentence correction rules the GMAT sets forward.

You will find many other examples in your studies of answers that are "GMAT correct" though you may not understand why. Try to forget what you see as 'common-sense' correct, and for one month only, begin thinking like a GMAT test writer.

Success Principle 5 - *Remember WHY You Want This!*

Studying for the GMAT is hard work. It takes a lot of commitment, patience, focus and determination. Sometimes we aren't going to feel pumped enough to sit down and study. There are days when we will think 'what's the point?". Think about *why* you want to spend the energy, time, and money on getting a great score on the GMAT. Think big, and think about the bigger picture (e.g. not "getting a 780" but "Get X career position so I can Y" or "Start X company so I can solve Y problem and live anywhere in the world" or "So I can support my family and spend more time with them") Keep this end goal in mind for your entire period of study.

Your motivation should be the first thing you think about when you wake up, the last thing you think about when you sleep, and on your mind at least once every hour that you spend studying.

Envision where these opportunities could take you- the many paths that simply having an MBA and the network you achieved in business school could unfold for you. Even though preparing for the GMAT is a lot of hard work, remember that there is light at the end of the tunnel. And the tunnel is leading you to a much better place where you can fully enjoy your life and pursue your dreams. An MBA degree not only helps you financially, it also opens doors for you and gives you endless career possibilities.

Suddenly, the work you are putting in to your GMAT preparation no longer seems like such a waste of time does it?

The GMAT Test Structure

The GMAT is divided into four sections: the Analytical Writing Assessment, the Integrated Reasoning Section, the Quantitative Section, and the Verbal Section.

The exam starts with the **Analytical Writing Assessment (AWA)**. You will have 30 minutes to write one Analysis of an Argument essay.

Then you move on to **Integrated Reasoning.** This section is also 30 minutes long and consists of 12 question prompts, each of which can have multiple questions to answer. The questions are verbal and quantitative.

The **Quantitative Section** starts after an optional ten-minute break and contains 37 multiple-choice questions. You have 75 minutes to complete this section. The questions are categorized into two groups: Problem Solving and Data Sufficiency. We will talk about both types of questions in more detail.

The **Verbal Section** starts after another optional ten-minute break, and contains 41 multiple-choice questions. You have 75 minutes to complete this section. The questions are categorized into three groups: Reading Comprehension, Critical Reasoning, and Sentence Correction. We'll also talk about these questions in detail.

Analytical Writing Assessment

This section consists of two essays, an Analysis of an Issue and an Analysis of an Argument. You have 30 minutes to finish each essay, and you are marked on a scale from 0 to 6. Two readers read an essay and grade it in half-point (0.5) increments. If the two scores from the readers are within one point of each other, then the average of the two is used. If a more than one-point difference exists, then a third reader grades the essay.

Now, when we talk about readers, we are not only talking about humans. The first reader is Intellimetric, a computer program that analyzes your writing and syntax abilities. The second and, if needed, third readers are humans who evaluate the quality of your ideas, your organizational ability, and how you develop and express your ideas.

The evaluators understand that English is not always the first language for test takers, and minor errors and mistakes are often expected. There is no need to worry about your essay being grammatically perfect. You will also find that most of the business schools that you apply to do not care much about this portion of the test. For them, the verbal and quantitative sections are the most important. Therefore, focus the majority of your preparation time on these two sections.

Integrated Reasoning

The Integrated Reasoning section attempts to measure your skills related to the use of both quantitative and verbal information. The information in the questions is provided through text, tables, graphs, flowcharts, budgets, spreadsheets, and more. Some questions contain only one source of information and some contain multiple. And even though the test claims to only have 12 questions on the Integrated Reasoning section, many questions contain multiple parts, which means you really have to answer closer to 20 questions. The topics range from business applications to sociological studies to scientific research, and they may combine verbal and quantitative information within a single question. Although there may be subject matter with which you are unfamiliar, no external knowledge is needed to answer the questions. All questions can be answered with the information provided. Among the tasks you will have to complete are:

- Drawing conclusions, predicting trends, and making inferences

- Evaluating information for accuracy, consistency, and sufficient supporting evidence

- Calculating probabilities, rates, and basic statistics

- Identifying relationships and correlations among various sources of information

- Making strategic judgments and decisions about potential courses of action

The Integrated Reasoning section is scored on a scale of 1-8 in single digit intervals and is not factored into the overall 800 score.

Quantitative Section

This section contains 37 multiple-choice questions and you have 75 minutes to complete the entire section. You will find two types of questions: Problem Solving and Data Sufficiency. You can score between 0 and 60 points on this section, although scores outside the 7 – 50 range are extremely rare.

Problem Solving

This type of question measures your quantitative reasoning ability (arithmetic, algebra, and geometry) by presenting a series of multiple-choice problems in either plain math format form or more complex word / sentence form. Sometimes, the questions use diagrams, but be careful as they are not always drawn to scale.

Data Sufficiency

Data Sufficiency questions test your ability to analyze and identify the information required to solve a quantitative problem. It starts with a question and two statements that contain information related to the question. You have to decide whether the two statements are sufficient to solve the question. The answers to this type of question are always presented as follows.

- Statement (1) ALONE is sufficient, but statement (2) is not sufficient.

- Statement (2) ALONE is sufficient, but statement (1) is not sufficient.

- BOTH statements TOGETHER are sufficient, but NEITHER statement ALONE is sufficient.

- EACH statement ALONE is sufficient.

- Statements (1) and (2) TOGETHER are NOT sufficient.

Verbal Section

The verbal section contains 41 multiple-choice questions and you have 75 minutes to complete this section. You will find three types of questions: Reading Comprehension, Critical Reasoning, and Sentence Correction.

You can score between 0 and 60 points in this section, although scores outside the 9 – 44 range are extremely rare.

Sentence Correction

This part of the test focuses on correct expression (grammar and structure) and effective expression (clarity and concision). The questions consist of a sentence and five associated answers. You choose the best way to restructure the sentence to express the same meaning, and you want to choose the answer that creates the clearest and most exact sentence without changing its meaning.

Critical Reasoning

Critical Reasoning questions test your reasoning skills. Understanding the logic behind the assumptions and conclusions is crucial for these questions, as is your skill in evaluating the strengths and weakness of the argument. For some of the questions, you may find that more than one answer is correct, and you need to select the "best" answer out of all of the "correct" answers.

Reading Comprehension

This section tests your ability to read critically and answer questions related to the passages presented. The passages are on a range of topics, from sociology and sciences to business. The questions test how well you understand not only the topic of the passage, but also the message that the author is trying to convey and the methods he uses to that end. No specific knowledge about the topics is required to answer the questions.

Typically, passages in this section are up to 350 words, with three or more questions based on their content. This section evaluates your ability to:

- Understand expressions, statements, and sometimes quantitative concepts in the passages;

- Understand the logic and arguments presented in the passages; and

- Infer facts and statements based on the information contained in the passages.

Your Score

Now we come to what really matters: your score. **Your GMAT score is calculated from the quantitative and verbal sections, and does not include the Analytical Writing Assessment or the Integrated Reasoning sections.** Your score will fall between 200 and 800.

Questions are dynamically selected as you take the test. The GMAT is called a computer-adaptive test, as it uses your answers to questions to determine the next questions to present to you, allowing you to obtain a score that reflects the level of difficulty of the questions that you answer correctly. If you answer a question correctly, the next question will be harder. If you answer a question incorrectly, the next question will be easier. The strategy here is to spend a little more time on the earlier questions so that the system places you at a higher rank, and continues to give you harder questions. This will, in the end, give you a better chance of getting higher scores.

REMEMBER TO SPEND MORE TIME ON THE EARLIER QUESTIONS!

An important thing to remember that cannot be stressed enough is:

LEAVING A QUESTION BLANK WILL HURT YOUR SCORE MORE THAN IF YOU ANSWER A QUESTION INCORRECTLY!

This is very important to remember. The GMAT is not like the SAT, which has a penalty for answering questions incorrectly. Always guess if you don't know the answer to a question, or if you are pressed for time.

Retaking the Test

If you need to retake the GMAT, you may do so once every 31 calendar days and no more than five times within a 12-month period.

Ready? Let's dive into the study schedule

STUDY SCHEDULE

Study Schedule

Let's get started!

In this section we'll take a look at how to efficiently use the time you have to study over the next 30 days. The goal of the study schedule is to help you plan your preparation to make the best use of your limited time. I will keep everything simple, short, and easy to digest. Information overflow is never efficient or effective, and reading a lot of words doesn't mean that you are absorbing what you need to know.

I recommend allocating 3-4 hours a day for your GMAT studies if possible. I studied four hours a day when I was preparing for the GMAT, and I strongly recommend that you also try to study four hours a day. Of course, this might be unrealistic with your current job and other commitments. But try to spend at least three hours a day studying. With only 30 days to prepare, this intense study is necessary. Decide on how much time each day you can spend studying and set aside a fixed period during the day for this. You should be studying roughly at the same time each day to help you stay focused and on schedule with your study plan. Use a timer to make sure that you put in the amount of time that you have committed to.

What Else You Need

1) Official GMAT Guide. Try to practice with official questions as much as possible. Although questions from other sources may be good, using the official questions will:

- Help you understand exactly what to expect on test day.

- Help you focus on real questions from past exams by reducing information overflow.

I see little value in trying to emulate these questions or to create "GMAT-style" questions here when you can get authentic questions directly from the source that creates the actual GMAT questions. Instead we will focus on planning your study schedule and on **what** you need to learn and how.

I recommend the three official GMAT books for practice questions, and reference various questions from the Official Guide for GMAT Review throughout this book.

You should get the first one. Then, decide whether you need more practice and get the other two.

- **The Official Guide for GMAT Review** (includes access to 50 online Integrated Reasoning practice questions)

- The Official Guide for GMAT Verbal Review

- The Official Guide for GMAT Quantitative Review

2) A notebook, preferably one with a calendar. This is one of the most important tools that you will use throughout your preparation. Find a notebook that is easy for you to write in and easy to carry around, as it will be central to your studying. Make sure to get a notebook that you like because you will spend the entire month with it. It will also be the most important test preparation material that you bring to the test center on test day. I recommend that you find a larger notebook so that you can write clearly; a larger notebook will also be easier to read.

3) A timer. This serves two purposes:

- Measures your test taking time;

- Keeps you on schedule with your study plan and makes sure that you are putting in enough hours both studying and getting rest.

4) Relaxation tools. Books, video games, TV/DVD/Blu-ray, hot baths, etc. Anything that can help you relax within 30 to 60 minutes. You will need some kind of entertainment tool to help you relax during this one month. Non-stop studying without taking a break will result in diminishing returns on your efforts. Get yourself a relaxation tool as a reward for completing sections of your preparation.

5) Determination. Determination. Determination! The GMAT is not easy, and even if you have all of the help that the world has to offer, you still need to put in the hours studying for it. Starting today for one month, all of the non-fiction books that you read should be related to the GMAT, and the only information that you absorb into your head should be related to the GMAT. Don't plan on having much of a social life for the next four weekends, turn off your cell phone and give up social media! This will be one of the toughest months of your life, but then anything worth doing requires a struggle, and at least this method is a short-lived version of GMAT pain!

You will live and breathe the GMAT. You will get tired and feel stressed. But when you come out of the test center one month later, you will thank yourself for making these sacrifices. Committing yourself to prepare for the GMAT this month will be one of the best investments that you make in yourself. A high GMAT score opened a wealth of opportunities for me, both in terms of career and self-growth. And it can do the same for you!

Everyone is different and so should his or her study plans be. To customize a study plan for you, I have structured the book into several parts. You will jump back and forth among chapters and study according to the study plan we create together.

DO NOT READ THIS BOOK FROM THE FIRST PAGE TO THE LAST!

Follow the instructions and study accordingly. Go for it!

Phase I - Self Evaluation

Here is the schedule for phase 1 - the first 10 days of the month. The group names will make sense to you later on in the chapter.

Day 1	Day 2	Day 3	Day 4	Day 5
Phase I: 1st Practice Test, Setting Priorities	Scheduling, Test Review	*Group D* Practice Test, Re-view	*Group D*	*Group C*

Day 6	Day 7	Day 8	Day 9	Day 10
Group B	*Group A, Rest*	*Group D*	*Group C*	*Group A, Group B*

Note: If you have more or less than 30 days to study, then you can adopt this schedule accordingly. For example, with 60 days to study, reduce the work load by half; with 15 days, double it.

DAY 1 (1st Practice Test, Setting Priorities)

My first mistake when preparing for the GMAT was not knowing what to study. Like most people, on the first day of studies, I opened a study guide and started reading. At the end of that day, I felt clueless and lost, and had no idea what I had just learned and what I should study the next day. To avoid confusion and wasting time, let's first define our direction before starting our journey.

Before you do any studying, take a practice test today. The goal here is not to get a high score – great if you do, but that's not the point. The goal here is to find out your weaknesses. Everyone has different strengths and weaknesses. You may already be good at parts of the test and need more time preparing for other parts. Today, the goal is to identify what you find most difficult and plan your study accordingly. This will maximize your study return on investment (ROI). Don't worry about not knowing anything about the GMAT yet. The more problems and difficulties that we you can identify today, the better. So get out your stop timer and the Official GMAT Guide, set aside 75 minutes for the verbal section and 75 minutes for the math section, turn off your cell phone, and find a place where you will not be interrupted. Later on you'll take full length practice tests with the Analytical Writing Assessment and the Integrated Reasoning Sections, but for now, just focus on what you need to do to reach your target score on the 800 scale.

Constructing the Test

If the practice question material you have contains fully constructed tests, you can skip this paragraph. The Official GMAT Guide series of books (which I recommend using for your practice questions) have many practice questions but do not come with full tests, so you will need to construct full sets of practice tests yourself with the questions supplied in these books. It's fairly straightforward - simply pick the number of questions according to the test structure:

37 Quantitative questions:

- 24-25 Problem Solving questions

- 13-14 Data Sufficiency questions

41 Verbal questions:

- 14-15 Sentence Correction questions

- 4 passages - 12-14 Reading Comprehension questions

- 14-15 Critical Reasoning questions

Remember to mark down on your books which questions you've used.

Alternatively, you can take a free practice test on the websites of reputable test preparation companies. Some good options are:

www.kaptest.com/gmat

www.manhattangmat.com

www.princetonreview.com/business

These established businesses produce high-quality practice content, but be cautious about pulling practice resources off random websites. There is a lot of GMAT content on the web that doesn't represent realistic questions.

Come back to this section after you take the test but before you check your answers. We want to discuss your test-taking experience before you check your answers.

Go ahead and take the practice exam now. And remember to time your-self.

------ take the full test ----- 2.5 hr

or

------ take either the full verbal or math test ----- 1 hr and 15 min

and take the other test on day 2

----- return here after the test -----

Congratulations, you have just finished your first GMAT experience. Don't check your answers yet. We will do that in a bit. First, let's discuss your test-taking experience.

Take out your notebook and write down the first answer that comes to mind to the following questions (don't think too hard on these):

1. Which did you find harder, the math section or the verbal section?

Ex. VERBAL

2. From your answer above, what part of that section was the most difficult? Rank the parts of the section in order of difficulty level (most difficult to least difficult).

Ex. Sentence Correction => Critical Reasoning => Reading Comprehension

3. From the other section of the test, rank its parts in terms of difficulty.

Ex. Data Sufficiency => Problem Solving

4. How much of the test were you able to complete within the time limit (answer in a percentage)?

Ex. About 50% completed.

5. Write down any other environmental, physical or mental issues that you noticed while taking the test.

Ex. My eyes got really dry after the first hour. Maybe it's my contact lenses.

Now, check your answers against the correct answers for the test. Rank the sections according to how well you did percentage-wise, and write this in your notebook. For example:

Brandon's Sample Ranking

(SC) Sentence Correction: 70% correct

(CR) Critical Reasoning: 60% correct

(RC) Reading Comprehension: 80% correct

(PS) Problem Solving: 85% correct

(DS) Data Sufficiency: 80% correct

Ranking: CR => SC => DS/RC => PS

Now let's prioritize your study plan. Look at the ranking before and after you checked your answers. Let's compare your comfort level with each section versus your performance on each section. You'll do this by dividing the question into the four groups that are part of your study schedule.

A. **Comfortable, good performance (Group A)** You have a good grasp of the material being tested, and feel confident when being tested on these sections. Let's not worry so much about these sections right now.

B. **Uncomfortable, good performance (Group B)** You might feel nervous about these sections, probably because you are not familiar with the test or the format/style of these sections. But with the existing knowledge that you have, you can do quite well. We will focus on familiarizing you with the formats and styles of these sections, and will not worry so much about knowledge related to these sections.

C. **Comfortable, poor performance (Group C)** You are confident about these sections, maybe because you had prior experience with similar topic. But you have obviously forgotten some of the material that you need to know to ace these sections. We will need to focus on getting your knowledge back in place for these sections.

D. **Uncomfortable, poor performance (Group D)** These sections are your top priority. You are not familiar with the form of the sections, and you need a lot of work on learning the knowledge related to these sections. These sections are a TOP PRIORITY!

Each section should belong to either A, B, C or D. And, each letter should have at least one section assigned to it (one of the letters will have two sections assigned). We will focus your study from Group D back to Group A. Mark your findings in your notebook.

Brandon's Sample Study Plan

Group A: Problem Solving

Group B: Reading Comprehension and Data Sufficiency

Group C: Sentence Correction

Group D: Critical Reasoning

Brandon's Tip

I made a big mistake while I was studying. I was so overly confident with the math sections, specifically the problem-solving section, that I completely ignored them until three days before the exam. I was caught off guard during the exam and got stuck on a few problem-solving questions, costing me precious exam time and resulting in a lower math score than my verbal score. Despite my high comfort level with math, I did better on the verbal section than on the math section. This is why I asked you to rank the sections twice, once according to your comfort level and once according to your performance. Considering both when prioritizing your study is crucial to creating a winning study strategy.

Thought for Day 1.

Good job today. You have finished your first day of studying! For many students getting started is the most difficult part. Try to cultivate a positive attitude towards studying by replacing thoughts such as "I can't do this" with "This is a work in progress and I'm making progress!"

While it can be frustrating uncovering your weaknesses at this early stage, that's really the main goal here. Look at it this way; the more weaknesses you find, the more progress you can make!

By making sure that you are extra prepared for the sections you are already confident in, you can ensure that your GMAT strategy is rock solid.

Aim to get a good rest tonight, as we will dive into the materials tomorrow with the blueprint that you have just created.

DAY 2 (Scheduling, Test Review)

Ready for the second day of your GMAT journey? Yesterday we established your priorities for studying for the GMAT based on the A-D group system that we developed. Remember the last two questions that you answered right after your took the test:

- How much of the test were you able to complete within the time limit? (state in a percentage)

- Write down any other issues that you noticed during the test.

If you weren't able to complete the test in time and answered less than 30% of the questions, let's indicate "time" in Group D as a priority. If you noticed any other issues during the test that might have a major impact on your score, keep them in mind (and in your notebook). We need to handle these issues before test day.

Brandon's Tip

Remember you have 75 minutes to answer 41 questions in the verbal section, which equals roughly 1.8 minutes per question (1 minute and 48 seconds). And, you have 75 minutes to answer 37 questions in the math section, or roughly 2 minutes per question. Keep this in mind at all times! We will talk more about time management in phase III.

Our next step is to plan our study schedule. Since we only have 29 days left, we need to plan accordingly to ensure that we use our time efficiently. Remember, the goal is not to absorb the greatest amount of information, but rather to absorb the information most relevant for you. This is what an effective study schedule achieves.

Macro Schedule (10 day increments)

We will divide our study into three major phases. In Phase I (the first 10 days), we will familiarize ourselves with the **logic of the GMAT** to basically learn how the writers of the test think. The GMAT does not test your knowledge of the world; it is, as is any other standardized test, a test of how well you understand the test itself. We need to abandon our own thinking at times and adapt to the "GMAT way of thinking."

We will spend 10 days on this phase to train our brain for this purpose. And we do this by spending the majority of the time studying individual questions and answers in an attempt to understand why the answers are considered "GMAT correct." This can often go against what we consider to be 'common-sense' correct.

In Phase II (the second 10 days), we will dive into **various techniques and tips** for taking the test. There are millions of test-taking techniques, and learning all of them simply isn't possible given the amount of time that we have. Instead, I will tell you about the techniques that worked for me when I took the test. Some of them are simple, and some may seem trivial and obvious. But keep in mind that we are not trying to become scholars. We want effectiveness, and the best techniques for you are the ones that are simple to implement and, at the same time, give you the greatest improvement on your scores. We will spend 10 days during this period learning and mastering these techniques.

In Phase III (the final three days), we will do only two things:

1. Review what you learned.

2. Get ready for the test day.

It is useless to continue learning new techniques when you are near the test day. The pressure will be too great for you to absorb any new information. Instead, we will make sure that we remember everything that we have learned, and ensure that we are physically and mentally ready for the test. As woo-woo as it may sound, your mind and body can have a big impact on your test performance.

As we progress, you will gradually spend less time on the planning part of the book and more on the skill-building part that follows this section.

Micro Schedule (daily)

Having a fixed daily study schedule will force you to study. It will also get your body accustomed to following fixed schedules—something you will need to do on test day. Let's take a look at your micro schedule for Phase I.

Phase I Study Cycle: The first 10 days in detail

Our goal in Phase I is to familiarize you with the test. Therefore, you will spend three to four hours each day on one "cycle" that focuses on the test and the test review. One cycle consists of three sessions and is defined as follows:

- 10% – Test Preparation + Review Previous Test

- 50% – Practice Test

- 40% – Test Review

If you can spend four hours a day studying, your cycle will be broken down roughly as follows:

- 30 minutes – Test Preparation + Test Review (of the previous test)

- 120 minutes – Practice Test

- 90 minutes – Test Review

If you spend three hours a day studying, your cycle will be broken down roughly as follows:

- 20 minutes – Test Preparation + Test Review (previous test)

- 90 minutes – Practice Test

- 70 minutes – Test Review

Session Definitions: How One Study Session Should Be Divided

Test Preparation (10%)– Study GMAT prep materials and review previously studied materials. Review the mistakes that you made on the previous day if you weren't able to finish the test. Participate in online forums to learn about the common mistakes that people make and the questions that most people find difficult to answer. In Phase I, as we familiarize ourselves with the test, spend most of your time reviewing explanations for answers from the Official Guide and less time on the techniques. In Phase II, start to shift your focus to the various test-taking techniques. If you have time, participate in online forums starting in Phase II.

Practice Test (50%) – Take one full practice test, or do the practice questions for the sections you are studying that day. Time yourself during the practice test, and circle all of the questions that you find difficult. If you are unsure about the answer to a particular question but were able to narrow your answer down to two or three choices, circle that question as well. Make notes to differentiate the questions you didn't understand at all from the questions that you mostly understand, but may just need a little help with. Doing so will help you realize where you need to invest the most time and where you are improving as you take subsequent practice tests.

Test Review (40%) – Check your answers against the correct answers provided by the book. Circle the ones that you answered incorrectly. After checking the answers, review all of the questions you marked as difficult, and all of the questions that you answered incorrectly. Carefully review each one of them and write down in your notebook anything that you learned. Keep in mind that the goal is not to write down a lot of information; just note the most important principles and key findings. In Phase I, we will spend some time in the beginning of the cycle each day to review the test you took on the previous day if you weren't able to finish reviewing it.

On the weekends, you should do two cycles each day. You only have four weekends before the test so let's not waste them.

Remember the study blueprint that you designed yesterday? We'll spend the rest of today reviewing the sections in Group D – the sections that are uncomfortable and difficult for you. If you have more than one section in Group D, select only one section for today. Review the selected section carefully from the practice test you took yesterday. For each question that you answered incorrectly, study the explanations in the *Official Guide* and spend as much time as it takes for you to understand "why" the answer you picked wasn't correct, and why the "correct" answer is correct. Read the explanation multiple times and try to familiarize yourself with how the authors of the *Official Guide* think. Even if the explanation doesn't make sense to you, try not to argue with it; rather, rationalize that answer and get used to "GMAT Correct" and the logic presented in the *Official Guide*.

Use your notebook to write down things that you find new or particularly difficult, especially idioms or commonly tested phrases. Don't worry if you can't find many of them, this is only your first test.

Many people argue that the explanations in the *Official Guide* are no good and that other test-taking methods are more effective. I don't disagree with studying other test-taking methods, but I have found that the combination of studying the "official logic" and the "test-taking secrets" helped me to quickly achieve a high GMAT score.

Brandon's Tip

I kept myself to this schedule for a month, non-stop and it was very difficult at first - I'm not going to lie! There were so many other things that I would rather have been doing, and forcing myself to stay focused wasn't easy. But after the first week, it became easier and easier. I was able to train myself to focus on the test and the prep materials. Persistence will be your key to success, so commit to this schedule and do the best that you can. Remember, you are doing this for yourself, and you will thank yourself very soon for being committed. Keeping your motivation levels high is going to be very important this month!

The key for today is to start to understand the logic behind GMAT questions. There is no better way to do this than studying the explanations in the *Official Guide*, since these are, well the official questions! You will have a very difficult time understanding them right now, because you are just getting started and because the logic behind GMAT questions isn't always obvious. But with the time that you spend studying for the GMAT, you will quickly become familiar with them and be able to easily spot the correct answer choices.

After reviewing your priority section, review the rest of the sections quickly using the same approach but spend less time on them if you get stuck. I suggest that you do not use up too much of your energy today.

Thought for Day 2.

Being organized, prepared and familiar with the "GMAT way of thinking" will help you far more than being the smartest cookie in the box will.

If you're finding something hard, it's important to get to the root of why it's hard for you. Ask yourself and try to find the answer. Maybe you don't understand the test process well yet? Maybe you're stressed because of the time pressure? Maybe you simply don't know the answer. It's still early days, and knowing why you find the test difficult is half the battle won. You still have plenty of time to conquer the other half!

DAY 3 (Group D, Practice Test, Review)

Let's continue working on our goal for Phase I – to learn the logic of the GMAT. Yesterday, if you weren't able to finish reviewing a section from Group D, review it now and come back when you are finished.

Today will be the first day of your "regular" days in which you exercise one study cycle. In the next couple of days, you will follow roughly the same study schedule. You will also spend much less time using this book on this section and more time on practice tests.

Let's now jump to the study material sections of this book (in the later part of this book - sections following Study Schedule). We will start with your priority 1 section (Group D) based on the priorities that you set on the first day. This section should also be the same one as you reviewed yesterday. Remember not to read for more than 25% of the time allocated for studying today because we still have to take our practice test and do the test review. The goal is not to read a lot, but to memorize a few points that can be useful for you. Make sure that you understand what you read.

Re-read anything that you find confusing, and don't skim through the materials. Quality is more important than quantity at this point. Again, write down in your notebook what you find difficult or hard to remember. Return here after studying.

OK, let's take a short five- to ten-minute break before we start the practice test. Drink some water and make sure you are well hydrated; over 70% of our daily fatigue is caused by a lack of adequate water intake. You can also try drinking coffee or tea to see if they will have any effect on you when taking the test. It's good to know these things in advance!

Depending on the time that you have allocated and your level of knowledge of the GMAT, you can take one full test, only the verbal section, only the math section, or selected parts of the test. We can be more flexible during Phase I of studying, so you don't necessarily need to do full sets now. We will start taking full sets later when we take time management into consideration. (during phase III)

For the practice test today, start with sections from Group D and/or Group C. We want to focus on your weakest points. Spend as much time as you need to on each question, and thoroughly consider your answer. Circle all of the questions that you find difficult. Also circle the answers that you are unsure of. If you think that answers A and C are both good answers for a particular question, circle the question, answer A, and answer C. This will help you determine what to study for and where your weaknesses are during your reviews.

Go ahead and take the test now. Return here and continue reading after you have finished.

Time for the review. First, check your answers against the correct answers and circle the questions that you answered incorrectly. Don't read the explanations until you've finished checking all of your answers.

Now, review all of the questions and answers that you circled today. These include questions that you found difficult to answer during the test, and the questions that you answered incorrectly. Review each one carefully, and try to understand the explanations as best as you can using the principles we discussed yesterday. See if you can identify questions that can be solved using techniques that you learned today. Also, don't forget to use your notebook! Write down anything you learned while reviewing the test today. This will be so helpful in phase III when you are reviewing your progress.

Again, spend as much time as it takes on your priority sections and really try to understand them. Don't worry too much about time management. After you've reviewed your priority sections, if you still have some time, quickly review the rest of the test.

Great! You have completed your first study cycle. Give yourself a pat on the back and get ready to do this again tomorrow.

Thought for Day 3.

If you don't understand something you read, note it down so you can come back to it later and then master it. Continue in that way. This grants you the calm to know that you will be tackling a problem when the time is right and you don't have to get stuck on it now.

Every correction is a big achievement - never forget that! Remind yourself of your achievements, and remember that knowing what your priorities are is already a great achievement. It will go a long way in improving your test score.

DAY 4 (Group D)

Today we will again focus on your priority sections from Group D. If you have more than one section in Group D, study the other section today. Since you completed one study cycle yesterday, you know the drill. We will do the same exercise today.

Remember; 10% of your time on Test Preparation, 50% of your time on the Practice Test, and 40% on Test Review. If you weren't able to finish reviewing the test yesterday, review it now before going into the study materials. Again, don't try to read everything today. Instead, spend your time understanding the materials and focusing your energy on just a few things.

After studying the materials, pick sections from Group D and/or Group C for today's practice test. Spend as much time as you need on each question, and think thoroughly about your answer. Circle all of the questions that you find difficult during the test. Also circle the answers that you are unsure of.

After the practice test, take a five- to ten-minute break. Now check your answers against the correct answers and circle all of the questions you answered incorrectly. Review all of the questions and answers that you circled today. Again, these should include questions that you found difficult to answer and questions that you answered incorrectly. Review each one carefully and try to understand the explanation. Write down in your note-book anything that you learned while reviewing the test today.

Again, spend as much time as it takes for you to understand the questions and answers. If you have difficulty agreeing with a particular explanation, my advice is to simply accept the explanation and try to adapt to the logic behind it. It might not be the most logical answer to you, but it is the most logical answer according to the GMAT. That reason alone is enough for us to adapt to this logic. After your priority sections, quickly review the rest of the test.

Thought for Day 4.

Be strict about timing while you are taking the test, but take as much time as you need to understand the explanations later. Also be sure to stay well hydrated and eat healthily. Taking care of your mind and body can go a long way to help your concentration, focus and ensures that you perform better. Keep a large glass of water next to you at all times during your studies!

By the way, are you feeling proud of yourself? It's already day 4, and you definitely should be!

DAY 5 (Group C)

Today we're on the same schedule as yesterday, but will focus on the section(s) in Group C – the sections you feel comfortable with but do not perform well on. You may have prior experiences with these sections in Group C, but don't overlook these questions. Some GMAT questions may seem easy, but don't be fooled! They often require much more thinking if you want to answer them correctly. Often, people can improve their scores in Group C by learning to be careful. I hope that you also do that today, and practice being patient with questions that appear simple.

Again, spend 10% of your time on Test Preparation, 50% on taking the Practice Test, and 40% on the Test Review.

Thought for Day 5.

If you find yourself getting distracted during the test, will yourself to concentrate even more. Concentration is a skill that needs work, but you can exercise it.

If you feel that something is attracting your attention that needs handling right away, have a break and deal with it. Remind yourself that you can concentrate when you have to. You can do it!

By circling all the questions on the test that gave you trouble, you are preparing and learning in a methodical and effective way. This beats the test takers who employ no rhyme or reason to their studies. You're kicking ass already!

DAY 6 (Group B)

You are probably pretty familiar with the schedule of phase I by now. Today we will focus on Group B – the sections of the test where you feel uncomfortable but actually performed well. You most likely know the materials well, but do not have sufficient practice in these areas. Today should be relatively easy for you.

Same drill: 10% Test Prep, 50% Practice Test, and 40% Test Review.

Thought for Day 6.

By being aware of which sections of the test you need to work on most, you have already made a great deal of progress. Keep at it.

DAY 7 (Group A, Rest)

Today should be a piece of cake for you – Group A. You know the materials well and can achieve good scores in these areas. We just want to make sure that you are spending enough practice time in all areas of the test, so don't overlook today's study schedule.

Thought for Day 7.

You have finished your first week of intense study, and that is cause for a reward.

Relax and take a short break from your studies. This will help you to perform to the best of your ability and motivate you for the next week of study. Think of something that has helped you to relax in the past and go do it!

(Psst... You're a week closer to finishing!)

DAY 8 (Group D)

I hope you had enough rest yesterday. We are almost done with Phase I – understanding the logic of the GMAT. Hopefully, you are feeling a bit more familiar with GMAT style questions, their way of thinking and the logic behind the correct answers.

We are back on our regular 10–50–40 schedule today – 10% Test Preparation, 50% Practice Test, 40% Test Review. Today, we will go back to Group D and tackle the most difficult sections.

Thought for Day 8.

You should be getting well-versed in the language of the GMAT by now. You should feel more comfortable taking the test and your stress about taking the test should be subsiding as you gain familiarity with it. Maybe you've realized it's not the monster you once thought it was! You're showing self-discipline toward your studies, one of the hardest skills there is. Maybe you've even come to like studying?

Studying can make us feel incredibly satisfied and it is has a funny way of becoming enjoyable in a weird way. There's no need to admit that out-loud though, it can be our little secret! ;) Enjoy the feeling and take it through to your studies tomorrow.

DAY 9 (Group C)

Group C is the name of the game today. Last time we looked, this was the section where being a little more careful can really improve your performance. Continue with this principle and let's try these sections again today.

And remember, go deep with each question.

Thought for Day 9.

Today you should challenge yourself with a more difficult section. Challenges are called exactly that because they stretch you, make you feel uncomfortable; but you'll feel better on the other side.

If you start to feel lazy, try to motivate yourself to beat your laziness and study harder than ever. Studying is your biggest priority right now. It will serve you well in the future if you can focus your attention on it for a brief period of time. You should be pretty proud of your self-study and motivation thus far – and by following this plan you can achieve your goals and dreams. You'll look back on this time as a big achievement in your life.

DAY 10 (Group A, Group B)

Today is the last day of our study Phase I, and we will focus on Group B and Group A sections – the areas where you performed well. Let's finish your study cycle first and then do a quick review of your first ten days of GMAT preparation. Come back after you finish the study cycle for today.

After today, we will have completed 30% of our GMAT preparation. How do you feel about the test after ten days of studying? You should have a pretty good sense of how the questions are structured and how most answer choices are constructed. Your notebook should also contain quite a few notes that you have written down during the past ten days. These notes are personalized and specific to you - your own GMAT advisor! Don't underestimate their value, you can learn a lot from them.

Tomorrow, we will start Phase II of your GMAT preparation. Phase II will focus more on the study materials and various test-taking techniques. If you didn't finish reading the study materials for all of the sections, we will finish them in the next ten days. We will also review other materials to help you prepare for the test.

Before we finish for today, review your notes and circle the points that you still feel unfamiliar with. And then get a good rest tonight!

After ten days of studying, we have established three things:

1. You are now familiar with the test format.

2. You are now familiar with the test logic.

3. You are now familiar with the study schedule.

In the next ten days, we will try to achieve the following three things:

1. Learn the most effective GMAT techniques;

2. Understand your GMAT level (score);

3. Participate in study groups or online forums (don't spend too much time on this and watch out for information overflow.)

We will first focus our study on various GMAT test-taking techniques. You have already studied some of them in Phase I. In Phase II, we will spend a lot more of our energy on learning and using these techniques to improve your scores.

Brandon's Tip

While I was studying, I found out that having someone else studying alongside with me was a great help. I participated in various GMAT forums in which members helped each other better prepare for the test. Not only can you find difficult questions discussed on these forums, you will also be more motivated knowing that others like you are working hard to prepare for the GMAT. Just like you, most business school candidates are highly motivated individuals, and having these people around you will help you not only with preparing for the GMAT, but with all other aspects of applying to and surviving B-school. You can find popular online GMAT forums by searching for "GMAT FORUM" on a popular search engine. Remember, a forum is only as good as its members, so try a few different ones to find a community that fits your study and communication style. Some good ones to try first are:

http://www.manhattangmat.com/forums

http://forum.kaplangmat.com/

www.beatthegmat.com/forums

Thought for Day 10.

Your studies are 1/3 complete. You're becoming a GMAT prep pro!

By comparing yourself with the beginners (or yourself 10 days ago) you can see your progress. You can help explain to others about the process of the test. If you're more familiar and better at answering questions now, imagine how you will be in a few days. You should look forward to seeing your future progress. For now you deserve a good rest.

Phase II - Balanced Study with Techniques

Day 11	Day 12	Day 13	Day 14	Day 15
Phase II: *Group D*	*Group D*	*Group C*	*Group A, Group B*	Integrated Reasoning and Essay, Rest

Day 16	Day 17	Day 18	Day 19	Day 20
Group D Start spending less time on individual questions.	*Group D*	*Group C*	*Group A, Group B*	Integrated Reasoning and Essay, Rest

DAY 11 (GROUP D)

Thought for Day 11.

You've made it to phase II. Now you need less time for planning and more time finding and experiencing the techniques that will improve your test score. Your progress should be becoming more obvious every day.

You have completed the first phase, and if you still answer some questions incorrectly, that's OK. You have plenty of time ahead.

You should be pretty familiar with our study schedule from Phase I. The study cycle in Phase II is similar – you will just spend slightly less time reviewing tests and a bit more time learning techniques.

In Phase II, one cycle is defined as follows:

- 25% – Test Preparation

- 50% – Practice Test

- 25%– Test Review

If you spend four hours a day studying, your cycle will be:

- 60 minutes – Test Preparation

- 120 minutes – Practice Test

- 60 minutes – Test Review

If you spend three hours a day studying, your cycle will be:

- 45 minutes – Test Preparation

- 90 minutes – Practice Test

- 45 minutes – Test Review

As you can see, your daily study cycle is now 25–50–25. We have increased the time allocated for Test Preparation to allow time to learn test techniques. You will also spend more time on the skill-building part of this book and less on the planning part. Starting today, you will exercise this study cycle for ten days and will study the following sections/groups:

Today we focus on your Group D section(s). Start your test preparation now and head over to the skill-building part of the book to learn and review test-taking techniques for these section(s). Then start taking practice questions for Group D section(s). Try to apply the techniques that you learned today. Review the practice test afterwards.

DAY 12 (GROUP D)

(Daily Study Cycle = 25 - 50 - 25)

Stick to the same routine as yesterday, again focusing on Group D. From today, you can start participating in the online forums suggested above after test review, but remember not to spend too much time comparing your performance with other people. Remember to focus on your own studies - other people can easily throw you off balance. We get the right - and wrong - kinds of energy from others.

Thought for Day 12.

It's important to remember that you are not alone in this GMAT journey, and that's why the GMAT forums are great. There are many others just like you, studying and working hard to prepare for this test. You are a part of a community.

You can share your experiences of studying with other students, but it's better to not spend time comparing results. Everybody has different weaknesses and strengths and this doesn't indicate the final test results.

You still have plenty of time to correct your errors. It's better that you find errors now so that you can correct them and learn.

DAY 13 (GROUP C)

(Daily Study Cycle = 25 - 50 - 25)

Today, we will learn some techniques for Group C by reading the relevant section in the latter part of the book.

Thought for Day 13.

I hope you are using and appreciating your notebook! It really is a little gem containing your goals, priorities, corrections and achievements. Continue to use and review your notebook and you'll soon be able to visualize the important points that you're jotting down in it.

DAY 14 (GROUPS A AND B)

(Daily Study Cycle = 25 - 50 - 25)

Focus on Groups A and B today, the sections you are most familiar with. If you find yourself finishing early, spend some time reviewing your notes to see if you are happy with the way you are organizing information.

Thought for Day 14.

Today is an easier day spent working on more familiar topics. That should feel good! They weren't familiar at the beginning but now they should be much easier for you. If you're feeling a bit lazy it might be because you are finding the questions easy. Be proud of yourself and try to focus and keep thinking clearly today.

DAY 15 (INTEGRATED REASONING, ESSAY, REST)

On Day 15, you should practice some Integrated Reasoning questions. Up until this point, you haven't really worked on those questions. The reason for this is that the Integrated Reasoning section doesn't really test any different concepts than do the regular verbal and math sections. You will see questions on percents, statistics, and algebra, you will see critical reasoning questions, and you will see some reading comprehension. But since the section functions differently (you have access to a calculator!) you want to spend some time familiarizing yourself with the question types and features, so today is the day to do that.

It's also time to start working on the essay. Even though the essay score does not count toward your 800, it is still important to do well. But you can't do well without practicing! Flip to an essay prompt in the back of the *Official Review* and start writing.

Thought for Day 15.

Good news*! You have passed the half way mark. You are two weeks closer to your goal, whoop!*

Try to rest well tonight. A rested mind and body process information more effectively the next day.

DAY 16 (GROUP D)

Starting on Day 16, we will spend slightly less time on each individual question or answer, and will transition our efforts from understanding the test to efficiently managing our time during the test.

Start timing yourself when taking your practice test and compare that with the time allowed for each section.

We are back to Group D again for today and tomorrow. You should feel much more comfortable with your Group D section(s) after tomorrow given all of the practice that you have had. This is going to boost your score significantly.

Thought for Day 16.

Practice improves your score, and timing the process develops your time management skills which is a huge part of the test. With practice you will become a lot less stressed about completing on time.

Soon you will be so familiar with the test that time management will come much easier to you.

DAY 17 (GROUP D)

No need for further introduction, as you are working on Group D again today. You know that you are conquering this section by now so try to enjoy it!

Thought for Day 17.

Let's have a little check in, shall we?

It's very possible that today, or yesterday, or tomorrow you are/ will feel overwhelmed or stressed out. That wouldn't be uncommon; any period of study is stressful and this has been a particularly intense one.

But it's important to know that you do have a certain amount of control over these thoughts and feelings you are experiencing. You can choose how to respond to them, and you can choose whether you focus on the positive or the negative. The positive: You chose a study plan that puts you ahead. You made it this far. You still have time to improve your score. You know more now about your potential and what you can achieve in just a couple of weeks. You're improving all the time. That should feel great.

Direct your thoughts and focus on these things, and keep on keeping on. If it feels like a mammoth task, break it down and start small. You got this.

DAY 18 (GROUP C)

You should feel quite comfortable with Group C by now. Remember to time yourself against the allowed two minutes per question, if possible. Time management is your focal point at this time. A genius with bad time management will never ace the GMAT. It's key.

Thought for Day 18.

Even though you are becoming familiar with the test, or maybe you're sick of the test, be sure not to get lazy now. Nothing feels as good as finishing something to completion. It's the habit of champions. Bring as much ener-

gy and focus to this last homestretch and finish strong - it's the difference between winners and losers!

Concentrate on the bigger picture here and the purpose of you taking the test in the first place.

DAY 19 (GROUPS A AND B)

Focus on Groups A and B today, the sections you are most familiar with. If you find yourself finishing early again, review your notes and focus on what you've forgotten.

Thought for Day 19.

By now you have probably broken any bad habits like procrastination, and replaced them with good planning habits. Can you see how organizing your time and planning helps get things done? This is what should motivate you for the remainder of the study schedule. ☺

DAY 20 (INTEGRATED REASONING, ESSAY, REST)

Spend your time today practicing more Integrated Reasoning questions and writing another Analysis of an Argument Essay. Afterwards, review your notes and all of the questions that you have highlighted over the last four days. Remember, your notebook is the textbook that you customized for yourself. Thus, it is the most important tool when it comes to test day. Make sure that you are familiar with every note that you have taken and keep your notebook well organized.

Finally, feel free to rest and relax a little today. We are going into the final ten days of studies and you want to be physically and mentally ready.

Thought for Day 20.

It's a cliché, but practice makes perfect, really!

Phase III - Full Sets, Time Management, Final Review

Here is your schedule for the final ten days:

Day 21	Day 22	Day 23	Day 24	Day 25
Full Set	*Full Set*	*Full Set*	*Review*	*Full Set*

Day 26	Day 27	Day 28	Day 29	Day 30
Full Test	*Full Test*	*Review*	*Review*	*Review*

DAY 21 TO DAY 25 (TIME MANAGEMENT, FULL SETS)

Congratulations! You've finished two-thirds of the course and are now well equipped with the techniques required. We have roughly ten days from today until your test day. We can accomplish a lot in that time.

In the first half of Phase III, one cycle is defined as follows:

- 60% – Practice Test

- 40%– Test Review

In the first half of Phase III, your daily study cycle should look like this:

- 150 minutes – Practice Test (75 minutes Verbal, 75 minutes Math)

- 90+ minutes – Test Review

If you don't have the time to do a full set every day, do half a set every day and alternate between the verbal and the math sections.

Do a full set during the Practice Test period, and then check the answers during Test Review. Also during Test Review, review the materials that you've learned. We are putting all of our efforts into getting ready for test day, and doing these full sets will help you get familiar with how the actual test will be. In Phase III, we will do only two things:

1. **Review what you learned.**

2. **Get ready for test day.**

If you couldn't finish some materials from the previous ten days, don't worry. We have some time for you to study them. However, try to finish all of the materials by day 26 or 27 (five to six days from today) if possible, and leave the last few days for just reviewing materials and getting ready for test day. You want to feel relaxed and prepared by then.

Time Management

The concepts tested on the GMAT do not go beyond high school Science, Math or English grammar.

So why are people finding the GMAT so hard to beat?

One explanation is the issue of time management. Blowing the timing is one of the most costly, and unfortunately common mistakes students make. The GMAT is as much of a test of time management as it is a test of content. If you have fantastic content knowledge but poor timing, you will be outperformed by those who have far from perfect content knowledge but excellent time management. This is the nature of standardized tests!

You need to be strategic with your timing. For example, for the quant section there are 37 questions to be answered in 75 minutes. So it makes sense to spend 2 minutes on each question, right? Well, what is really important to know is that 2 minutes is just an average, a rule of thumb. Some questions you might be able to figure out in 10 seconds, others might take three or four minutes.

One of the top skills of the GMAT is recognizing when those extra seconds are worth spending on the question, or recognizing that you should just guess and move on.

This is something that perfectionists and overachievers in particular have a hard time with – they cannot just leave a question without finishing it, and end up taking too long on it. No matter how tempting it might be to keep plugging away at a question if you feel like you are "really close!" - let go of your stubbornness and move on.

Do not let your ego jeopardize a fantastic score!

Thought for Days 21-25.

You're in phase III and three weeks closer to your goal. You've come a long way, baby!

Everyone *feels stressed during the final days before the GMAT, so know that any anxiety you are feeling is entirely normal. You have a certain amount of control over that anxiety though. Take care of yourself and don't let it spiral out of control. Recognize when you need a break, and when you can use the stress to study even better. Remember that not all stress is bad stress; we all need a bit of stress in our lives to get stuff done.*

These last days are for making you feel more sure about yourself, and to solidify the facts you have already learned. You may not feel like it, but you're ready already.

Brandon's Tip

Time management, huh? Managing your time during the test is one of the most important factors that will affect your score. No matter how prepared you are for the verbal or math sections, poor time management can prevent you from getting your desired score.

Spend no more than four to five minutes on each question early in the test, and no more than two minutes later on in the test for the same section. As discussed, the earlier part of the section will have a greater impact on your final score than the latter part of the same section, so focus and spend more time on the early parts.

*Don't think too much about any one question when working on the latter part of the section. You will have less time for each question, so if you can't figure out an answer during the latter part of the section, just guess. **Unlike other standardized tests such as the SAT, the GMAT will not penalize you for guessing wrongly.***

Now go ahead and start the final push for test day. Remember to time yourself and try to simulate the actual test environment when you take the full sets. If you notice anything bothering you during the test-taking session, write that down in your notebook and try to find a way to avoid the annoyance on test day. You have **75 minutes for the verbal part of the test and 75 minutes for the math part** of the test.

On Review days, spend the full three to four hours reviewing the questions you highlighted before and the review techniques in your notebook and in the textbook. Participate in the online forums during the Review days if you feel that they are useful to you. You should also rest properly during this period, as taking these full sets can be stressful. Keep your mind sharp by getting enough water, sleep and fresh air.

Day 26 - Day 27 (FINAL REVIEW): 5 DAYS BEFORE THE TEST

Take a full practice test each of these days, starting with the essay and completing all 4 sections in one sitting. This will take a long time and some serious commitment, but it is important that you have the complete 3.5 hour GMAT experience before test day.

Thought for Days 26-27.

Are you experiencing thoughts such as 'I'm running out of time for the test!'?

Stop that already. You've had enough time and you've used it perfectly. You've learned as much as you could have possibly learned and you are well-prepared for the big day.

Now is the time for final review. You have a few more days, enough time to comfortably practice for the test. You should feel confident, and know that you can do it, and do it well. You have prepared well so relax and use all that you have learned.

Day 28 - Day 30 (FINAL REVIEW): 3 DAYS BEFORE THE TEST

The final three days!

We are almost there. There is only one thing that you should do in these final three days – review. You will most likely forget any new information that you cram into your brain now because you are too close to the test day. Don't do it, no matter how tempting it is!

Instead, focus on consolidating what you have studied, and make sure that you understand the answers and reasoning to all of the questions that you previously answered incorrectly. Go back to the techniques you have used and quickly read through them to see if you missed anything.

Review your entire notebook and spend time on your most difficult subjects. Don't feel stressed out about studying. Feel free to cut down on your study hours if you are comfortable with the topics. Use these three days to ready yourself mentally for the test. This involves staying calm, building your confidence and feeling positive.

Adjust your body to get ready for the test by sleeping well, eating right and getting enough fresh air and exercise. And try not to stay up too late!

Thought for Days 28-30.

You have achieved a lot of things over the last 30 days and can now take the test with confidence. You know how to concentrate, and how to man-

age your time. You should be calm in order to easily recall the techniques and strategies we talked about. Go show them – and yourself – what you got!

TEST DAY!

Finally, the test day has arrived.

Wake up early and have a good breakfast. Pack a bag with water, snacks, a pen and your notebook. Leave ample time to get to the test center, find parking and have a breather/ bathroom break before your appointment.

Briefly review your notes before the test, but don't spend too much time trying to memorize everything.

Take a deep breath before you start the test. Remind yourself that you can do it.

There's a message for you on page 376 that I'd like you to read right before the test. If today is your test day, you can turn to that page now. If not, wait until test day to turn to it.

Relax and enjoy the ride!

GMAT VERBAL

GMAT Verbal

"The difference between good and great is just a little extra effort".

- Duffy Daugherty.

For the rest of the book, we will look at the different sections to help you learn how to score high marks. We will try to understand how the test works and clarify what you need to watch out for.

In this section, you will learn how to prepare for the verbal portion of the exam. We will be looking at the fundamentals, so the examples are basic and simple. Understanding the fundamentals will help you answer more complex question based on the same rules.

This is not a guide that lists the answers to questions, nor is it designed to make the test a piece of cake without having to study. It is a guide designed to aid your study process - showing you how to pass the GMAT with flying colors. We focus on studying <u>smart</u> but you will still have to study <u>hard</u> (though only for 30 days and then you can have your social life back!)

Taking the Verbal Portion

First things first. There are many ways that you can take the verbal test to make things easier on you as a whole. The following are just a few of the strategies that will help you:

1.   **Organization** is the key to passing the verbal portion of the GMAT. You are starting the test with the harder questions; this is where you need to shine, so work systematically to ensure that you put forth your best answers. Do not be afraid to scratch down thoughts to keep them organized during the test. Scratch paper is available for this purpose. If you keep your thoughts written down, you are less likely to make a careless mistake. Look at the question with a rational mind and determine the answers that simply cannot fit. The first 15 questions on the GMAT verbal portion are the most important, as they will determine the overall flow and score of your test, so take your time with them. If you answer several of these questions in a row wrongly, your score will start plummeting, so don't rush.

2.   **Use the process of elimination.** This is one of the most important techniques for taking the GMAT! By using this process, you will be surprised at how easy it is to eliminate the answer options that just "don't belong." Instead of looking for the "right" answer, eliminate the wrong answers from the choices and narrow down your options. Even if you can only eliminate one or two choices, your chance of guessing the right answer improves. So identify what's wrong with a choice, cross it off on your scratch paper or white board, and do this for all of the answer choices to increase your chance of choosing the right answer.

3.   **Don't rush**. Rushing is one of the worst things that you can do to hurt your score. "Driving" the GMAT is like driving too fast down a road, trying to steer and navigate obstacles. It just won't work – you'll make mistakes. If you race through the test the same applies. As "they" say, slow and steady wins the race!

4.   **Don't waste time.** Even though you don't want to rush, you also don't want to waste too much time on the hard questions. There will be

questions that you will have trouble answering, so just answer them as best as you can. You have a 20% chance of answering them correctly, so always give them a shot. Remember that the next question may be one you understand better, so you'll want to have enough time to answer it without rushing.

5.   **Don't let the clock distract you.** Some people find clocks distracting, especially during a test. The GMAT has a clock that you can turn off if you need to, so that you can focus on the test at hand. But if you turn the timer off, be careful not to run out of time. You must answer all the questions in each section to do well. Remember:

WHATEVER YOU DO, DO NOT LEAVE A QUESTION

UNANSWERED!

Brandon's Tip

Also realize that some of the hard questions that you see on the tests are experimental and do not count towards your final scores. Keeping this in mind can help you stay calm and focused even when faced with the most difficult of questions.

---

6.   **Stay calm.** This test is only a test and if you have studied hard, you will do fine. Do not get stressed out about it - stress will have a negative impact on your performance. If you feel yourself starting to panic, just sit back, breathe, and take a moment—even a minute or two—to relax and refocus on the test. Remember:

STRESS IS THE ENEMY!

Sentence Correction

"Go confidently in the direction of your dreams. Live the life you have imagined." - Henry David Thoreau

In most cases, sentence correction questions follow a standard format. **Some part of or all of a sentence will be underlined; this is the part you need to focus in on.** Your job is to determine whether there is an error and, if there is, to choose the best correction from the choices provided. If you feel that there isn't an error, select the first answer choice - this is the same as the original sentence.

When you are trying to figure out the best answer choice, the following technique can help you decide:

- **First, go over the original question in your head.** If you notice anything that doesn't sound right or natural, eliminate the first answer choice since it's always the same as the original. If you are a native English speaker or confident with your English language skills, you can also eliminate other answer choices that sound unnatural, even if you don't know exactly what the error is.

- **Next, try to identify the error in the sentence.** If you are able to find the right way to correct the error immediately, then trust your instincts. If not, compare the answer choices and look for differences among the choices you are given. Sometimes the same error will occur in multiple options. In this case, eliminate all of the options with the same error. Eliminate the answers with errors and settle on one, or at the most, two options. It is very important that you don't second-guess yourself in this situation.

Understanding GMAT English

Thankfully, GMAT Sentence Corrections do not test every grammar rule there is, which makes things much easier on you. Here are the five rules that you do need to understand when dealing with GMAT English:

1. Basic Sentence Structure

If you took elementary English and remember any of it, then you should know what a verb is. Essentially, a verb is the action the subject is performing in a sentence. For example, consider the following sentence:

- Layla ran home.

In this sentence, *Layla* is the subject and *ran* is the verb because it describes the action that the subject is performing. Sometimes, a verb consists of two parts: the auxiliary, or helping verb, and the main verb. Take this sentence for instance:

- Layla's house is burning.

In this case, the subject is now *house*, while *is burning* is the verb. *Is* is the auxiliary verb while *burning* is the main verb.

Remember that verbs must agree with their subjects. A singular subject requires a singular verb, and a plural subject requires—yep, you guessed it—a plural verb. This rule is a popular one on the GMAT and one that will trip up many a test-taker. Follow these rules, so it doesn't happen to you:

Correctly identify the subject and verb of the sentence

Contrary to popular belief, the verb does not always follow the subject. Sometimes the verb comes first. Although this isn't normally the case, it will show up on the GMAT as a way of throwing you off base. Many sentences that begin with the words "here" or "there" have this kind of inverted construction. The key to this type of question is spotting the subject and verb. Once you've done that, just make sure they agree. It's really that simple. Let's look at some examples:

- Here (is, are) the invoices you requested.

- There (is, are) the spotted dog we saw at the park.

To the untrained eye, both of these sentences may appear to require a singular verb since the words *here* and *there* appear singular. The problem with this theory is that *here* and *there* aren't the subjects of the sentences; therefore, they have no impact whatsoever on the verb. The best strategy is to find the verb and plug it into the following question:

What _____?

(verb)

The answer to that question will be your subject. In the above sentences, the answers are *invoices* and *dog*. One is plural and one is singular, and they both require verbs that agree in number. Therefore, *are* is the correct verb in the first sentence whereas *is* is appropriate for the second. The words *here* and *there* are inconsequential to the answers. If you see these words on a question asking you to identify the verb, it might be a good idea to cross them out right away to prevent them from influencing your answer.

Look out for collective and compound subjects

Sometimes subjects can be tricky, especially when they come in the form of collective nouns which may be singular even though they refer to more than one person or object. If this rule doesn't make sense to you, don't despair—you don't have to agree with it; you just have to follow it. It is what we can call "GMAT correct," not "common-sense correct." Let's examine some sentences including collective nouns acting as subjects.

- The team (win, wins) the game against Green Oak every year.

- The price of eggs is rising; a dozen eggs (cost, costs) nearly two dollars nowadays.

In both of these sentences, the subject refers to more than one person or object. The *team* in the first sentence is probably comprised of twenty or more players, but since we are referring to them collectively, the noun is singular, at least in the grammatical sense. Therefore, *wins* is the correct verb in the first sentence. In the second sentence, you may be tempted to select the plural verb *cost* because it immediately follows *eggs*. However, the subject is really *a dozen*, which is an intangible concept and is singular. Therefore, the correct verb is the singular *costs*. Another easy way to tell that you need a singular verb in this instance is the article *a*. *A* only precedes singular or uncountable subjects. The exception to this rule is the phrase *a number of*. This is a plural construction.

- A number of cars on my street are parked illegally.

Like collective subjects, compound subjects can also throw you a curveball when it comes to finding an agreeable verb. By definition, a compound subject is one that is comprised of two or more nouns joined by the conjunction *and*. A compound subject always takes a plural verb. Take, for instance the following examples:

- Bill and Ted (like, likes) hiking.

- The lion and the giraffe (is, are) my favorite animals at the zoo.

In both of these sentences, the word *and* joins two otherwise singular subjects. Since they are connected, however, and have the same verb, they are considered plural and require a plural verb. Therefore, the answer for the first sentence is *like*, and the answer for the second sentence is *are*.

Some conjunctions can be slightly more confusing. The count of subjects with the conjunctions *either...or* and *neither...nor* varies. But the rule is simple – you only have to look at the subject closest to the noun.

- Either my sister or my brothers (is, are) going to visit me on Thanksgiving.

- Neither the houses nor the church on my block (is, are) well-maintained.

In the first sentence, *brothers* is the subject nearest the verb, so select *are*. In the second sentence, *church* is the subject nearest the verb, so select *is*.

Be aware of pronouns

When answering a question dealing with subject-verb agreement, it's also important to be on the lookout for pronouns, especially indefinite ones. Some are always singular such as: someone, no one, everyone, nobody, and everybody. Some of these singular indefinite pronouns, like *everyone* and *everybody*, for instance, sound plural, so be especially careful with these. Look at the following examples:

- Everyone (is, are) happy to be here.

- No one (is, are) uncomfortable.

Even though the subject in the first sentence appears to refer to more than one person whereas the subject in the second refers to not even one, both are considered singular, grammatically speaking, and require a singular verb. Therefore, the verb *is* is correct for both of the above sentences.

There are some pronouns that vary in their count according to what they represent. *All* and *none* are the pronouns in this case that can play tricks on you. Look at the following examples:

- All of the pizza (was, were) eaten by the time I arrived.

- All of the students (was, were) prepared for the exam.

In both sentences, the word *all* is the subject. But since *all* can change from plural to singular, you need to look at the entire subject phrase. In the first sentence, the key word is *pizza*, which is singular, so you should select the verb *was*. In the second sentence, the key word is *students*, which is plural, so you should select the verb *were*.

Phrases that separate a subject from its verb

The GMAT is notorious for complicating subject-verb agreement questions by separating the verb from its subject. They typically do this by throwing in a prepositional phrase, appositive (see box below), or a relative clause. As long as you are adept at identifying the subject and verb in a sentence, this potential distraction shouldn't be a problem for you. Just for good measure, though, let's examine some sentences with intervening phrases:

- Mrs. Jones, the teacher who assigns the most writing assignments, (is, are) always the last to leave school for the day.

- The child who is wearing the pink shoes (take, takes) the bus home every day.

- The frogs on the lily pad (jump, jumps) to and fro.

In the first sentence, the subject *Mrs. Jones* is separated from the verb by the appositive, *the teacher who assigns the most writing assignments.* Even though *assignments* is the noun closest to the verb, it is not the subject; therefore, it has no impact on the verb. The subject of the sentence is the singular *Mrs. Jones*; therefore, the sentence requires the singular verb *is*.

A ***Prepositional Phrase*** a phrase that begins with a preposition and ends with a noun or a pronoun. For example, By the window, Near the car, On your head, Under the tree, Above it, Over there.

An ***Appositive*** is a noun phrase in which a noun that identifies or renames another noun by following it after a comma, or by proceeding it before a comma at the beginning of a sentence. For example, Andy, *the guy next door*, won the lottery. In this sentence, "the guy next door" is the appositive. An example of an appositive at the beginning of a sentence would be: *The guy next door*, Andy won the lottery. Here again "The guy next door" is the appositive.

The second sentence contains the ***relative clause*** (see the box below), *who is wearing the pink shoes* which separates the subject *child* from the verb.

Since the subject is singular, the verb must also be singular, so the correct answer is *takes*.

A *relative clause* is used to modify a noun or pronoun and give more information about the noun or pronoun. It begins with relative pronouns such as *who, whom, whose, which,* and *that,* or relative adverbs such as *when, where,* and *why.*

- Dogs **that have strong olfactory systems** make good police dogs.
- There is a new movie **that introduces the science of global warming to children.**
- A pub is a place **where people go to enjoy a drink but mostly to socialize with other local people.**
- The movie theatre **at which we saw *Inception*** has now closed.

More on relative clauses in the next section.

In the third sentence, the prepositional phrase *on the lily pad* separates the subject *frogs* from the verb. Although the noun closest to the verb in this sentence is *lily pad*, since it is not the subject, it has no bearing on the verb. Therefore, the plural noun *frogs* takes the plural verb *jump*.

More examples of this:

- Each of the musicians (was, were) paid in advance

- A series of Loch Ness Monster sightings (has, have) turned Scotland into a tourist destination.

- There (is, are) a number of different ways to cook oysters.

In the first example, since *each* is singular because it refers to the individual musicians, *was* is the correct answer. In the second example, *series* is always singular and is the subject, not *Loch Ness Monster sightings*. Therefore, *has* is the correct answer. Keep your eye out for tricks in which subjects like "series", "spate", and "succession" are followed by prepositional phrases containing plurals (in example *a.* the prepositional phrase containing plurals is "of the musicians" and in example *b.* "of Loch Ness Monster sightings"). These subjects are still singular! Also be careful of words, such as *series*, that end in the letter *s* but are really singular. In the last example, *a number of different ways* is plural because it means several. Therefore, the correct answer is *are*.

2. Pronouns and Modifiers

The second grammatical rule that you need to follow on the GMAT deals with pronouns and modifiers. Before we get to the examples, let's quickly review pronouns. Essentially, a pronoun substitutes for a noun (you, they, she, he, it...etc). Looking at the following sentence will make this much clearer:

- Robert gave his steak to Mindy

In this case, all three nouns (Robert, steak, Mindy) can be replaced by pronouns; for example, He gave it to her. If Robert, the steak, and Mindy have all been mentioned before, then the reader can deduce what the pronouns he, it, and her refer to.

Other examples of sentences that use pronouns include:

- Take it or leave it.

- I love you.

- She stared at them.

- That reminds me of him.

Make sure that pronouns refer to only one thing, and that modifying phrases are positioned in the sentence as closely as possible to what they are modifying. If a pronoun is underlined, find out what the pronoun is replacing, and make sure it agrees in number with its antecedent (the noun it is replacing)

Also, make sure that it is clear which noun the pronoun is replacing.

Let's look at two sample sentences to further understand this:

- The company promised to maintain operating factories inside the county, but (it, they) later reneged on the commitment.

- If the couple cannot resolve their differences, the court will do (it, so).

Company is a collective noun, as is group, crowd, etc., and requires a singular pronoun. Therefore, "it" is the correct answer. In the second sentence, we do not know what "it" refers to. It could refer to custody of the children, the house, the car, and the terms—we simply do not know. Ending the sentence with "it" would cause confusion on the part of the reader since "it" has no clear antecedent. Therefore, "so" is the correct answer as it signifies the court will conduct the action "resolve their differences."

Since we also mentioned modifiers in this rule, we will take a look at them in an example sentence.

Modifiers are **adjectives** or **adverbs** with the ability to change the meaning of a noun, pronoun, or verb. Adjectives modify nouns or pronouns, whereas adverbs (these often end in –ly) modify verbs. In other words, adjectives tell what something is like, whereas adverbs tell how something was done.

- The napkin was lying (flat, flatly) on the table.

In the above example, the correct answer is *flat* (an adjective) because the modifier is describing what the napkin (a noun) is like and not the action, *was lying,* that was done to it. However, if the sentence read:

He laid his napkin (careful, carefully) on the table, the correct answer would be the adverb *carefully (an adverb)* because it describes how the napkin was placed on the table, that is, how the verb was performed.

An **adjective phrase** is a group of words that act as an adjective to modify a noun. Example: Lenny is a man *of kind nature*. The phrase "of kind nature" is an adjective phrase that modifies "man". Similarly, an **adverb phrase** is a group of words that act as an adverb to modify a verb. Example: It was *on this spot* he proposed. The phrase "on this spot" modifies the verb "proposed."

We mentioned relative clauses earlier. **Relative clauses** are also often used to modify nouns - similar to adjective phrases. There are two types of relative clauses: restrictive relative clauses and non-restrictive clauses.

Restrictive clauses identify and limit the noun they modify and are not offset by commas. On the other hand, the information in the non-restrictive clauses don't restrict or limit the noun it modifies, and are separated from the main clause by commas. Non-restrictive clauses does not help in the identification of the noun, but only provide information about it.

A quick way to find out if relative clause is restrictive or non-restrictive is by removing it and see if the meaning of the sentence is still clear and specific. If the meaning of the sentence becomes unclear after you remove the relative clause, the relative clause is restrictive. If the meaning of the sentence is still clear after you remove the relative clause, it is a non-restrictive clause.

It's easier to understand this with some examples:

- I was sitting next to the man who travels the world every year.

The relative clause in this sentence "*who travels the world every year*" is a restrictive clause as it identifies the man to be one specific person with the information that this man travels the world every year. If we remove this clause, the sentence will be unclear as the man isn't identified. The clause provides information to identify the noun.

- I was sitting next to the King, who travels the world every year.

In this sentence, the relative clause "*who travels the world every year*" is a non-restrictive clause as it merely contains additional information about the King. If we remove this clause, the meaning sentence is still clear because the man is identified as *the King*. The clause provides additional information but is not necessary to identify the noun.

Whether they are adjectives or adverbs, adjective phrases or adverb phrases, or relative clauses, **modifiers must be placed as close to the word or phrase that they modify as possible**. Misplaced modifiers cause sentences to be awkward and even confusing. For instance, consider the following sentence:

- Sitting under the tree, a nut fell right on Leroy's head.

The modifying phrase in the sentence, *sitting under the tree*, obviously describes what Leroy was doing when the nut fell, but because it is placed closer to another noun—in this case, nut—it appears to describe the nut's actions instead. Since we all know that a nut can't sit, it's clear that the modifier is misplaced. To correct the error, you can either move the modifier or the noun it modifies. Here are the options:

- Sitting under the tree, Leroy felt a nut fall on his head.

- A nut fell on Leroy's head while he was sitting under the tree.

As you can see, it is sometimes necessary to reword the sentence a bit to make it flow smoothly. The important thing here is to put the modifier and the noun or phrase it modifies as close together as possible.

Other modifier errors include the differences between *greater* and *more*, and between *fewer* and *less*. *Greater* is used when describing numbers while *more* is used when describing a number of things. For example, the number of people in the classroom is *greater* than 20; there are *more* than 20 people in the classroom. For *fewer* and *less*, use *fewer* if you can count the objects, and use *less* if the objects are not countable.

For example, *fewer* apples and *less* air. The same rule applies to *number* and *amount*, where *number* is used for countable objects and *amount* is used for uncountable objects, as in the *number* of participants and the *amount* of effort.

One side note: numbers can be counted but percentages cannot. For example:

- Fewer than 30 people showed up. ("Fewer" is used because a number is countable.)

- Less than 30 percent of the people showed up. ("Less" is used because percentages cannot be counted.)

3. Parallel Structure

The next rule is on parallel structure: a) making sure that similar items in a list have a similar construction, and b) only elements of the same sort are being compared. No matter what nouns, verbs, or other elements are in a sentence, if they are of the same importance, they should be expressed the same way. See the following sample sentences to understand parallel structure.

- The downward trend of the hockey team comes from mismanagement, poor performance, and (star players relocating, relocation of star players) to other teams.

The correct answer is *relocation of star players* because the other objects of the preposition *from*, namely *mismanagement* and *performance* are nouns similar to *relocation*. Use of the gerund form *relocating* would be a deviation from the parallel construction of the sentence. If the gerund forms, *mismanaging* and *performing* had been used instead, then the logical and parallel choice would be *relocating*.

The **Gerund Form** refers to the usage of a verb (in its -ing form) as a noun. An example would be, the verb "teaching" in this sentence: "Teaching is a great skill to have".

- I remember my uncle making moonshine and (playing, that he would play) the banjo.

Since the verb *making* is used in the first part of the sentence, *playing* is the best choice in order to maintain parallelism.

- To visualize excellence is not the same as (to achieve, achieving) it.

The use of the infinitive *"To visualize"* in the first part of the sentence sets the structure of the sentence and necessitates the use of *"to achieve"* in the latter part. You can't compare apples to oranges, and you have to make sure that your comparisons are logically similar to each other. Remember that in parallel structures and comparisons, you can only compare similar words.

4. Idioms

Using correct idioms can be difficult, and knowing the "right" way of saying something is not always easy. You might not be able to guess the meaning of an idiom as it has more of a figurative meaning than a literal one. When you say, *He kicked the bucket*, people who speak the English language understand that he did not literally kick the bucket, but that he died. Not all idioms are figurative, however. Some are simply defined as how something is said in a certain language. There are no rules that make it so; that's just how it's done. Let's look at a few examples:

- Wayne Gretzky is regarded (as, to be) one of the greatest   NHL hockey players.

- Pollution from greenhouse gases is generally (considered, considered as, considered to be) a major threat to the environment.

- It took me twice as long to build the shed collaboratively (as, than) it would have taken by myself.

Idioms can also be used in comparison and, as a result, must be followed by parallel constructions.

- Neil Young is not just a great singer, (and also, but also, but is also) a legendary musical icon.

Looking at the first example, the correct answer is as; "regarded as" is the correct use of idiom and not "regarded to be".

The correct answer for the second example is *considered*. Although *considered to be* is also grammatically correct, it will not be considered idiomatically correct on the GMAT.

The infinitive "to be" is implied and therefore stating it explicitly is redundant.

As is correct in the third example, because *as long* was used earlier in the sentence. You use *than* when it is preceded by an -er word, while you use *as* when it is preceded by *as*. For example: "I am *taller than* her." "I am *twice as tall as* her."

The last statement uses *but also* because the format for parallel construction with this idiom is:

not only ... but also ....

These idioms cannot be explained by grammar or logic, but the good news is that the more you practice them, the more familiar they will become.

See the cheat sheet - a list of idioms at the end of the chapter - for a further review of idioms commonly found on the GMAT.

5. Avoid Redundancy and the Passive Voice

Avoid redundancy and do not use unnecessary words. Also, do not use the passive voice if you can avoid doing so.

Many errors come from using ineffective expressions and problems with style. The most common of these on the GMAT is the use of far too many words to get the point across. The most common style problems are:

- unnecessary words

- redundancy

- using a passive voice when the sentence needs an active verb.

The passive voice is a sentence construction in which the subject is being acted upon rather than performing the action (passive rather than active). It is sometimes okay to use, such as in instances when the object is more important than the subject, but generally speaking, it should be avoided. The passive voice can be easily changed to an active voice by making the subject perform the action in the sentence.

- The kitchen is cleaned by Mary's housemate once a month.

- Mary's housemate cleans the kitchen once a month.

Questions of style can be tricky since the original sentences are not necessarily wrong, but could be written more clearly and concisely.

Let's look at these sentences and see how they could be rewritten:

- There are many children who believe in the Easter Bunny, but there are few adults who do.

- The largest pyramid is at least 4,000 years old or older.

- The Lord of the Rings has been bought and read by millions of readers since it was first published in 1951.

The first sentence could read as:

- Many children believe in the Easter Bunny, but few adults do.

Repeating *there is/are* makes sentences too wordy.

In the second sentence, saying *at least* and *or older* is redundant. At least implies that the minimum age is 4,000, so it may be much older, so stating this explicitly is redundant and unnecessary. The revised sentence should read:

- The largest pyramid is at least 4,000 years old.

The third sentence should read:

- Millions of readers have bought and read The Lord of the Rings since it was first published in 1951.

In the original sentence, the verb phrase *has been* is in the passive voice and should be revised.

Things to Remember...

- **Always start by examining the question carefully.** Try your best to find errors and problems with the original sentence before looking at the answer choices. If you find an error in the original sentence, go through the answer choices and eliminate all the ones that contain the same error. If you don't see an error in the original sentence, proceed to the choices and decide whether the original sentence is the best choice - if so, choose the first answer choice.

- **Don't try to fix the original sentence** if it's not broken!

- **Always put your final choice into the underlined portion of the original sentence** and double-check to see if there are any errors that you hadn't noticed before. The correct answer should not introduce a new error.

- **Use the process of elimination to save you time** and avoid confusion. When you find an error in a sentence, eliminate all choices that contain that same error either in the original question or in any of the choices.

- The three basic elements of any sentence are **subject**, **verb**, and **object**. Always know where these three elements are in the sentence so that you have a good understanding of its structure. First, check for consistency among these three elements and make sure that they all agree with each other. Subjects, verbs, and objects are often separated from each other by phrases, so pay attention to them throughout the entire sentence.

- **Understand that idioms don't follow rules.** The best way to deal with idioms is to simply memorize them. Throughout your practice sessions, make a list of the idioms that you are not familiar with, and review the list frequently.

- When you see a sentence with parallel components, which are usually created by the use of "and," "or," "but," "similar to," "in contrast to," "as well as," "like," "unlike," and others, **make sure that the parallel components are consistent in grammatical structure.**

- **A pronoun is a word that replaces a noun.** Words such as he, she, it, who, are pronouns.

- If you cannot be sure which noun a pronoun refers to, or if the pronoun could refer to multiple nouns, then an error exists.

- **Avoid the passive voice where possible.** The passive voice is usually not as clear or effective as the active voice. That said, using the passive voice does not immediately create a grammatical error, and if no grammatically correct alternative exists, then consider the passive voice. The passive voice can also be used when it is impossible or inappropriate to state the subject of the action.

- If omitting words/phrases makes the sentence unclear, the words/phrases should not have been omitted and should be put back in. On the other hand, the infinitive phrase *to be* is often unnecessary, so when you see it in a sentence, check the sentence for other unnecessary words.

- **Eliminate an answer choice immediately if you find a grammatical error.** Although this section asks you to consider the effectiveness of the choices, the correct choice will never contain a grammatical error. On the other hand, don't expect to always find the perfect answer for the sentence, as the point is to pick the best choice among the answer choices provided, and not to construct a perfect sentence. In the case where you find all the answer choices flawed, simply pick the best choice available and move on.

Sample Questions

Now that you've mastered the key grammatical concepts tested on the GMAT, it's time to try your hand at some real life GMAT-style sentence correction questions. Good luck!

1. A recent study conducted on middle and high school students suggest that participation in competitive team sports has a positive effect on overall health and well-being.

    A. suggest

    B. suggests

    C. suggested

    D. will suggest

    E. have suggested

Knowledge of subject-verb agreement and verb tense is necessary to answer this question correctly. Using our techniques to successfully identify *study* as the subject of the sentence, we can then determine that a singular verb is necessary and eliminated options A and E because they have plural verbs. Then, eliminate C and D since the remainder of the sentence is in present tense and a shift in tense is unnecessary. Therefore, B is the correct answer.

> ➤ **More Practice from the GMAT® Review 13ᵗʰ Edition:** Questions 16, 30, 62, 83, 133

2. According to a recent survey, atheists are more knowledgeable about religious topics than the people who believe in Christ.

A. the people who believe in Christ

B. the Christ-followers

C. are Christians

D. those who believe in Jesus

E. church-goers

This question tests your knowledge of parallel comparisons. As we reviewed earlier, items being compared should be stated in similar terms. In this case, the sentence is comparing the knowledge level of "atheists" and "those who believe in Christ." Although the phrase "those who believe in Christ" is not grammatically incorrect, it is not the most effective means of expression stylistically. Eliminate A and D because they are too wordy. Next, in order for the comparisons to be parallel, you need to repeat the verb "are." If you do not repeat the verb, the sentence implies that atheists know about two things: religious topics and the people who believe in Christ. Repeating the verb applies the phrase "are knowledgeable" to both subjects. Therefore, option C is correct.

> **More Practice from the GMAT® Review 13th Edition:** Questions 11, 32, 85, 124, 132

3. Some <u>instructional professors</u> believe that alternative forms of assessment are more authentic ways of assessing student performance than are traditional exams.

A. instructional professors

B. educational professors

C. professors

D. instructive professors

E. didactic professors

This is a clear example of redundancy. The very definition of the word "professor" implies that such a figure is indeed "instructional," so this fact need not be stated explicitly. All other options exhibit the same error in redundancy, making them easy to eliminate. Therefore, C is the correct answer.

> **More Practice from the GMAT® Review 13ᵗʰ Edition:** Questions 24, 35, 56, 58, 137

4. <u>Focusing on the positive, setting achievable goals, and the ability to keep a singular vision for the future</u> are the true keys to success.

   A. Focusing on the positive, setting achievable goals, and the ability to keep a singular vision for the future

   B. Focusing on the positive, setting achievable goals, as well as the ability to keep a singular vision for the future

   C. Focusing on the positive, setting achievable goals, in addition to one's ability to keep a singular vision for the future

   D. Focusing on the positive, setting achievable goals, and having the ability to keep a singular vision for the future

   E. Focusing on the positive, setting achievable goals, and keeping a singular vision for the future

This question deals with parallel construction and items in a series. In this sentence, the first two items in the series are gerund phrases; therefore, it stands to reason that the last item should also be expressed as a gerund phrase. Eliminate options A, B, and C.D fixes the error but is not as concise as E, so E is the GMAT correct response.

> ➢ **More Practice from the GMAT® Review 13ᵗʰ Edition:** Questions 26, 38, 51, 116, 121

5. The extinction of so many endangered species in North America has been attributed with a general lack of concern for wildlife.

   A. has been attributed with

   B. had been attributed with

   C. had been attributed to

   D. has been attributed to

   E. has been attributed by

This question challenges your knowledge of verb tense and idiomatic expressions. There are no words of time or other past tense verbs that indicate you should switch from "has" to "had," so eliminate choices B and C. Next, focus on the change in prepositions in the answer choices. These changes indicate an idiom error. In English, speakers use the preposition "to" after the verb "attribute" to indicate a catalyst or cause for an event or phenomenon. Therefore, D is the correct answer.

> ➤ **More Practice from the GMAT® Review 13th Edition:** Questions 5, 12, 34, 69, 95

Idioms Cheat Sheet

Here is one of the many sets of notes I prepared while studying for the test. This note is rough and in its original form without much editing because I want to show you exactly what worked for me and how I took notes in my notebook. I found it extremely useful to have this notebook with me whenever I was studying to write down things that were difficult. The notebook was the only thing I took with me to the center on the day of the test and it proved to be excellent material to read right before the test.

"due to" vs "because of"

    due to - modifies nouns.

        Her failure was due to poor study habits.

    because of - modifies verbs.

        She failed because of poor study habits.

"concur with" a person, "concur in" a decision

    I concur with John. I concur in this decision.

A series of... has...

series, string, spate, succession --> all singular.

also: company, committee, group, gang --> all require singular pronouns.

"a number of" = "several" --> always signals a plural subject.

    A number of apples were stolen.

"the number of" --> singular

The number of apples stolen was five.

Neither... nor (noun)... were/was | Either... or (noun)... were/was

were/was depends on the noun following "nor" as it is the subject of the sentence.

Neither you nor John was able to finish the race.

Either the boy or the girls were really loud last night.

"among" vs "between"

"among" is used when referring to three or more units, while "between" is used when referring   to two.

It was very difficult for me to choose between coffee and tea.

Among the three choices, tea was the healthiest drink.

watch out for "Because... so..." and "Because... therefore..." --> redundant sentence structure and often incorrect.

... is "credited with (verb-ing)"... --> "with" is correct

...is "credited for (verb-ing)"... --> "for" is incorrect

"just as... so..." - Just as interest in climate change increased, so the number of hybrid cars sold increased.

"more than" - I certainly have more confidence now than five years ago.

"the reason... was because..." --> incorrect. This is redundant because the word "reason" already means "because." Likewise, "the reason why" would be redundant. The correct idiom is "the reason that."

"between... and..."   ex. between Los Angeles and San Francisco "from... to..." ex. from Los Angeles to San Francisco

"... insist that ... (original verb-form) ..."

Airlines insist that each passenger pass through a metal detector.

"require to" - You are required to bow when you accept someone's business card.

"if... then..." -If you go, then I will go.

"the -er ... the -er ..." - The drunker he gets, the funnier he becomes.

"as" vs "like"

"like" is used to compare nouns while "as" is used to compare actions and is often followed by a clause.

Life is like a box of chocolates.

Life surprises you everyday, as a box of chocolates often does.

"decide to" - I couldn't decide whether to take the job or not.

"credit with" - The Beatles are often credited with starting the 1960's pop movement.

"double"(verb) vs. "twice"(comparison)

The landlord tried to double the rent on our house.

That would mean paying twice as much as we do now.

A person is irritated. A situation or condition is aggravated.

"each other" (2 things) vs. "one another" (3 or more things) -

> The pear and cheese compliment each other.

> The pear, cheese and walnuts compliment one another.

"associate with" - People often associate Japan with sushi.

"extent to which" - I was surprised at the extent to which the student's listened to their teacher.

"considered to be + (noun)" will never be correct on the GMAT. It should be "considered + (noun)"

> The Segway was considered a failure.

"fewer" (countable) vs. "less" (uncountable) - I want fewer work hours and less stress.

"continue to" - They can't continue to live like that without serious damage to their health.

"just as.. so too..." - Just as a car needs gas, so too does the body need food.

"forbid to" - We are forbidden to wear high heeled shoes to school.

"from... to" - From her beautiful face to her great sense of humor, I love everything about her.

"There is/are" sentences are often needlessly wordy and could be more concise. For example, "There is a fly in my soup." is not as concise as "A fly is in my soup."

"in danger of" - If the supermarket opens across the street we are in danger of going out of business.

"-er than" - California's winter is much warmer than Boston's.

"link to" - Overexposure to sun has been linked to skin cancer.

"define as" - A genius is defined as someone with an IQ of over 160".

"not ... but rather/merely ..." - it is not fun but rather tedious walking the dog each morning.

"believe ... to be ..." - I believe the bag to be fake.

"distinguish between... and..." - It is hard to distinguish between John and Jack.

"so as" is never correct on the GMAT

"so... as to be..." however is often correct

"perceive as" - Can a robot be perceived as a developing creature?

"native to" (plants, animals, etc.) vs. "native of" (people's birthplaces) -

The kangaroo is native to Australia.

Pamela Anderson is a native of Canada.

"prohibit from" - Kids are prohibited from entering this venue after midnight.

"either... or..." - I could either go to the movies or finish my homework

"like" vs. "such as"

"such as" is used for examples, while "like" is used to demonstrate similarities.

He loves outdoor sports such as hiking an camping.

This place smells like curry.

"resistance to" - Vitamin C increases one's resistance to catching a cold.

"range from ... to ..." - The ages of people working in this factory range from twenty to fifty.

"same as" - The book he is holding is the same as the one on that table.

"likely to" - If you study effectively, you are likely to do well.

... is **"estimated to be"** ... --> "to be" is correct

... is **"estimated as"** ... --> "as" is incorrect

This church is estimated to be over 250 years old.

"try to" - Why don't you try to do it too?

Reading Comprehension

"They can because they think they can" - Virgil

Reading for the GMAT is easy once you understand how the passages are constructed. This part of the GMAT primarily tests your ability to understand the main ideas in a short article.

The passages only span four genres (humanities or social science, physical science, biological science, and business) and all follow one of four styles (defining, comparing/contrasting, advocating, and refuting). You'll be very familiar with these genres and styles after you've gone through some practice passages and questions.

Don't try to understand every little detail in the passages because the goal is not comprehension, but rather finding the right answer choice!

The Scope of the Text

There is a common saying: can't see the forest for the trees. This applies to evaluating the text in the Reading Comprehension part of the GMAT. When you first read the passage, you need to look at it from afar before analyzing its details. Pay attention to the scope of the passage and try to understand its overall intent; that is, read with the goal of understanding the main idea, the author's tone, and the purpose. If you are able to grasp these basic elements, you have won half the battle as many of the reading comprehension questions on the GMAT will probe your understanding of these fundamentals. After you have a good idea of the scope of the passage, you can start analyzing it in more detail.

Break it Down

Now that you have looked at the entire passage as a whole to understand the scope, begin to break it down into smaller parts. This doesn't mean that you need to break down each sentence and comprehend every little detail. At this point you are just looking for the major supporting details.

Remember that not every sentence will be critical to answering the questions; there will be only into a few key pieces of text that need to be noticed. You should look primarily for these important sentences, although you may also find that some secondary sentences help you understand the key concepts of the passage. Sadly, you don't have a lot of time to go over the passages, analyze them, pick out the good points and the bad points, and understand the concepts. After all, the test is timed, so you have to work quickly and efficiently. Not all sentences are equal. Some are important, while others are not. Identifying which is which will help you a lot. Here are a few tips that should help you.

1. **Focus on the topic sentence in each paragraph.** Topic sentences can be identify with key words such as: therefore, main, most important, in conclusion

2. **Read the important stuff very carefully to fully understand it.** Important sentences are generally those that are set off by transition words such as: yet, so, while, although, despite, in fact, first,

3. **Only glance over the secondary and pointless details of a passage.** These sentences tend to be the ones that are bogged down with details and scientific words. They support the topic sentences and main points, but aren't necessary to read to get the general idea.

Things to Remember…

- To quickly answer most of the questions, make sure that you understand the key points of the article and ask yourself: **Why was the article written?** Keep these in mind when you read the passage. Do not get sucked into trying to figure out the details. Grasp the main ideas first. Read the entire passage, as the main idea and key points may not be obvious unless you do so.

- Always quickly scan the entire passage to get a rough idea of what it is about. Then, create a mental image of how the passage is structured and the key points in each paragraph. Do not try to memorize details, but do try to summarize the key points of each paragraph into one or two sentences. As long as you understand the structure of the passage and know that you can find information, you can always go back to sift through the details if necessary.

  Again:

  1. Scan the passage;

  2. Grasp the main ideas, author's intent, and key points;

  3. Understand the paragraph structure;

  4. Go back to find details only when a question requires details.

- Spend no more than five minutes reading the passage and roughly one minute per question. Since some passages are long, be sure that you are comfortable with the speed at which you read them.

- Read the questions carefully and don't be confused by answer choices that contain the same words or phrases as those in the passage. This is a common trap used in Reading Comprehension questions to trick you into selecting the wrong answer. Pay attention to the <u>meaning</u> of the answer choices and not how the sentence is constructed.

- If the passage contains a lot of technical terms (for example, scientific language), do not panic! The GMAT does not require you to have any knowledge in specific fields. All of the information you need is in the question. There is no need to panic. Attack these passages with the same tactics as you use for other passages and get a good understanding of the key points and the structure of the paragraphs.

- Understand that the information needed to answer questions containing references to a line will not be far from that particular line in the passage. This is also why you don't have to memorize details but can instead refer to the passage to find the information you need.

- Pay extra attention if you see a question or answer choice that uses information from different parts of the passage, as this is a common trap. Most of the time, the information needed to answer the question will be located close to that part of the passage. So, answer choices using information from different parts of the passage are likely not the correct answers.

Sample Passages

Let's examine some sample reading passages. The first one is a **compare and contrast** humanities passage.

Eastern theories of health and medicine are quite different from their Western counterparts. Whereas Eastern health practitioners attribute a person's overall health to factors related to a person's physical, emotional, and spiritual health, this holistic view of medicine often stands in opposition to Western doctors who typically blame biological factors alone for a person's ailments.

Over the past two decades, the prevalence of cancer has increased dramatically. Eastern medical professionals attribute this increase to the fast-paced and stress-filled nature of modern life whereas Western researchers are quick to blame environmental and nutritional causes.

When an Eastern doctor is confronted with a patient complaining of stomach pain, he does not simply prescribe an antacid as a Western doctor might. Instead, he may suggest that in addition to taking medicine, the person change his diet, practice relaxation techniques, and examine the health of his closest relationships.

Eastern doctors also differ in their beliefs about preventative medicine. While it is true that Western doctors will advise their patients to maintain a healthy lifestyle including exercising regularly and adhering to a healthy diet, Eastern practitioners go one step further and believe that maintaining a healthy spiritual balance is also an important tool in warding off physical illnesses.

As mentioned earlier in this section, the first step to tackling reading comprehension questions is to find the scope of the passage —that is, to identify the main idea, the author's tone and intent, and the major supporting details of the passage.

Scope

Main idea (why the article was written): The main idea of the passage is the difference between Eastern and Western approaches to medical diagnoses and treatment.

Author's Tone and Intent: The author's tone here is very matter-of-fact and informative, and that tone is aligned with his overall purpose, which is to objectively compare Eastern and Western medical philosophies.

Major Supporting Details: The details which best support the main idea of this passage are: the details regarding how each philosophy explains the rising cancer rates and the one which explains how an Eastern and Western doctor would respond to a patient with stomach pain.

After analyzing these three main components, the next step is to break down the passage to better understand its structure. This will help you find important information quickly when referencing the passage to locate answers. The best way to do this is to scan back through the passage and read the first sentence of each paragraph. This first sentence will typically reveal the main point of the paragraph.

Now that we have a good understanding of the scope and structure of the passage, let's break it down to determine the overall structure.

Structure

1ˢᵗ Paragraph- The first paragraph of this passage introduces the main idea by presenting Eastern and Western medical approaches in opposition to one another and explaining their differences in very general terms.

2ⁿᵈ Paragraph- The second paragraph introduces the first major supporting detail—the discrepancy in how the two medical approaches explain the rising cancer rates.

3ʳᵈ Paragraph- The third paragraph introduces the second major supporting detail—an anecdote describing how Eastern and Western doctors differ in their approaches to patients and their symptoms.

4ᵗʰ Paragraph- The fourth paragraph concludes the passage by offering yet another supporting detail—the disparity that exists between Eastern and Western philosophies of preventative medicine.

Having identified the scope and structure, we're now ready to answer the questions:

1. *The author is primarily concerned with*

   A. *identifying the cause of rising cancer rates*

   B. *tracing the history of Eastern medicine*

   C. *the need for a more holistic approach to medical practices*

   D. *the difference between Eastern and Western medical philosophies*

   E. *helping people decide whether an Eastern or Western approach to health and wellness is the best fit for them*

Since we've already determined the main idea and the author's intent, the answer to this question should seem obvious. Although all of the other selections contain elements of truth, the only one that clearly identifies the *primary* focus of the author is choice "D," the difference between Eastern and Western medical philosophies. Still, let's examine the other choices:

A. identifying the cause of rising cancer rates

Although this seems like a noble cause, there is only one mention of the rising cancer rates in the entire passage; therefore, it cannot possibly be the author's primary concern.

B. tracing the history of Eastern medicine

This is probably the choice you eliminated first since it is the weakest selection. Although Eastern medical philosophy has a long and interesting history, it's not mentioned at all in this passage.

C. the need for a more holistic approach to medical practices

Because the author's overall intent is to merely compare Eastern and Western medicine, not to make a judgment as to which is better, this choice isn't logical.

E. helping people decide whether an Eastern or Western approach to health and wellness is the best fit for them

This selection is very similar to the previous one, a fact that in itself suggests elimination of both choices. Remember that the author is making an objective comparison, not expressing an opinion. Although the information he presents may indeed help someone make an educated decision regarding health care, this is not the author's primary concern.

2. *Why does the author use the example of a patient who visits an Eastern doctor for stomach pain?*

    A. *To illustrate the difference between Eastern and Western medical treatment*

    B. *To suggest that stomach problems may arise from stress or relationship problems*

    C. *To criticize the Western tendency to simply prescribe a pill to solve every medical ailment*

    D. *To ridicule the superstitious nature of Eastern practitioners*

    E. *To recommend a change in the way doctors treat their patients*

Knowing the author's intent is also helpful when answering this question. Since we know that the author is simply describing the difference between the two philosophies, not making an evaluation or recommendation, the only logical choice is "A," to illustrate the difference between Eastern and Western medical treatment. Let's take a look at the other choices:

B. To suggest that stomach problems may arise from stress or relationship problems

Although the author implies that the Eastern philosophy of medicine may suggest that stomach problems arise from stress, he is merely making an observation about this philosophy, not expressing his own opinion. This is a very important distinction to make, and one that will help you arrive at the correct answer.

C. To criticize the Western tendency to simply prescribe a pill to solve every medical ailment

Although the passage does note that a Western doctor might prescribe an antacid for a stomach problem, it doesn't criticize this practice; it simply exposes the practice as a point of distinction between the two philosophies being compared.

D. To ridicule the superstitious nature of Eastern practitioners

This choice is fairly easy to eliminate since it is way off base. Both Eastern and Western medical philosophies are addressed respectfully in the passage, and the author doesn't ridicule either one.

E. To recommend a change in the way doctors treat their patients

Again, once you know that the author's intent is to merely describe differences, not express an opinion or bring about a change, choices such as this one are easy to eliminate.

3. *What does the author mean when he suggests that Eastern doctors take a more holistic approach to medicine?*

   A. *They focus more on spiritual aspects rather than biological causes.*

   B. *They take into account a variety of different sources (i.e. emotional, physical, spiritual) when making a diagnosis and prescribing treatment.*

   C. *They don't rely solely on the patient's own insight into the problem when making a diagnosis.*

   D. *They believe emotional causes are more significant contributors to illnesses than are physical factors.*

E. *Their spiritual beliefs prevent them from treating illnesses with traditional medicine.*

This question requires that you look back at the text at the author's use of the word "holistic." Certainly, it is helpful if you know the definition of this word, but even if you don't, the passage provides enough clues to lead you to the correct answer. If you're still unsure, you can always use the process of elimination to discard inaccurate answer selections. In the very first paragraph of the passage, the phrase "this holistic view" references the previous description of the Eastern philosophy as one that "attribute[s] a person's overall health to factors related to a person's physical, emotional, and spiritual health;" therefore, B is the correct answer. Just to be sure, let's analyze the other choices:

A. *They focus more on spiritual aspects rather than biological causes.*

This choice is tempting since the passage does seem to highlight Eastern doctors' emphasis on non-biological causes of illness. This emphasis is intended to illustrate the difference between the two approaches, however, not to suggest that the Eastern approach places more importance on any one factor.

C. *They don't rely solely on the patient's own insight into the problem when making a diagnosis.*

This choice is beyond the scope of the text. The passage doesn't address the differing ways Eastern and Western doctors might arrive at a diagnosis; it focuses instead on their beliefs regarding underlying causes and treatment of medical ailments.

D. *They believe emotional causes are more significant contributors to illnesses than are physical factors.*

This choice is very similar to choice A. Remember, when two choices seem so much alike that it's difficult to distinguish between them, they are probably both wrong, as in this case. Again, the passage indicates that the Eastern philosophy takes into account all factors regarding a person's overall health, but it does not imply that emotional causes are more important than physical ones.

E. Their spiritual beliefs prevent them from treating illnesses with traditional medicine.

This choice can be eliminated quickly since it is entirely inaccurate. There is no mention or implication in the passage that Eastern doctors avoid traditional treatment methods because of their spiritual beliefs.

The next sample passage is a social science passage, the intent of which is to advocate.

Jean Ayres, an occupational therapist and pioneer of a treatment approach called Sensory Integration, was one of the first to recognize that children traditionally referred to as simply clumsy or uncoordinated actually suffer from an ailment called Sensory Processing Disorder (SPD). SPD is a disorder characterized by a person's inability to interpret and respond to the sensory stimuli in their environment.

Ayres and her colleagues realized that in addition to difficulties related to the traditional five senses (i.e. taste, smell, touch, hearing, and sight), children suffering from SPD have trouble processing stimuli related to the vestibular and proprioceptive senses as well. The vestibular sense is governed by the inner ear and establishes one's balance and equilibrium whereas the proprioceptive sense is responsible for orienting the parts of one's body and how they relate to one another spatially. Therefore, in addition to having adverse reactions to loud noises or bright lights, children suffering from this disorder may also have difficulty performing age-appropriate tasks that require certain movements of the body.

There are a variety of treatment approaches available for SPD, one of which exposes the child to sensory-rich activities in an occupational therapy (OT) gym. Under the guidance of a licensed therapist, students engage in sensory activities with the use of specialized equipment designed to stimulate the child's senses. Other treatment approaches include cognitive behavioral therapy which focuses on teaching the child specific problem solving skills to enhance daily functioning. Current research supports the claim that the most effective approaches are the ones that include family members and take into account the family's lifestyle and routines.

The success of treatment depends largely upon the commitment of time and energy that the family is willing to make to help their child succeed. Often, the therapist will assign "homework" for a child to complete with *the parents' assistance. Furthermore, a sensory "diet" may be prescribed, consisting of certain sensory-rich activities that should be incorporated into the child's daily routine.*

In addition to therapy, children with SPD require interventions at school in order to perform well academically. Depending on the severity of the disorder, these children may be mainstreamed into the regular classroom, or they may require a special setting. The school's special education department should work with parents to develop an Individual Education Plan (IEP) which outlines specific interventions tailored to meet the child's specific learning needs. Accommodations and modifications to the curriculum might include alternate assessments, preferential seating, and extended time to complete assignments.

Although Ayres' research certainly increased awareness of SPD, it is still widely under-diagnosed and unrecognized by the general public and even medical professionals. If educators and parents were better able to recognize the signs of this disorder, they would be able to intervene and implement the steps that are necessary for the benefit of their children.

Let's try the same strategy on this reading passage:

Scope

Main Idea: The main idea of the passage is that children who suffer from Sensory Processing Disorder, a little known dysfunction that affects a person's ability to process the stimuli in his environment, can be helped through a variety of methods. However, those methods won't be implemented unless parents and educators can recognize the signs of the disorder.

Author's Tone and Intent: The author's intent is to persuade the audience that action needs to be taken to benefit SPD sufferers. Here the tone is one of concern and urgency.

Major Supporting Details: The major supporting details of this passage involve the explanation of SPD as a real disorder that affects a child's ability to process stimuli from the environment, the claim that the disorder is under-diagnosed as well as under-recognized, and the fact that there are treatment options and classroom accommodations available that could make life easier for children with SPD.

Structure

1st Paragraph: The first paragraph introduces the disorder and gives a brief history regarding its founder and the traditional misconceptions associated with it.

2nd Paragraph: The second paragraph goes into more detail about the disorder itself and explains how it interferes with the traditional five senses as well as two other senses that are often overlooked.

3rd Paragraph: The third paragraph describes two treatment options available for SPD: occupational therapy and cognitive behavioral therapy.

4th Paragraph: The fourth paragraph emphasizes the role of the parents in SPD treatment and describes some of the things parents will be responsible for doing at home.

5th Paragraph: The fifth paragraph outlines what steps need to be taken in the school setting to increase the child's academic performance.

6ᵗʰ Paragraph: The sixth paragraph concludes the passage with a call to action and a reminder that education and proper training are the answers to many of the problems children with SPD face.

Now that we've analyzed the scope and structure of the passage, we're ready to tackle the questions.

1. *The author seems to be focused mostly on*

   A. *the need for the general public to be more aware of the disorder*

   B. *the critical role of the parents in ensuring that the treatment their child receives is effective*

   C. *the steps that should be taken to enable SPD sufferers to succeed at home and at school.*

   D. *the accommodations and modifications that should be implemented in the classroom to give children with SPD equal access to the curriculum.*

   E. *the increased prevalence of SPD amongst school-aged children*

Since we took the time to carefully examine the author's intent as well as the main idea of the passage, this question is a cinch. Since we've already determined that the author intends to advocate for the child and that the main idea includes both parental and academic support, the obvious answer is C. There are some tempting answer choices though. Let's take a look.

A. the need for the general public to be more aware of the disorder

This choice is tempting because it is true that the author is concerned with the lack of awareness amongst the general population, but this is where it's very wise to read the question carefully. The question does not simply ask what the author is concerned with; it asks what the author is *mostly* concerned with. Since we've broken down the structure of the passage and determined the main ideas, we know that awareness is just one of the things the author mentions, not the entire focus.

B. the critical role of the parents in ensuring that the treatment their child receives is effective

Again, tempting, but our thorough analysis of the passage tells us that this concern is the subject of a mere paragraph, not the passage as a whole.

D. the accommodations and modifications that should be implemented in the classroom to give children with SPD equal access to the curriculum.

This option is very similar to option B in that it is true, but describes the focus of only one paragraph of the text. Therefore, it cannot represent the focus of the entire passage.

E. the increased prevalence of SPD amongst school-aged children

This choice is outside the scope of the passage. Although it may very well be true that SPD is on the rise, this is not even mentioned in the passage; therefore, it could not possibly be the main focus.

2. *According to the passage, why might children with SPD have trouble performing age-appropriate tasks related to movement?*

A. *Because SPD is a brain disorder that affects how the brain sends messages to parts of the body*

B. *Because SPD affects all five senses and children have trouble interpreting their environment as a result*

C. *Because parents and teachers are not educated about SPD and fail to provide the support children need to complete these tasks*

D. *Because SPD affects children's vestibular and proprioceptive senses which affect movement and balance*

E. *Because the treatment options available for SPD are limited and more research needs to be conducted to develop better therapeutic techniques*

This is one of those questions that require that we go back to the text and reread. This is not a problem though since we have already broken down the structure of the passage and know exactly where to look for the answer. The key phrase in this question is "according to the passage." That phrase gives the test-makers liberty to throw in other correct answers to trick you, so make sure that the answer you choose is based solely on the information provided in the passage. A look at the second paragraph of the passage will guide you to the correct answer. Towards the end of this paragraph, after a brief explanation of the commonly overlooked vestibular and proprioceptive senses, the author writes the magic word "therefore," and then explains that in addition to other symptoms, the child with SPD may have trouble making certain movements. Thus, we have our answer, answer choice D.

3. *The author implies that the role of the parents and family members of the child with SPD is to*

   A. *provide emotional encouragement to their child as he goes through therapy*

   B. *ensure that there are financial resources available to pay for specialized treatment*

   C. *find the most qualified therapist and choose an intervention plan that is well-suited to their lifestyle*

   D. *ensure that the school provides accommodations and modifications that will enable the child to perform to his full academic potential*

   E. *play an active role in the therapeutic interventions prescribed by the OT*

Because we have already analyzed the structure of the paragraph, we know that the fourth paragraph focuses on the role of the parents and family in SPD treatment. Even so, it is a good idea to scan the entire passage again to look for references to parents or family members. Doing so will reveal that the only other reference is in the concluding statement which reinforces the need for parents to be educated about the signs and symptoms of the disorder; therefore, we can rely on the fourth paragraph alone to inform our choice. After reading through the answer selections, carefully reread the entire fourth paragraph and then look back at the answer selections for a match. Since this paragraph makes references to "homework" assignments that the therapist may assign children to complete with the parents' assistance as well as a sensory diet that should be integrated into the child's "daily" routine, it is clear that the author believes the parents must take an active role in their child's treatment plan; thus, E is the correct answer. Just to be sure, let's look at the other options to eliminate them:

A. provide emotional encouragement to their child as he goes through therapy

This option is a classic example of how test-makers use answer selections that sound good, but are actually incorrect. Any reasonable person would assume that a child would need emotional support as he goes through any type of therapy, but the question is not asking you what a reasonable person might believe, it is asking you what the *passage* implies. Therefore, we have to base our answer on the passage alone.

B. ensure that there are financial resources available to pay for specialized treatment

Although, this is certainly a good idea, like the above choice, it is not textually based and therefore, can be eliminated as a viable answer.

C. find the most qualified therapist and choose an intervention plan that is well-suited to their lifestyle

This one is tricky because it uses terminology from the passage to tempt you. However, a close comparison of the answer choice and the passage reveals that a match does not, in fact, exist. Although the passage does state that the most effective treatment options are those that acknowledge a family's lifestyle, it says nothing of the parent's role in finding a therapist or choosing a therapy option.

D. ensure that the school provides accommodations and modifications that will enable the child to perform to his full academic potential

Like, choice C, this option uses information from the text to lure you in, but the paragraph on school accommodations does not mention parental responsibility; therefore, this option can also be eliminated.

Some of the passages on the reading comprehension section will be harder than others. Sometimes, the passage is based on something so unfamiliar and uses such specialized, technical vocabulary that it's easy to get overwhelmed. Before, you throw your hands up in frustration, take a deep breath, and rely on the same strategies that you would use for any other passage.

Remind yourself that you don't need to understand every word or even every sentence; you need only grasp the main idea, purpose, and overall structure. If a question asks you for anything other than that, you can always go back to the text to find the answer. Now let's take a look at one of these highly technical passages that defines a situation.

Scientists have discovered a new type of energy that calls into question Einstein's theory of relativity, a heretofore standard amongst the scientific community. This ground-breaking, new discovery called "dark energy" was acknowledged when scientists realized that the expansion of the universe was not decelerating in response to gravity's pull as Einstein initially suggested, but on the contrary, was growing at more rapid speeds than ever before. To explain this phenomenon, scientists have identified a force they dubbed "dark energy" which counteracts gravity's pull by forcing galaxies in opposite directions.

New technologies which enabled scientists to more accurately measure the Doppler effect and the redshift of certain supernovas were the catalysts for the unveiling of dark energy. Furthermore, the cosmic microwave background (CMB), an electromagnetic radiation which gives off a certain glow detectable only by radio telescopes, indicates that they universe is relatively flat. In order for this to be the case, however, a certain density must be achieved, and prior to the discovery of dark energy, there was no explanation for the lack of perceptible density. Dark energy fills this void, confirming its existence for many astronomers. Scientists now estimate that dark energy constitutes approximately 74% of the entire universe.

This recent discovery has prompted scientists to attempt to determine the new rate of cosmic expansion, something that can only be calculated through the "equation of state," a term used to describe the combination of pressure, temperature, and energy in any given area of space. This endeavor will cost NASA and the U.S. Department of energy close to 6 million dollars in research funding.

Even though the topic and specialized vocabulary in this passage may be intimidating, we can rely on the same simple strategy to break it down into more digestible portions.

Scope

Main Idea: The main idea of the passage is that dark energy, a force that pushes galaxies apart, confirms that the universe is flat and is expanding more rapidly than ever before, though more research is needed to determine the exact rate of cosmic expansion.

Author's Intent and Tone: The author's intent is to describe the new discovery and its implications in the field of astronomy. The tone is very objective and didactic.

Major Supporting Details: The major supporting details of the passage are 1) Scientists' realization that the universe was expanding at a faster rate than they previously predicted, 2) that dark energy was discovered by observing the Doppler effect and redshift of supernovas, 3) that dark energy supports CMB's hypothesis that the universe is flat, and 4) that more research has been funded to determine the rate of cosmic expansion.

Structure

1st Paragraph: The first paragraph introduces the topic of the passage — the discovery of dark energy, what it is, and how it refutes Einstein's theory of relativity.

2nd Paragraph: The second paragraph describes how dark energy was discovered and how it provides support for the theory that the universe is flat.

3rd Paragraph: The third paragraph discusses the topic of future research inspired by the discovery of dark energy.

Now that we've broken it down into its simplest, most fundamental parts, it doesn't seem nearly as bad, right? Kind of makes you wonder why they didn't just write it that way in the first place! On to the questions…

> *1. Which of the following can be inferred from the above passage?*
>
> > *A. Thanks to the discovery of dark energy, scientists now know exactly how large the universe will become.*
> >
> > *B. Dark energy can be detected by high powered telescopes.*
> >
> > *C. The increased rate of cosmic expansion has scientists rethinking Einstein's theory of relativity.*
> >
> > *D. Dark energy is responsible for diminishing the distance between galaxies.*
> >
> > *E. Dark energy has proven that the Earth is flat after all.*

Since this is an inference question and doesn't refer to a specific topic, it would be a good idea to read the answer selections carefully, eliminate the ones that you know are wrong, and then scan back through the passage to determine which choice is correct. The best technique for answering these types of questions is the process of elimination. Use the text as a reference to eliminate the wrong answer choices one by one and then match the right answer to the text just to be sure. Let's do that now.

A. Thanks to the discovery of dark energy, scientists now know exactly how large the universe will become.

You may be able to eliminate this answer right away since the very last paragraph, the one that should be freshest in your mind, states that more research is needed to determine the rate of cosmic expansion.

B. Dark energy can be detected by high powered telescopes.

This selection is tempting since it uses terminology in the passage, but do not be fooled; a look back at the text reveals that the telescopes are necessary to see the glow of the cosmic microwave background, not dark energy.

C. The increased rate of cosmic expansion has scientists rethinking Einstein's theory of relativity.

A look back at the first paragraph confirms that this answer is correct. The passage clearly states that the universe is expanding at a faster rate than expected and has caused scientists to reconsider the theory of relativity.

D. Dark energy is responsible for diminishing the distance between galaxies.

When you compare this answer selection to the information presented in the text, you will see that it is in direct opposition to the author's claim that dark energy is pushing the galaxies apart, resulting in universal expansion.

E. Dark energy has proven that the Earth is flat after all.

Hopefully, this answer selection was among the first you eliminated since it is by far the most absurd. The passage refers to the universe being flat, but makes no such assertion about the Earth.

2. *The passage suggests that dark energy will affect the rate of cosmic expansion by*

    A. *revealing the redshift of the certain supernovas*

    B. *flattening the universe*

    C. *pushing the galaxies apart*

    D. *contributing to the density of space*

    E. *contradicting Einstein's theory*

Again, the best strategy here is to read through all of the options, eliminate one or two that you are sure are incorrect and then compare the remaining choices to the passage. Let's take a look:

A. revealing the redshift of the certain supernovas.

A look back at the passage reveals that "new technologies," not dark energy, revealed the redshift of supernovas; therefore, this answer is factually inaccurate.

B. flattening the universe

This selection may be tempting since the passage mention that dark energy helps to confirm the flatness of the universe, but it does not say that it is actually contributing to the flattening process. This is an important distinction that will help you identify the correct answer to this question.

C. pushing the galaxies apart

A close reading of the first paragraph of the passage confirms that according to the author, dark energy is indeed pushing the galaxies apart, resulting in cosmic expansion. Therefore, this is the correct answer.

D. contributing to the density of space

This answer is tempting since it is true that dark energy contributes to the density of space. This is a good example of the need to read the question very carefully. The question asks how dark energy is contributing to cosmic expansion, not the density of space.

E. contradicting Einstein's theory

Again, this choice may seem appealing since we have already determined that dark energy does indeed contradict Einstein's theory. However, the act of contradicting a theory cannot possibly cause the universe to expand. Therefore, this answer is close, but not close enough.

3. *According to the passage, NASA and the U.S. Department of Energy are funding research ultimately intended to*

   A. *find out how much of the universe is comprised of dark energy*

   B. *discover more supernovas*

   C. *confirm the existence of dark energy*

   D. *determine the rate of cosmic expansion*

   E. *calculate the "equation of state"*

The fact that there is only one mention of the research funding in the passage makes this a relatively easy question to answer. Remember, you don't have to rely on your memory alone to answer the question correctly. The passage is right there in front of you, so use it! Look back at the paragraph that mentions "research" and you will see that the research is aimed toward determining the rate of cosmic expansion; therefore, D is the correct answer. There are some other choices that may appear viable, however, so let's look at how we can eliminate them:

A. find out how much of the universe is comprised of dark energy

You probably eliminated this one right away since the passage already states that dark energy comprises up to 74% of the universe. Surely, NASA and the U.S. Department of Energy wouldn't spend six million dollars trying to find out something that has already been determined.

B. discover more supernovas

This one is also a no-brainer since supernovas are only mentioned once and not in relation to research.

C. confirm the existence of dark energy

You probably didn't even have to go back to the passage to eliminate this one. The entire passage is about dark energy, and if you read it carefully the first time around, you should know that its existence has already been confirmed.

E. calculate the "equation of state"

Now, this one is truly tempting and if you answered this question incorrectly, you probably chose this answer. The research goal does include calculating the equation of state since that's the only way of determining the cosmic rate of expansion, but if you look carefully, the question is not asking about just any goal; it's asking about the "ultimate" goal, and the equation of state is not the ultimate goal. Therefore, this answer selection can also be discarded.

4. *The author mentions the cosmic microwave background because*

   A. *it was instrumental in discovering dark energy.*

   B. *it is what propels further inquiry into the mysteries of dark energy.*

   C. *it helps support the case for dark energy by exposing it as the missing link between the CMB and the heretofore unexplained lack of space density.*

   D. *it is the basis of Einstein's theory of relativity and is therefore under scrutiny as a result of the discovery of dark energy.*

   E. *it gives us a better picture of the universe itself and deepens our understanding of dark energy.*

Since we have already analyzed the structure of the passage, we have a leg up on this question. Even if the term "cosmic microwave background" does make us sweat, at least we know just where to look in the passage for information on it. This question asks us to determine why the author mentions this concept which is just another way of asking how it relates to the topic of the passage—dark energy. Therefore, our strategy is to look back at the passage to figure out what the cosmic microwave background has to do with dark energy. Since the passage suggests that the existence of dark energy helps to explain the shape of the glow emitted by the cosmic microwave background, we can say with confidence that C is the correct answer. Let's look at the other choices just to be safe.

A. it was instrumental in discovering dark energy.

A look back at the passage reveals that technologies which helped scientists measure the Doppler effect and the redshift of supernovas were largely responsible for the discovery of dark energy, not the cosmic microwave background.

B. it is what propels further inquiry into the mysteries of dark energy.

This choice has its appeal since the cosmic microwave background   and dark energy are related, but there is nothing in the passage to suggest that the CMB directly prompted further inquiry.

D. it is the basis of Einstein's theory of relativity and is therefore under scrutiny as a result of the discovery of dark energy.

Hopefully, you were quick to eliminate this answer selection since it is way off base. Not only is it factually inaccurate, but there is nothing in the text that connects the theory of relativity to the cosmic microwave background in any way.

E. it gives us a better picture of the universe itself and deepens our understanding of dark energy.

This choice sounds nice but is so vague that it says practically nothing at all and certainly doesn't answer the question.

As you can see, even the most technical of passages on the GMAT can be tackled with ease when you break in down into smaller parts and look for the key components. Remember not to give up just because you see a few difficult words. It's not important to understand everything, just the key concepts. Zero in on the text for questions that call for specific details, and most importantly, stay calm. You can do this!

> **More Practice from the GMAT® Review 13th Edition:** Use the following matrix to make sure that you practice a variety of passage types. Note that not all combinations are available because some just don't occur very frequently. This doesn't imply that you won't see a given combination on your test, but if you have practiced enough, you will be able to work with any combination. The numbers refer to the page numbers in the *Official Guide*.

	Define	**Compare/ Contrast**	**Advocate**	**Refute**
Humanities and Social Science	390	394	368	372
Physical Science	370	not available	406	not available
Biological Science	364	not available	408	not available
Business	402	not available	378	366

Critical Reasoning

"We are still masters of our fate. We are still captains of our soul."
- Winston Churchill

Critical Reasoning is a favorite of people who love to argue. Here, your talents at arguing, breaking apart reasoning, and finding weak points to attack or defend will shine.

This section is one of the most important on the GMAT. Anyone who can argue persuasively by logically evaluating an issue on its merits and responding to its strength and weaknesses has the critical thinking needed to be a good business manager.

Business managers must evaluate arguments and proposals with a critical eye because not all business deals recognize their parties equally. Sometimes you have to argue your point to be heard.

This section accounts for a full 30% of your verbal section score, and contains 12 to 13 questions.

Understanding Critical Reasoning Questions

To answer questions correctly in this section, it is very important to identify the various parts of critical reasoning questions.

The Question

Critical reasoning questions are easy to understand as they are very short and usually begin with the following instructions: *For each question, select the best of the answer choices given.* A critical aspect to answering the questions lies in the instruction itself. Note that you are not told to select the *perfect* answer, but to select the *best* answer available from the choices given. This is an important distinction since you don't want to immediately discount any one choice simply because it doesn't coincide perfectly with the ideal answer you may have in mind.

Having said that, it is a good idea to answer the question in your head before looking at the answer choices. This can help you solidify your thinking before being influenced by the sometimes tempting answer selections. Remember, though, if you don't find a perfect match, quickly reevaluate the question and look for the *best* answer from the available options.

The Short Passage

The next part of the question is the short passage. The passage is drawn from a variety of areas including casual conversation, natural sciences, and more. You may have no experience with the topic, but that is okay, as you do not need outside knowledge to understand the question. In fact existing knowledge can mislead you or bias your answer. So try to understand the question based on the information provided.

There are several different types of critical reasoning questions. You may be asked to identify a point that will strengthen or weaken the argument, or to make a deduction from the passage.

Choosing the right answer can be difficult, especially when some questions have two or more correct answers; one will be superior over the other though Again, the goal is to choose the *best* answer, Here are a few steps that can help.

1. **Before you read the short passage, read and understand the question as thoroughly as possible** because your understanding of the short passage will depend on the question. If you know what

you are supposed to look for before reading the short passage, you will be able to take a more logical approach while reading.

2. **Once you understand the question, read the short passage.** Most critical reasoning questions require you to identify parts of the argument, so read the passage actively and critically. Understanding the strengths and weaknesses of the argument will help you answer the question accurately.

3. **Since you know the question and have read the passage, do yourself a favor by first answering the question without looking at the answers provided.** For example, if the question wants you to find a statement to weaken the argument, review the passage and determine what could weaken it.

4. **If you were able to determine an answer, then look at the answers provided for a match.** If you couldn't come up with an answer, skim through each answer provided, keeping the passage in mind. Quickly eliminate the answers that do not apply. Once you select an answer, reread the question and the passage to be certain about your answer.

Splitting Up the Argument

Of course, reading a passage and drawing your own conclusions is one thing; reading the answers and figuring out the best one in relation to the passage is another thing altogether.

For Critical Reasoning, understanding the logic behind the argument is imperative in order to answer the questions. Doing this involves identifying the different components of the passage. On the GMAT, the argument is a claim supported by reasoning.

- The Earth is flat because it looks flat.

This was a common argument centuries ago, and it carries the same components that an author uses when pushing across his or her argument. The three main components of an argument are: the conclusion, the evidence, and the assumption(s). We'll deal with the conclusion and evidence first since they are the easiest to identify.

1. The conclusion: This is the author's claim or the point that he or she is trying to make. In this example, *the Earth is flat* is the conclusion.

2. The evidence: this is what the author uses to back up his or her claim. Here, *It looks flat* is the evidence.

While reading Critical Reasoning questions, it is important that you identify the conclusion from the evidence provided. First, despite its name, the conclusion does not always comes at the end of a passage as in the above example. It may come at the beginning, it may follow the evidence, or it may, in fact, be at the end.

As a result, finding the conclusion in a long passage can be difficult. Thankfully, a few keywords can ease the process. The words *therefore, us, as a result, hence, clearly, so,* and *consequently* are examples of conclusion keywords. We know this because their meanings essentially signal the beginning of a conclusion.

- When I look around I see flatness, (therefore, thus, as a result, hence, so, consequently) the Earth is flat.

- Clearly, the Earth is flat because all I see around me is flat ground.

These two sentences show how certain keywords signal the conclusion. In the first sentence, the words *therefore, thus, as a result, hence, so*, and *consequently* are interchangeable since they all signal the conclusion *the earth is flat*. In the second sentence, the word *clearly* signals the conclusion.

Likewise, evidence keywords help you identify the evidence. The words *because, since*, and *for* are examples of evidence keywords.

- The Earth is flat because all I see around me is flat ground.

- Since all I see around me is flat ground, the Earth is therefore flat.

- The Earth is flat for all I see around me is flat ground.

The use of the words *because, since*, and *for* signal the evidence in the above sentences. Obviously, these are very easy questions to answer correctly because they contain just one line, one quick piece of evidence, and one quick conclusion.

However, searching for evidence keywords can be effective for longer passages. The following sample passage helps us understand how.

Global warming is a serious problem for our planet. All around us, the Earth is heating up to record temperatures, which can seriously affect our way of life. Since global warming became a problem after the advent of the automobile, it can clearly be ascertained that the invention of the automobile has caused global warming. Only the elimination of the automobile will then fix the problem of global warming.

This relatively long passage includes some fluff and secondary points. Where is the evidence and conclusion? Let's look again, with the evidence keywords underlined.

> *Global warming is a serious problem for our planet. All around us, the Earth is heating up to record temperatures, which can seriously affect our way of life. <u>Since</u> global warming became a problem after the advent of the automobile, it can <u>clearly</u> be ascertained that the invention of the automobile has caused global warming. Only the elimination of the automobile will then fix the problem of global warming.*

Now we see why identifying an easy passage like *the earth is flat because all I see is flat ground* is such an effective tool to use to figure out a passage. While reading the above passage, take out everything that is not needed and condense it into a short sentence that includes the evidence and the conclusion.

If done properly, your short sentence should read something like this:

- Since global warming became a problem after the automobile was invented, it is clear that the automobile is the cause of global warming.

We have taken a complicated passage and condensed it into a short sentence, eliminating the useless information. This method uncovers the conclusion and evidence quickly and easily.

Now that we understand the conclusion and the evidence, let's look at the third element of an argument:

3. The assumption (s): This is what the author assumes to be true when formulating evidence for the conclusion. We will discuss how to identify an assumption a bit later.

Although only one type of Critical Reasoning question specifically asks you to identify the assumption, this step is an important part of understanding the argument itself, and is therefore crucial to answering any of the critical reasoning questions.

Brandon's Tip

So, what exactly is an assumption? An assumption is anything the author assumes is true and uses to support the argument. This assumption is often pertinent to the validity of the argument, and if proven to be untrue, would completely destroy the entire argument.

Let's look at our argument about the Earth being flat. We've already determined that the evidence the author uses to support the argument is the fact that it looks flat. So, what is the assumption behind the author's decision to use this particular piece of evidence? To answer this question, ask yourself why the evidence supports the conclusion, and put your answer in statement form so that it looks like this:

- The evidence supports the conclusion because _____.

Your answer to this question will be the assumption of the argument. In our example, the statement will read:

- The fact that the Earth looks flat supports the argument that the Earth is flat

The assumption behind the argument is the idea that what something looks like and what it actually is are always the same. Of course, anyone who has ever heard the expression, "don't judge a book by its cover," or has discovered that a seemingly loyal friend has betrayed him knows that this isn't true; nevertheless, it is the assumption that this particular argument is based on. Assumptions do not have to be true, but the strength of the argument will depend on the believability of the assumption(s) behind it.

Some of the arguments on the GMAT will have more than one assumption. Let's look at another example:

3-D movies draw in twice as many audience members as their standard counterparts even though they are more expensive. Robots from Outer Space is a 3-D movie. It will make twice as much money as Monkeys of Madrid despite the bad economy.

Let's use our technique to determine the underlying assumptions of the argument.

First, we must identify the conclusion and evidence. Remember, the conclusion is what the author is trying to prove. Despite the absence of keywords, it is clear that the author wants you to believe that the 3-D movie Robots from Outer Space will make twice as much money as Monkeys from Madrid despite the bad economy. To support this claim, the author provides the following evidence;

- Robots from Outer Space is a 3-D movie.

- 3-D movies draw in twice as many audience members as their standard counterparts even though they are more expensive.

To determine the assumptions that this argument is based on, we must ask ourselves why the evidence supports the claim. In other words, what else has to be true in order for this argument to make sense. Let's fill in the blank.

The fact that 1) Robots from Outer Space is a 3-D movie and 2) 3-D movies draw in twice as many audience members as their standard counterparts even though they are more expensive supports the argument that Robots from Outer Space will make twice as much money as Monkeys from Madrid despite the bad economy because: _____.

That's a mouthful and probably wouldn't pass a grammar check, but it serves our purpose of identifying the hidden assumptions. Here, you should have filled in the blank with some variation of the following:

The fact that 1) Robots from Outer Space is a 3-D movie and 2) 3-D movies draw in twice as many audience members as their standard counterparts even though they are more expensive supports the argument that Robots from Outer Space will make twice as much money as Monkeys from Madrid despite the bad economy because: 1) The dimension of the movie is the only factor one considers when deciding which one to watch and 2) The economy has no effect on how much money one is willing to spend on a movie ticket.

Now that we have covered the scope of the questions and how they can be broken up into smaller bits to help you to make an informed decision, we will move on to the types of critical reasoning questions that you will be asked on the GMAT.

Assumption Questions

The first type of question is the assumption question. In this type of question, the author makes an assumption about something, and it is up to you to select the best of the answers provided based on that assumption.

Assumption questions are often presented in one of the following ways:

- *Which of the following is an assumption...*

- *The argument depends on which of the following assumptions?*

- *The conclusion drawn above is based on the assumption that...*

- *The conclusion above is properly drawn if which of the following is assumed?*

First, find anything that goes beyond the scope of the argument. Often, each argument is written within a narrow set of parameters. The wrong answers go beyond these simple parameters.

Second, wrong answers to assumption questions often use extreme language that goes beyond the claim of the author.

Lastly, wrong answers do not support the argument. Remember, an assumption must support the argument, and an assumption must be true for the argument to be valid.

To determine where the author is going with the assumption, ask yourself the following 3 questions;

1. Which of the following, if added to the passage, makes the conclusion more valid?

2. Which of the following does the author assume?

3. The validity of the argument depends on which of the following?

Let's look at a few examples.

The class action suit against Walkers claims that the company failed to give its employees adequate break times. Since it is true that workers were only allowed a thirty minute break for every six hours of labor, the class action suit is more than justified. After all, it takes more than half an hour to get in one's car, drive to the nearest restaurant, stand in line, and get back to Walkers.

The argument above is based on which of the following assumptions:

A. *Most people bring their lunches to work because leaving the office for lunch is so time-consuming.*

B. *The amount of time an employee gets for a break should be based upon the total amount of time it takes to go out for lunch.*

C. *Laws are in place that mandate that employers give their employees at least an hour break for every six hours worked.*

D. *Employers should always follow company policy when deciding upon break times; location of nearby restaurants and personal employee preferences should not be a factor.*

E. *Since so many employees decided to be a part of the class action suit, it must be a valid claim.*

The author's argument here that the class action suit against Walkers regarding break times is a valid one since the workers barely have enough time to go out to lunch and return before their thirty minute break is up. Since the only piece of evidence the author presents is the amount of time it takes one of Walker's employees to go get take-out, we have to assume that this is the underlying assumption of the argument. If there was any doubt, a look at the other choices should confirm B to be the correct choice:

A. Most people bring their lunches to work because leaving the office for lunch is so time-consuming.

Eliminating this first choice should have been a no-brainer. Since the main piece of evidence the author uses deals with the amount of time it takes to go *out* for lunch, this statement regarding the number of people who prefer to eat in is in direct opposition to the author's claim.

C. Laws are in place that mandate that employers give their employees at least an hour break for every six hours worked.

This choice is tempting because if it were true, it would certainly strengthen the argument, but remember, this is not a strengthen question, it's an assumption one. Since this information is not even mentioned in the argument, it cannot possibly be the basis for the argument,

D. Employers should always follow company policy when deciding upon break times; location of nearby restaurants and personal employee preferences should not be a factor.

This option also opposes the author's claim. The purpose of the passage is to explain why Walker's is legitimately being sued; this choice supports Walker's company policy and can be immediately eliminated.

E. Since so many employees decided to be a part of the class action suit, it must be a valid claim.

This option goes beyond the scope of the argument. There is no mention of how many people are part of the class action suit; therefore, it cannot possibly be the foundation for the argument.

> ➤ **More Practice from the GMAT® Review 13th Edition:** Questions 41, 48, 77, 83, 96

Strengthening and Weakening Questions

These are the most common types of critical reasoning questions that you will face on the GMAT. Obviously, these questions are pretty easy to understand. You need to analyze what may strengthen or weaken the argument made by the author. As with the previous type of question, and any other critical thinking question on the GMAT, breaking the passage apart is the first step.

Strengthen questions are often presented in one of the following ways:

- *Which of the following, if true, most strongly justifies the claim...*

- *Which of the following, if true, provides the most support for the argument above?*

- *Which of the following, if true, would most strengthen the conclusion drawn?*

- *Which of the following, if true, provides the strongest grounds for...*

Weaken questions are often presented in one of the following ways:

- *Which of the following, if true, most seriously weakens the argument above?*

- *Which of the following, if true, most seriously calls into question...*

- *Which of the following, if true, casts the most serious doubt on the argument above?*

- *Which of the following, if true, most strongly indicates that the logic of the prediction is flawed?*

When trying to strengthen the argument, pick out the choice that will best fill in the key assumption and give it more merit. When you want to weaken an argument, pick the choice that will undercut the key assumption.

Let's look at an example:

The claim that fast food contributes to obesity is simply absurd. I personally eat fast food every day and am well within the normal range for weight and body mass index. As long as you exercise regularly and eat fast food in moderate portions, there's no reason to worry about fast food restaurants making you gain weight.

Which of the following, if true, would strengthen the argument above?

- A. *People who eat out three times a week are no more obese than those who eat at home.*

- B. *Fast food restaurants have recently made an attempt to offer healthier choices.*

C. *Research shows that exercise and moderation are the most im-portant factors in maintaining a healthy weight—more important even than the kinds of food one eats.*

D. *Some people abstain from fast food but are still obese.*

E. *Some fast food is actually healthier than home-cooked meals.*

The author concludes that since he has a normal weight and BMI and eats fast food every day, then fast food does not cause obesity. He goes on to say that as long as one eats in moderation and exercises, then fast food will not have an impact on his/her weight. Although his personal experience with fast food is not enough to make such a broad generalization, if it is true that research has proven that exercise *and moderation are more important factors than the nutritional value of the food one eats, then his claim is valid.* Answer C is correct.

Now, let's look at the other choices:

A. *People who eat out three times a week are no more obese than those who eat at home.*

This choice introduces weak, anecdotal evidence that lacks the specific details needed to strengthen the argument. We have no clue who these people are, where they are eating out three times a week, what portion sizes they're consuming, or whether or not they exercise. Therefore, this "evidence" proves nothing in relation to the potential impact of fast food on weight.

B. *Fast food restaurants have recently made an attempt to offer healthier choices.*

Again, this choice lacks the detail and specificity needed to strengthen the argument. It may be true that fast food restaurants are making attempts to offer healthier choices, but we don't know how healthy they are, whether consumers are taking advantage of these options, and if they are being consumed in moderation or in conjunction with adequate exercise. Therefore, this detail has no bearing on the argument in question.

D. Some people abstain from fast food but are still obese.

This choice offers a faulty comparison. Just because some obese people eat things other than fast food doesn't mean that fast food cannot have an impact on weight.

E. Some fast food is actually healthier than home-cooked meals.

Even if this is true, we have no way of inferring from the statement which types of fast food are healthier. Furthermore, just because some types are healthier does not mean that fast food in general does not cause obesity. This choice is much too vague to impact the argument.

Now, consider this question:

The "Kids' Night" promotion at Burgers-n-More, a local fast food restaurant, has been a huge success. The last time I visited the restaurant on Kids' Night, the place was packed with parents looking to get a free meal for their children. This promotion will no doubt increase Burgers-n-More's overall profits.

Which of the following, if true, would most seriously damage the argument above?

A. *Burgers-n-More gives out an average of 150 free meals during each Kids Night.*

B. *More parents attend Pizza King on Kids Night than Burgers-n-More.*

C. *The same total number of patrons visit Burgers-n-More now as before the promotion began, but more come on Kids Night to take advantage of the promotion.*

D. *In a recent survey, kids reported that they prefer Burgers-n-More to any other fast food restaurant.*

E. *Burgers-n-More recently stopped promoting its Kids Night on the local radio station.*

The author concludes that the Kids Night promotion will increase the overall profits of Burgers-n-More. Although there are no key words that indicate this is the conclusion, it is what the author wants you to believe. It has not happened yet – the author uses the word *will* - so there can be no concrete evidence. From the author's perspective, the more parents that buy food from the restaurant, the higher the profits for Burgers-n-More.

But, of course, things aren't always that simple. There are other factors that could influence the success of the promotion. For instance, if the promotion is simply steering its regular customers to visit the restaurant on a certain night when free food is available, rather than drawing in new customers, as proposed by choice C, then that would seriously weaken the author's argument...and Burgers-n-More's bottom line. Choice C is correct. Let's examine the other choices:

A. *Burgers-n-More gives out an average of 150 free meals during each Kids Night.*

Although that does seem like a lot of free food to be giving away, we can't derive a conclusion from this fact alone. We don't know how many adult meals, soft drinks, or other profit-makers the restaurant sold in addition to giving away the free kids meals.

B. *More parents attend Pizza King on Kids Night than Burgers-n-More.*

This is a classic case of a faulty comparison thrown in as a distraction. Although it doesn't sound good for Burgers-n-More that parents prefer Pizza King's promotion, that doesn't eliminate the possibility that Burgers-n-More's Kids Night is increasing its own profit margins.

D. *In a recent survey, kids reported that they prefer Burgers-n-More to any other fast food restaurant.*

You probably eliminated this choice first as it seems to strengthen rather than weaken the argument. Keep in mind, though, that just because kids report that they prefer a restaurant doesn't mean their parents plan on taking them there. This answer neither weakens nor strengthens the conclusion.

E. *Burgers-n-More recently stopped promoting its Kids Night on the local radio station.*

Although it would stand to reason that the more publicity the promotion received, the more patrons would attend the promotion, we have no proof of how effective the radio promotion was in increasing sales. Therefore, it is not the best choice.

➢ **More Practice from the GMAT® Review 13th Edition:** Questions 11, 23, 40, 67, 118 (strengthen)

➢ **More Practice from the GMAT® Review 13th Edition:** Questions 25, 32, 37, 58, 62 (weaken)

Flaw Questions

Flaw questions ask about the structure of the argument, rather than the topic. They look at the way terms are defined, the way the premises support the conclusion, or omissions made by the author.

Flaw questions are often presented in one of the following ways:

* *The argument is flawed in that it ignores the possibility of...*

* *Which of the following points is the most serious logical flaw in the argument?*

* *The argument is most vulnerable to criticism on which of these grounds?*

* *The argument is most vulnerable to the objection that it fails to...*

Do not confuse flaw questions with weakening questions. Although they may seem similar, in weakening questions you are supposed to find additional information to weaken the argument if it is true. In a flaw question, the evidence is not very supportive of the conclusion, and you as the test taker must explain why.

As usual, break up the argument to find out how best to determine why it is flawed.

Here is an example:

Proponents of the law against texting and driving attribute up to 20 percent of all accidents to sending text messages while operating a motor vehicle. This alarming statistic must be true since many accidents are caused by teenagers, and adolescents text more than any other segment of the population.

Which of the following indicates the most serious flaw in the author's reasoning?

    A. He clearly has a moral issue with the teenage population.

    B. He does not take into consideration other possible causes of teen accidents.

    C. He doesn't include information about why texting causes accidents.

    D. There are no specific examples to support his claim.

    E. He fails to acknowledge the rights of teenagers.

The author makes the argument that since many accidents are caused by teenagers, and teenagers text more than any other age group, then texting must be to blame for 20% of all accidents. This sweeping overgeneralization fails to mention other causes of teenage accidents, which is the major flaw of the argument, as indicated in option B.

Let's analyze the other choices:

A. He clearly has a moral issue with the teenage population.

Although it may seem that the author is biased against teenagers, he makes no comment that could be construed as a moral criticism.

C. He doesn't include information about why texting causes accidents.

Although information about why texting causes accidents may be helpful, it would do nothing to prove or disprove the argument - that texting causes 20% of accidents.

D. There are no specific examples to support his claim.

Specific examples are not necessary for statistical claims. Stories about individual car accidents would do nothing to support the argument.

E. *He fails to acknowledge the rights of teenagers.*

Although it may be true that the author doesn't address the rights of teenagers, this is an irrelevant observation since it has no impact on the basic assumption of the argument- that texting is to blame for a fifth of all accidents.

Here's another…

There is definitely not a behavior problem at Gateview High School as implied in the editorial in yesterday's newspaper. I am an Honors student at GHS and take all advanced classes, so you can take it from me when I say that the kids in my class pay attention and work really hard. In fact, all my friends are so concerned with earning high grades that we don't have time to misbehave.

Which of the following statements best reveals the absurdity of the above argument?

    A. *It is a personal account and therefore offers a narrow point of view.*

    B. *The author attends the high school in question and is therefore biased, making her argument invalid.*

    C. *Since the author is admittedly enrolled in all upper-level courses, she is only aware of the behavior of the most advanced students at her school.*

    D. *The author bases her argument only on her own behavior, not the behavior of her classmates.*

    E. *The author is clearly misrepresenting the truth since all high schools have some sort of behavior problem.*

The author of this passage argues that since none of the students in her advanced classes at Gateview High School misbehave, then there is not a behavior problem at the school. Because this student has classes with only the top-performing students at the school, she is not in the position to make such a broad statement about Gateview's overall student population. Therefore, C is the correct choice.

Let's look at the other choices:

A. It is a personal account and therefore offers a narrow point of view.

This answer is very similar to the correct answer and is therefore, tempting. However, a close examination of the wording reveals its inaccuracy. The use of the word "therefore" in the answer selection states that the point of view in the argument is too narrow *because* it is a personal ac-count. This is not true. Since the author of the passage attends the high school, her personal account would be valid if she attended regular classes at the school. It is her enrollment in *only* upper level classes that limits her perspective, not the fact that her argument is a personal account.

B. The author attends the high school in question and is therefore biased, making her argument invalid.

Although it is true that the author may be biased toward the school since she is a student there, there is nothing in the passage itself that implies bi-as, and it is not the *major* flaw of the argument.

D. The author bases her argument only on her own behavior, not the be-havior of her classmates.

We can immediately eliminate this answer choice on the basis that it is simply not true. Although the author does reference her own behavior, she also talks about the behavior of her classmates.

E. The author is clearly misrepresenting the truth since all high schools have some sort of behavior problem

A careful reader will have no problem eliminating this answer either since it is an opinion statement, is not based on the argument, and makes a gross over-generalization—that "all high schools" have behavior problems.

> ➢ **More Practice from the GMAT® Review 13th Edition:** Ques-tions 2, 8, 20, 51, 100

Inference Questions

There will be a few inference questions on the test. These questions do not require you to distinguish the evidence from the conclusion when you read the passage. In fact, the entire passage consists of evidence and your task is to select a proper conclusion.

Inference questions are often presented in one of the following ways:

- *Which of the following conclusions can be most properly drawn from the information above?*

- *Which of the following most logically completes the passage below?*

- *If the statements above are true, which of the following must be true?*

- *The statements, if true, best support which of the following as a conclusion?*

Let's look at a few sample questions.

When people experiment with hard drugs such as cocaine or heroin, there is no certainty that they have also tried softer drugs such as marijuana. There are a great many factors that could lead a person to experiment with hard drugs. Nevertheless, many opponents of legalizing marijuana claim that it is a gateway drug, one that leads its users to try progressively more dangerous substances.

If the statements above are true, which of the following must be true?

A. *If marijuana were legalized, drug use in general would become a bigger problem.*

B. *If a person abstains from marijuana use, he or she will not try other, more serious drugs either.*

C. *Preventing a young person from trying marijuana increases the likelihood that he'll try other drugs.*

D. *A decrease in marijuana use would cause a decline in other types of drug use as well.*

E. *Marijuana is sometimes inaccurately determined to be the cause of hard drug use.*

The main idea of the passage is that marijuana use contributes to the likelihood that a person will try other, more serious drugs. It does not argue that this is the only contributing factor, however. This distinction is important and can help us in eliminating some of the wrong answers. Let's take a look:

A. If marijuana were legalized, drug use in general would become a bigger problem.

Although the passage does indicate that some people believe marijuana use leads people to try other drugs, the passage also indicates that this is not always the case. There are too many factors that the passage does not discuss to be able to draw such a conclusion.

B. If a person abstains from marijuana use, he or she will not try other, more serious drugs either.

This answer choice is also too extreme. Although the author implies that abstaining from marijuana can decrease the likelihood that a person will try other drugs, he does not rule out the possibility of other contributing factors that may cause a person to try other drugs.

C. Preventing a young person from trying marijuana increases the likelihood that he will try other drugs.

This option was probably the first one you eliminated because it directly contradicts the argument offered in the passage. The passage implies that preventing a person from trying marijuana will decrease, not increase, the likelihood that he will try other drugs.

D. A decrease in marijuana use would cause a decline in other types of drug use as well.

This statement is too broad a generalization to make from the argument presented in the passage. As we already mentioned, the author does not rule out the possibility of other factors that may contribute to drug use; therefore, we cannot state that a decrease in marijuana use would necessarily decrease drug use in general because we cannot control these other factors.

E. Marijuana is sometimes inaccurately determined to be the cause of hard drug use.

The passage says that there are many causes of hard drug use, and that prior marijuana use is not a certainty despite the tendency of some people to believe it is. Therefore, this is a valid conclusion.

Here's another inference question:

Preschool children are the targets of most of the advertisements run during morning and daytime television. In fact, some of the most successful ad campaigns are those directed towards small children. Corporations spend millions of dollars per year creating commercials that appeal to children under the age of five. More often than not, this is money well-spent and contributes to mass profits for these companies.

If the statements in the passage above are true, which of the following must also be true?

   A. *When children see an item advertised on a commercial that immediately precedes their favorite television show, they are much more likely to express a desire for this item.*

   B. *Childhood obesity rates will rise in proportion with the number of fast food commercials run during morning and prime time hours.*

   C. *Children who are easily influenced by television commercials will make poor financial decisions as adults.*

   D. *Parents and other caregivers sometimes give in to children's demands for items advertised on television.*

   E. *Parents will be able to save more money per month if they limit the amount of television their children are allowed to watch during morning and prime time hours.*

The author of this passage makes the case that commercials targeted towards preschool children are very successful and result in big profits for corporations. Since children of this age are not capable of earning money or going to the store themselves to purchase items they've seen on television, it stands to reason that parents and caregivers must be giving in to their children's demands. Therefore, D is the correct answer.

Now, let's examine the other choices and use some of our strategies to eliminate them:

A. When children see an item advertised on a commercial that immediately precedes their favorite television show, they are much more likely to express a desire for this item.

This choice is too specific to be the correct answer. Although the argument does say that children are influenced by commercials played during certain hours, it says nothing of the timing of certain commercials in relation to a child's favorite shows. In addition, to say the commercials that *precede* are more effective is unsupported. They could be during or after.

B. Childhood obesity rates will rise in proportion with the number of fast food commercials run during morning and prime time hours.

Remember, one of our strategies is to eliminate answer selections that go beyond the scope of the text; this is one of those choices. The passage says nothing of childhood obesity rates and does not provide enough information related to fast food commercials or nutritional values in order to make this inference.

C. Children who are easily influenced by television commercials will make poor financial decisions as adults.

Again, this selection goes way beyond the scope of the passage and can be eliminated immediately. Remember, even if you agree with the answer choice and believe it to be true, do not let this influence your choice. Stick to the text!

E. Parents will be able to save more money per month if they limit the amount of television their children are allowed to watch during morning and prime time hours.

This choice is much too broad to be the correct answer. Although it is loosely tied to the subject of the argument, it is not well-supported by the passage. There are way too many other factors influencing a family's ability to save money to make such a claim. It also assumes that all parents give in to their children's demands for items they've seen on television, and the strategies we've learned tell us to eliminate such over-generalizations.

> ➢ **More Practice from the GMAT® Review 13th Edition:** Questions 26, 38, 66, 91, 103

Explanation Questions

These questions are completely different from the other types of questions for the very reason that they present no argument. Instead, the passage, which usually contains the argument, will describe a situation with two or more contradictory facts. Answering the question means explaining how the two contradictory facts can actually be true. You will find that incorrect answer choices typically touch upon only one fact, make the decision even more ambiguous, make a pointless comparison, or fail to address the scope.

Explanation questions are often presented in one of the following ways:

* *Which of the following, if true, would most help to explain...*

- *Which of the following, if true, does the most to explain…*

Here's an example:

Parental education initiatives and social programs designed to boost a child's chances for proper brain development are at an all-time high. Even so, there are more cases of children with learning disabilities today than there were twenty years ago.

Which of the following, if true, contributes most to an explanation for the apparent contradiction noted above?

A. *Brain disorders among the elderly are also on the rise.*

B. *Teachers are better equipped to handle children with learning dis-abilities today than they were twenty years ago.*

C. *Increased awareness of learning disabilities has led to an increase in diagnosed cases.*

D. *Children with learning disabilities have more opportunities than ever before.*

E. *Parents let their kids watch too much TV these days.*

The passage introduces the contradiction that despite increased efforts to promote proper brain development amongst children, there are still many more children with learning disabilities today than there were twenty years ago. Choice C is the only answer that explains this contradiction in a logical way, noting that along with prevention efforts, there have also been campaigns to increase awareness of learning disabilities, which has no doubt led to an increase in diagnosed cases.

Now, let's look at the other choices and analyze why they are wrong:

A. Brain disorders among the elderly are also on the rise.

This answer choice goes outside the scope of the issue presented in the passage. We are not concerned with the rise in brain disorders amongst the elderly, unless it somehow explains the rise in learning disabilities in children, which it does not, at least not by this answer choice.

B. Teachers are better equipped to handle children with learning disabilities today than they were twenty years ago.

This statement, although it may be true and is certainly interesting, is also irrelevant. The fact that teachers are better prepared to teach learning-disabled children does nothing to explain the rise in prevalence.

D. Children with learning disabilities have more opportunities than ever before.

This option is very similar to the previous one, a clue that neither of them are right, since you can only pick one. Again, the statement may be true, but it does not explain why learning disabilities have become more common.

E. Parents let their kids watch too much TV these days.

This choice is very tempting since it's easy to assume that watching too much TV can cause learning disabilities. Even if this assumption could be proven, it is not stated in the answer choice. Remember not to assume too much, especially when choosing amongst possible answers. The use of the phrase "too much" is also vague and subjective, making this option much too general to be the correct choice.

Let's look at another explanation question:

Seventy-five percent of customers surveyed on Food-Mart's coupon site reported that they would only purchase a full-price item at Food-Mart if they also had a coupon for that item. However, on an average day, Food-Mart sells more non-sale items without coupons than with coupons.

If the above statements are true, which of the following best explains the apparent discrepancy?

A. *The people surveyed on Food-Mart's coupon site are not representative of the average Food-Mart customer.*

B. *Food-Mart only redeems coupons at face-value whereas their competitor doubles coupons on Wednesdays.*

C. *The local economy has experienced a setback and Food-Mart's overall sales have declined slightly.*

D. *More sale items are purchased on an average day at Food-Mart than non-sale items.*

E. *Customers who spend more than $100 per shopping trip are less likely to use coupons than those spending less than $100.*

The author makes the argument that a paradox exists between the results of the survey on Food-Mart's coupon site and the actual amount of coupons used on non-sale items. The critical issue that he fails to address is that the customers who would take a survey on the coupon site are much more likely to use coupons than the average customer. Therefore, the survey is not a reliable indicator of overall coupon usage. This is the missing link that explains the discrepancy. Thus, A is the correct answer.

Now let's examine the wrong answers:

B. Food-Mart only redeems coupons at face-value whereas their competitor doubles coupons on Wednesdays.

This is a classic case of the kind of faulty comparisons often found in incorrect answer choices. The passage speaks only of coupons used at Food-Mart; therefore, the information about Food-Mart's competitor is irrelevant.

C. The local economy has experienced a setback and Food-Mart's overall sales have declined slightly.

You probably eliminated this choice first since it not only fails to explain the discrepancy, it complicates it further. If the economy is faltering, it would stand to reason that more people would use coupons, especially on non-sale items.

D. More sale items are purchased on an average day at Food-Mart than non-sale items.

This answer selection goes beyond the scope of the argument. The issue here is how many non-sale items are purchased with and without coupons. A comparison between the sales of full-price and sale items is irrelevant.

E. Customers who spend more than $100 per shopping trip are less likely to use coupons than those spending less than $100.

Since this selection fails to mention the major focus of the argument—coupon usage as it pertains to non-sale items—it cannot possibly explain the apparent paradox.

> **More Practice from the GMAT® Review 13ᵗʰ Edition:** Questions: 17, 24, 57, 61, 94

Evaluate Questions

The last type of question that you will find on the GMAT is an evaluate question. These will contain evidence and a conclusion, but the task you have to complete can vary a lot from question to question, Sometimes you will need to analyze the evidence for flaws or assumptions, sometimes you will need to think about what is missing from the argument, and sometimes you will need to analyze the structure of the argument. It is important that you read the question carefully and understand the task before you jump into the answers.

Evaluate questions are often presented in one of the following ways:

- *In evaluating the argument, it would be most useful to...*

- *Which of the following would it be most useful to determine in order to evaluate the argument?*

- *For purposes of evaluating the argument, it would be most useful to establish which of the following?*

- *Which of the following must be studied in order to evaluate the argument presented above?*

Here's an example:

For similar food products within a single grocery store, brand names items have always cost more than the generic items have. However, market research indicates that the cost of the ingredients that are used to make brand name and generic items are identical. Therefore, companies that manufacture brand name food products have a greater profit margin than do companies that manufacture generic food products.

In evaluating the argument it would be most useful to compare

A.   *the average quantity of brand name items compared to generic items over a certain time period*

B.   *labor and equipment costs for the two different types of companies*

C.   *the sale prices of similar food items in other grocery store chains*

D.   *consumer preferences for brand name items over generic items for certain food products*

E.   *the profit margins for brand name and generic household goods*

The evidence is that the prices between the two items are different, with brand name prices being higher. Since the cost of ingredients is the same, the author wants you to believe that the difference in price represents profit for the brand name companies. However, there may be other factors that affect profit margins. Answer B brings in some of those other factors. If labor and equipment costs are the same for brand name and generic companies, then the extra revenue is more likely to represent a profit.

Now, let's look at the other choices and analyze why they are wrong:

A. the average quantity of brand name items compared to generic items over a certain time period

This answer is tempting because if more generic items are sold than brand name items, the generic companies may earn more money in the long run. However, the conclusion drawn is about *profit margin*, not overall profits. Profit margin is only concerned with the "per item" revenue and cost. This answer will not help you evaluate the argument.

C. the sale prices of similar food items in other grocery store chains

If you examine the prices in other grocery store chains, you bring in a new variable. There could be other factors that influence prices in different grocery store chains. To evaluate whether an argument is logical, you should keep as many variables constant as possible.

D. consumer preferences for brand name items over generic items for certain food products

Consumer preferences are not linked closely enough not to profit margin. Preferences do influence how much a company can charge for item, but this answer is similar to the other wrong answers in that it brings in other variables and is more relevant to overall profits than profit margin.

E. the profit margins for brand name and generic household goods

Profit margins for household goods are not relevant to profit margins for food products.

Let's look at another evaluate question:

After the city of Bellingham installed more than 40 new bicycle lanes on major streets at the request of the citizens, the administration expected to see a sharp decrease in morning traffic congestion since the citizens now had a safe and cheaper alternative than driving their cars to work. That expectation was clearly unfounded. A survey of more than 1,000 citizens in Bellingham revealed no significant change in morning driving behavior.

Which of the following would be most useful to determine in order to evaluate the argument?

    A. *Did the citizens surveyed drive a lot in the mornings already?*

    B. *Do the citizens who tend to drive in the afternoons, rather than mornings, drive less now than they did before?*

    C. *What types of vehicles are driven by the citizens who were surveyed?*

    D. *Do the citizens surveyed bike more now that they did before?*

    E. *Did the citizens specify the reason they wanted the bicycle paths?*

The author makes the argument that the city administration should not have expected a decrease in morning traffic despite all the bicycle lanes. The bicycle lanes built at the request of the citizens, so one would expect the citizens to use the bike lanes. However, the evidence never indicates for what exact purpose the citizens wanted the lanes. If the reason were known, you would be able to evaluate the argument to determine whether the conclusion is logical. The correct answer is E.

Now let's examine the wrong answers:

A. Did the citizens surveyed drive a lot in the mornings already?

The level of traffic prior to the availability of bicycle lanes is not relevant because a *sharp decrease* is relative to whatever level previously existed.

B. Do the citizens who tend to drive in the afternoons, rather than mornings, drive less now than they did before?

Knowing whether the bicycle lanes had their intended effect on afternoon traffic does not help you evaluate an argument that draws a conclusion about morning traffic.

C. What types of vehicles are driven by the citizens who were surveyed?

The type of vehicle is only loosely linked to the argument. You could rationalize this answer by thinking about the cost of gasoline and whether biking to work is really necessary for owners of fuel-efficient cars, but you would be getting to far away from the given information. Remember that the question specifies *most useful* and answer E is definitely more tightly linked to the argument than is this choice.

D. Do the citizens surveyed bike more now that they did before?

This question does not specify the time of day, so it is not helpful in evaluating an argument whose conclusion is about morning traffic.

> **More Practice from the GMAT® Review 13ᵗʰ Edition:** Questions: 15, 27, 36, 47, 70

Things to Remember...

- **Pay attention to the assumption, evidence, and conclusion for each question.** The questions are likely to be long and have complicated sentence structures. Don't let that distract you from understanding the argument presented by the question. The conclusion should be supported by factual evidence, while the assumptions need to be true if the conclusion and the entire argument are to be solid.

- **All facts not stated in the question should be treated as assumptions.** Remember that the GMAT does not require you to have knowledge in any specific field, and you shouldn't have to use any knowledge/facts related to specific fields when answering any questions. Therefore, treat any knowledge that you obtained outside of the test as assumptions that need to be qualified before you can use them as facts when answering questions.

- **How do you know if an assumption is necessary?** One quick way to find out is by denying the assumption and determining whether the argument still holds. If the argument falls apart, the assumption is necessary and cannot be omitted or changed.

- **On questions regarding percentages and ratios, be careful not to confuse ratios with numbers and quantities.** If ratios confuse you, assigning actual numbers to the ratios may help. For example, if the question says "56% of American people," first assume that the entire population consists of 100 million people and then convert "56% of American people" into "56 million American people." Be careful of the new assumption that you made, and make sure that it does not conflict with the statements in the question.

- **Pay extra attention when presented with a survey or with research,** as these often test you on how to draw the correct conclusion from them. Examine all assumptions carefully and make sure that the groups represented in the results are comparable.

- **Watch for a question that changes the scope of an argument.** The question may draw general conclusions about an entire group from a specific smaller group. Be careful about generalization.

- **Make sure that you understand the difference between causation and correlation.** Correlation indicates that a relationship exists between two things but it does not specify cause and effect. Just because something happens before another does not automatically make it the cause. Also keep in mind that sometimes one piece of evidence can be the cause for multiple possible outcomes, and one particular outcome can have more than one cause. For example, consider this argument:

More ice creams are sold on sunny days. More children drown in the sea on sunny days. Therefore eating ice cream causes drowning.

This is incorrect and is an example of mistaken correlation for causation. In this case, both the increase in ice creams sold and the increase in drowning are results of the warm weather. The increase in ice cream sold and drowning are two correlated events, but one does not cause the other to happen.

GMAT MATH

GMAT Math

If you are planning on applying to and attending a graduate business school, you are probably familiar with the vast majority of the math concepts that you will see on the Quantitative section of the GMAT. In fact, if you went to junior high school in the United States, you have probably studied this kind of math at some time in the past. The Quantitative section of the GMAT largely tests your knowledge of arithmetic (approx. 50 percent of all questions), algebra (25 percent or so), and geometry (generally less than 15 percent). There are a few more specialized concepts that make up the final 10 percent or so but you can prepare for them as well with targeted study on specific topics. Mastering the less-difficult questions for mastery will take you a long way toward acing the GMAT.

In short - the math content of the GMAT is not as difficult as you may think. You'll probably find that a review of the main question topics and formats will go a long way toward increasing your comfort level with these sections. Certain types of questions come up on every test. Since the makers of the GMAT strive to standardize scoring from one test to the next, you'll see the same question types expressed the same way each time. **Becoming familiar with the predictable wording and phrasing of these question types will put you at a significant advantage** over those who have to figure everything out during the test.

Here are some question topics that you can expect from the Quantitative section of the GMAT, as well as some brief reminders that should help you brush up on the basic math skills that you'll see on test day:

- **Adding, subtracting, multiplying, and dividing**
  - Whole numbers
  - Fractions
  - Positive/negative numbers
- **Converting fractions to decimals and decimals to fractions**
- **Forming and solving basic algebraic expressions**
- **Calculating a percentage value using the percentage formula** (*Part = percent × whole*).
  - Example: What is 50 percent of 40?
  - Setup: Part = $\frac{50}{100} \times 40 = 20$

- **Calculating percent change.** $\frac{\text{difference}}{\text{original}} \times 100$. If a question asks by what percent a value increased, put the positive difference of the two values in the numerator, and the smaller of the two values in the denominator. If a question asks by what percent a value decreased, put the positive difference of the two values in the numerator, and the larger of the two values in the denominator.
- **Calculating a simple average.** Average = *sum of terms / number of terms*
- **Calculating certain measures for shapes:**
  - Rectangles/squares
    - area = length × width
    - perimeter = 2 × (length + width)
  - Triangles
    - area = $\frac{1}{2}$ (base × height)
    - perimeter = side A + side B + side C
  - Circles
    - area = πr^2
    - circumference = πd
- The remainder will consist of more difficult questions on topics such as **simple probabilities** and **standard deviations**. (Review

these topics only if you have extra time – remember: these make up less than 10 percent of the total questions)

Let's look at some of the most effective tools used to handle the types of math questions that you will encounter on the GMAT.

Brandon's Easy Reference Math Terminology

You probably learned these concepts back in school, but hey, that was a long time ago! The following is a quick recap of the terms you need to know for GMAT Math. If you have trouble with any of these terms, write them down in your notebook so you can review them right before your test.

Integer - also known as a whole number. It may be positive or negative but it must be whole. 0 is considered an even integer.

A **Prime Number** (or a **Prime**) is a number that can only be divided by itself and the number 1. The first 10 prime numbers are 2, 3, 5, 7, 11, 13, 17, 19, 23, and 29. Note that 1 is not prime.

A **multiple** is the result of multiplication. 12 is a multiple of 3. Every number is a multiple of itself.

A **factor** is any number that can be divided into another and will give an integer result. 3 is a factor of 12. Every number is a factor of itself.

An **Exponent** is also known as an **index** or **power**. It is written as a small number to the right and above the base number, and it tells you how many times the base number is to be multiplied by itself. For example $5^2 = 5 \times 5 = 25$.

A **Numerator** is the number in a fraction that lies above the divide line.

A **Denominator** is the number in a fraction that lies below the divide line.

To **Reduce a Fraction** means to reduce it to its lowest terms by factoring both the numerator and denominator with their common factors. For example $\frac{6}{63}$ can be reduced to its lowest term by dividing both the numerator and denominator by their common factor, 3. So 6 divided by 3 = 2 and 63 divided by 3 = 21. The fraction is reduced to $\frac{2}{21}$.

To **Cancel** is to eliminate a number, quantity, or term from both the numerator and denominator of a fraction, or from opposite sides of an equation, because they are common and equal.

A **Variable** is a lettered term. Commonly expressed as x, y and z. A variable can change while a numbered term is constant. (In the example of 3x, x is a variable but 3 must remain constant).

Reciprocals are two numbers that when multiplied together equal 1. Most reciprocals on the GMAT can be found by inverting the fraction (switching the numerator and the denominator upside down). $\frac{3}{4}$ is the reciprocal of $\frac{4}{3}$.

The **Mean**, also known as **average**, of a set of numbers is calculated by adding up the set, and dividing that sum by the number of members in the set. With the set 4, 10, 16, the mean would be calculated with the equation $\frac{4 + 10 + 16}{3} = 10.$

The **Median** of a set is the middle value for the set. If the numbers are placed in order, the middle number represents the median. If there two middle numbers (in an even number of data points), taking the average of the two middle numbers represents a median value.

The **Mode** is the number that occurs most often in a set of data. It is possible to have more than one mode in a set of data, although bimodal sets are generally not seen on the GMAT.

The **Standard Deviation** is a statistic that tells you how tightly, in a set of data, various examples are clustered around the mean. A small standard deviation would mean that the examples are closely bunched together. If they are spread out, then the standard deviation is large.

A **Polynomial** expression is made up of constants (numbers), variables (letters) and exponents, which are combined using addition, subtraction and multiplication signs. It has one or more summed terms. An example would be 2x -7x + 3, or 4yz + xy - 3.

A **Binomial** is an expression that consists of two terms, such as 2x + 2z

A **Vertex** is a corner or a point where lines meet. The plural form of vertex is **Vertices**. Triangles have 3 vertices and quadrilaterals have 4.

An **Isosceles Triangle** is a triangle which has two sides of equal length.

A **Hypotenuse** is the longest side of any right angled triangle and faces opposite the right angle.

The **Pythagorean Theorem** (also known as **Pythagoras' Theorem**)

In any right angled triangle, the length of the sides follow the following equation:

$$a^2 + b^2 = c^2$$

where c represents the length of the hypotenuse, and a and b represent the lengths of the other two sides.

An **Operation** is an action or procedure that changes the value or create a new value from one or more values. Addition, Subtraction, Multiplication, Division are basic operations.

A **Product** is the result of a multiplication.

A **Quotient** is the answer to a division problem or equation. The quotient of $20 \div 5$ is 4.

A **Rational** number is a number that can be written as a simple fraction (i.e. as a ratio). It can be an integer, a terminating decimal, or a repeating decimal.

An **Irrational** number is a number that cannot be written as a ratio or fraction. An example of this is Pi. π = 3.1415926535897932 (etc). Pi cannot be written as a simple (accurate) fraction or ratio. Rational and irrational numbers are not generally tested on the GMAT.

A **Real** number is a number between positive and negative infinity without imaginary component, and it is either a **Rational number** or an **Irrational number**. The GMAT does not test imaginary numbers.

The Three Techniques You Should Know

Some questions are not what they seem! Many times, there are quicker ways of getting the answer to a GMAT math question than actually going through the usual (and often much longer) steps required to solve the problem as stated in the question. The following are the three basic techniques that you should use for solving GMAT math questions:

1. **Backsolving**

2. **Assigning values**

3. **"Drawing" the questions (for word problems)**

We'll start with a brief discussion of each technique and follow up with some practical applications and practice problems to show you the technique in action. Once you understand how each one works, we'll explain which techniques work best with the standard question types. Spending time understanding how to match techniques with question types now will ensure that you'll have one more step to breeze through during the actual test.

1. Backsolving

Backsolving is the first technique that we'll review. This technique is most effective for questions that have a clearly stated equation that might be difficult to solve when using standard methods (complex fractions and exponents are two examples). Instead of digging in to the ugly equation, you'll essentially work around it. This technique involves testing the answer choices provided to you for a given question. Basically, you'll select one of the five answer choices and then plug that corresponding value into the question to see if the answer is correct. If it's not correct, you quickly eliminate that choice and pick another one.

The great part about this technique is that there are only five possible choices. You can usually narrow your choices down somewhat based on the equation or the possible choices. Even if you have no idea at all, you still have a 20 percent chance of getting the right answer when you pick one choice at random! Of course, you'll know that this technique has worked if the choice correctly solves the math problem. This is a simple and effective technique for maximizing your use of time during the GMAT.

Brandon's Tip

An additional time-saver: if the answer choices are concrete values (meaning not fractions, decimals, percents, or ratios), try the middle value, choice (C), first. Since the answer choices for GMAT math questions are given in ascending order, you will probably be able to determine whether you should next try values larger or smaller than the middle value. If that first value is right, move on to the next question. If the first value is wrong but you know to go higher or lower from that point, you've still effectively narrowed your choices down from five to two – and the chance that your total guess answer will be right goes from 20 percent to 50 percent. It's techniques like this that will raise your score to the next level.

Here's backsolving in action:

What is the value of x if:

$$\frac{x+1}{x+2} - \frac{x+2}{x-4} = 1$$

    A. *-2*

    B. *-1*

    C. *0*

    D. *1*

    E. *2*

Since 0 is often an easy value to plug in, and it just happens to be choice C, let's try that first. Solving for $x = 0$ gives us:

$$\frac{0+1}{0+2} - \frac{0+2}{0-4} = 1$$

$$\frac{1}{2} - \left(-\frac{1}{2}\right) = 1$$

$$\frac{1}{2} + \frac{1}{2} = 1$$

$$1 = 1$$

Choice (C), $x = 0$ is correct. Sure, you could have gone through the process of cross-multiplying these complex fractions and solving for x. In this case, that option would have taken you longer and also introduced the possibility of making a computational error that would have led you to the wrong value in the end.

Let's try another one.

Which x value results in the lowest value for y in the following equation?

$$\frac{1}{x} + \frac{1}{x}^{-3} = 5x + y$$

    A. $x = 2$

    B. $x = 4$

    C. $x = 7$

    D. $x = 10$

    E. $x = 11$

In this case, answer C might not be the best place to start. Because you are looking for the lowest value of *y*, solving for answer C won't tell you anything. You are comparing the answers to each other. Since they are sequential, start with the highest or lowest and compare what happens to *y* as you change the value of *x*. Let's start with $x = 2$.

$$\frac{1}{2} + \frac{1}{2}^{-3} = 5(2) + y$$

$$\frac{1}{2} + \frac{1}{8} = 10 + y$$

$$\frac{5}{8} - 10 = y$$

$$-9\frac{3}{8} = y$$

Now let's increase the value of x to 4.

$$\frac{1}{4} + \frac{1}{4}^3 = 5(4) + y$$

$$\frac{1}{2} + \frac{1}{64} = 20 + y$$

$$\frac{33}{64} - 20 = y$$

$$-19\frac{27}{64} = y$$

As you can see, the value of y has decreased. You can continue to solve for the remaining choices, but you can probably tell that as the value of x increases, the value of y continues to decrease. Therefore, choice E (x =11) is correct.

Backsolving isn't useful for all question types, but recognizing the times when it is your best option will be a big help during the actual test. In this particular question, you may have been able to tell that $5x$ was the most influential factor on y because it gets subtracted from the left side of the equation. The left side will always be positive, so you want $5x$ to be as large as possible to make y negative. You could have selected choice E immediately and moved on. However, if you aren't comfortable with that estimation, backsolving is a great tool.

> ➤ **More Practice from the GMAT® Review 13ᵗʰ Edition:** Questions 51, 55, 72, 74, 83

2. Assigning Values

The next technique for handling GMAT math questions is similar to backsolving in that you are trying to find the answer without directly solving the question. **Assigning values** is something that many people do as a natural part of their routine when standard problem solving doesn't work or will be too time-consuming. What is useful about this technique is recognizing that for some types of problems it's easier to skip the initial problem solving altogether and go directly to assigning values.

Basically, you'll assign specific values to undefined terms in these questions. That will allow you to perform a simple calculation and then look at the answer choices to see which one makes sense. For example, if the question asks about integers, pick a few strategically-chosen integers (maybe a negative integer, a positive integer, and zero) and plug them into the question. If the question is asking about fractions of some quantity, choose a quantity that is a common denominator of the fractions so that they're easier to deal with.

By seeing the result that you get with each value assigned, you'll have a much better idea of which choice is correct. This technique should make working with variables and unknowns much easier. With practice, you'll get better at knowing which values to use for different questions. Assigning values will not directly give you an answer but will help you understand the question better and make choosing an answer easier.

Here's a good example of a question stem that lends itself to assigning values:

If x and y are odd integers, which of the following is an even integer?

    A. x (x + 6)

B. *3x + 7y*

C. *(x + 4) (y - 6)*

D. *xy + 6*

E. *x (y - 4)*

Of course, you could simplify some of these by multiplying through the parentheses and grouping like variables, but assigning values makes quick work of these choices. The question stem offers a simple set up – x and y are odd integers. Let's choose the easiest ones to plug in: x=3 and y=5. Assigning these values yields:

F. *27*

G. *44*

H. *-7*

I. *21*

J. *3*

The only value that's even is (B), 9+35=44. This type of question should be one to solve quickly so that you can move on. Saving time on questions like these will give you the time cushion you need in case you run into a really difficult question later in the test.

To make sure that you're comfortable with this technique, let's try it out with another question stem that involves number properties but is a little more difficult. This is a classic question type where assigning values will help to narrow down the choices:

If $\frac{n}{4}$ is an even integer, what is the remainder when n is divided by 8?

   A. 0

   B. 1

   C. 2

   D. 3

   E. 4

There are a few ways that this problem could be approached – we're going to go through the simplest one. You know that $\frac{n}{4}$ is an even integer. That means that n divided by 4 is an even number that has no remainder. You may intuitively realize that n must be a multiple of 4, but we can work through it to identify WHICH multiples of 4 might work. First, you would assign values to n:

$n=2$ gives you $\quad \frac{2}{4} = \frac{1}{2}$

  (not an integer)

$n = 4$ gives you $\quad \frac{4}{4} = 1$

  (an ODD integer)

$n = 8$ *gives you* $\dfrac{8}{4} = 2$

(an EVEN integer)

$n = 16$ *gives you* $\dfrac{16}{4} = 4$

(an EVEN integer)

Once you've established that n needs to be a multiple of 8, you may intuitively know the answer due to number properties. We can confirm this idea by testing these values. Divide by 8 to find the remainder for both:

n=8

$\dfrac{8}{8} = 1$ *(remainder 0)*

n=16

$\dfrac{16}{8} = 2$ *(remainder 0)*

The number of values assigned initially is really an arbitrary number. You should substitute as many as it takes for you to feel comfortable with the numbers that result, but keep in mind that you do have a time constraint. If you have assigned multiple values already and don't think you are closer to an answer, make an educated guess and move on. Remember that the question may be experimental and not even count, and the next question may be easier for you to answer.

> **More Practice from the GMAT® Review 13th Edition:** Questions 81, 89, 91, 96, 123

3. Drawing the Question

The math required to answer word problems is usually easier than that needed for straight math problems, but the added language means that you need a clear understanding of the questions. Understanding the exact setup of GMAT questions and the precise question that they are asking are necessary keys to correctly answering these word problems.

You'll have scratch paper to use during the actual test so it's useful to practice **drawing the question** on a piece of paper while you prepare for the test. This will probably help you think clearly without getting tangled up in the words and sentences. Many complicated word problems can be converted into simple math problems by simply using this technique. To do this, carefully read the entire question and identify the variables. Pay special attention to the actual question stem which identifies that central variable that the question is addressing.

Draw a graphical representation of the situation on paper in order to give it a clear context and to fully conceptualize what's being asked. Finally, translate the question into a math problem by turning sentences into equations while using your visual representation as a guide. This technique is especially useful for questions related to geometry, ratio, speed, rate, distance, and volume. Let's take a look at one of these questions to show you what we mean:

Doug pays 25 percent of his income in taxes and 15 percent of the re-mainder on his car payment. What percent of his income does he spend on his car payment?

A. *11.25*

B. *11.50*

C. *12.25*

D. *12.75*

E. *13.25*

At first glance, this appears to be a more difficult problem than it actually is. Test writers know that people see word problems with percentages and get anxious. When you see a word problem, you should be reassured because you know that once you unwrap the actual equation that's buried in the words, it will likely be easier to solve than one that's given directly to you.

There are many ways to draw this out but one of the simpler ones is just as a box representing 100 percent of Doug's income. Once you do that, it's easier to visualize what will need to be calculated.

25% taxes   75% remaining income

(Car payment is 15% of this portion)

From this drawing, we can see that the question is really looking for us to solve this simplified question stem:

Doug's car payment is 15 percent of Doug's remaining income. Since we know that his remaining income is 75 percent of his total income, we can substitute that into the equation. In words, we get:

Doug's car payment is 15 percent of (75 percent of Doug's total income).

Doug's car payment = 15%(75% of x)

= 0.15(0.75x)

= 0.1125 = 11.25%

In the end, this question ends up being a very simple multiplication problem. There's really no trick to this technique. It's simply becoming proficient at translating the (sometimes confusing) words into an equation. The key is to not be intimidated and know that the test takers who can push through the uncertainty to the equation will be rewarded with a higher score. Let's try another one:

The amount of water in an aquarium is halved by draining 20 gallons of water from it. If q gallons of water are then added to the aquarium, how many gallons of water are in the aquarium?

   A. 20+q

   B. 40-q

   C. 40+q

   D. 2q – 40

E. *q-20*

The key to getting a good start to this question is really in the first sentence. Some test takers might translate that sentence into an equation:

$$x - 20 = \frac{1}{2}x$$

$$2x - 40 = x$$

x= 40 gallons in the aquarium to start

You might find it more intuitive to draw it out like this:

This shows clearly where the starting and current level of the aquarium (and the associated values) can be found. Once you've gotten that far, it's not difficult to take the extra step to show the addition of q gallons into the tank:

This gets you to the correct answer: (A) *20+q*. An additional benefit of this approach is that it is less vulnerable to a computation error. The question writers will often choose answer choices that are based on common computation errors made by test takers. If you are moving quickly and fall into one of those traps, you may find an answer that matches up to your incorrect calculation, choose that answer and move on without realizing your error. When you draw or visualize the problem, you're less likely to make this type of error because you can clearly see (as in this problem) that some of the choices just don't logically make sense when compared with your drawing.

That's our final technique dealing with the math questions in the Quantitative section. As a reminder, the three techniques that we've discussed are:

1. **Backsolving**

2. **Assigning values**

3. **Drawing the questions**

It takes some practice to be comfortable applying them in the right situations. It also takes a bit of practice to really get comfortable with applying them quickly and effectively – that's the key to realizing the true benefit of these techniques. Simple repetition and application of easy, medium, and hard sample questions will guarantee that you won't be thrown for a loop during your actual test.

Hopefully working your way through these examples has been helpful for you. Each one that you can use proficiently will provide you with an additional tool in your GMAT Quantitative tool belt. Recognizing the question types and being able to use the most effective tool for each will help boost your score to the next level. Even when these techniques don't solve the problem completely for you, we've shown you ways that they will certainly improve (sometimes dramatically) your chances when you're in the difficult situation of having to guess at the correct answer and move on.

Since you're penalized by not answering EVERY question on the computerized GMAT test, you'll want to make at least an educated guess on every single question. This means that if the end of the test is approaching and several questions remain, you'll want to apply these techniques quickly and do what you can to increase your chances of guessing correctly. The end result of your practice with the techniques of backsolving, assigning values, and drawing the question will be twofold. You'll save time on the questions that you know how to approach and solve and they'll get you closer to the answers when you have to make an educated guess. The result will allow you to move faster and more confidently through these sections – and raise your Quantitative score.

Arithmetic

Expect to deal with arithmetic in some form or another during the math portion of the GMAT. As a result, you will need to understand basic arithmetic definitions.

Numbers

The following are the different kinds of numbers that appear on the GMAT.

- **Real numbers** are numbers on the number line. All of the numbers used on the GMAT are real numbers.

- **Rational numbers** are numbers expressed as the ratio of two integers, and include all integers and fractions.

- **Irrational numbers** are real numbers with non-terminating decimals places. They can be either positive or negative.

- **Integers** are numbers with no fractional or decimal areas. They are all multiples of one. The distinction between an integer and a number (which is not necessarily an integer) is important on the GMAT.

Operations

Operations essentially dictate how the entire mathematical sequence reads on paper. Operations include everything from parenthesis and exponents to simple arithmetic expressions.

The order for operations is as follows:

- Parentheses;

- Exponents;

- Multiplication / Division (from left to right);

- Addition / Subtraction (from left to right).

(An easy way to remember this is the acronym PEMA!)

Let's look at a sample equation that requires you to follow the above order:

$$27 + 5 \times 2^2 + (\frac{100}{5}) - 19 = ?$$

If we don't follow the order, and just work from left to right, the answer is 26.6.

However, doing it in correct operation order yields the following:

1. Solve the numbers in the <u>parenthesis</u> first: $\frac{100}{5} = 20$

2. Solve the <u>exponent</u>: $2^2 = 4$

3. Do the <u>multiplication</u> and <u>division</u> from left to right: $5 \times 4 = 20$

4. Now the formula is as follows: $27 + 20 + 20 - 19$

5. Now do the <u>addition</u> and <u>subtraction</u> from left to right

6. This yields the result of 48.

This answer is a bit different from the answer we got by not following the order of the operations.

Laws of Operations

You should remember the following mathematics laws and their operations so that you can correctly do the calculations.

Commutative Law

Addition and multiplication are commutative. This means that no matter what order they are done in, the result is the same.

$$10 + 15 = 25$$

$$15 + 10 = 25$$

$$9 \times 2 = 18$$

$$2 \times 9 = 18$$

Division and subtraction, however, are not commutative.

$$9 - 2 = 7$$

$$2 - 9 = -7$$

$$\frac{10}{2} = 5$$

$$\frac{2}{10} = .2$$

Associative Law

Addition and multiplication, as above, are also associative. This means that these operations can be regrouped in any way without changing the end result. Division and subtraction, on the other hand, are not associative.

$$(10 + 10) + 9 = 10 + (10 + 9) \quad (5 \times 5) \times 2 = 5 \times (2 \times 5)$$

$$20 + 9 = 10 + 19 \qquad 25 \times 2 = 5 \times 10$$

$$29 = 29 \qquad 50 = 50$$

Distributive Law

Distributive law allows you to distribute a factor among the terms that are added or subtracted, often seen as $a(b + c) = ab + ac$.

$$4(10 + 2) = 4 \times 10 + 4 \times 2$$

$$4 \times 12 = 40 + 8$$

$$48 = 48$$

Division can be done in a similar format.

$$\frac{3 + 5}{2} = \frac{3}{2} + \frac{5}{2}$$

$$\frac{8}{2} = \frac{3}{2} + \frac{5}{2}$$

$$4 = 1.5 + 2.5$$

$$4 = 4$$

Fractions

Fractions form a significant portion of the math portion of the GMAT. Let's review the basics of fractions, such as:

$$\frac{3}{5}$$

3 is the numerator, with the fraction bar below, meaning divided by, and 5 is the denominator.

There is more to remember than simply numerator and denominator, so let's get into the different types of fractions.

Equivalent Fractions

In this type of fraction, its fractional value remains unchanged when you multiply it by one. When dealing with fractions, multiplying the numerator and denominator by the same non-zero number is equivalent to multiplying them by one; the fractional value remains unchanged.

$$\frac{1}{2} = \frac{1 \times 3}{2 \times 3} = \frac{3}{6}$$

You also get the same result when dividing by the same non-zero number.

$$\frac{6}{9} = \frac{6 \div 3}{9 \div 3} = \frac{2}{3}$$

Canceling and Reducing

When dealing with fractions, especially on the GMAT, you have to work to put fractions in the lowest terms. This means that the numerator and denominator cannot be divisible by any other common integer except for one.

The best way to think about this is to look at $\frac{6}{24}$. This fraction can be reduced by dividing both the numerator and the denominator by 3, to get $\frac{2}{8}$. We can divide the numerator and denominator once more by 2, and get $\frac{1}{4}$.

An example of a question that you will face on the GMAT concerning this is this as follows:

Reduce $\frac{50}{110}$ to its lowest terms.

To do this, find a common factor of the numerator and denominator, such as 5, and divide by it to get $\frac{10}{22}$.

At this point, divide by another common factor, 2, to get $\frac{5}{11}$

Addition and Subtraction

You can add or subtract two fractions only if they have the same denominator. We first need to find a common denominator, which is generally the lowest common denominator. The common denominator is an important concept in understanding fractions.

$$\frac{4}{5} + \frac{1}{3} - \frac{3}{4}$$

Here, the denominators are 5, 3, and 4. To find the lowest common denominator, you can usually just multiply the denominators together.

$$\text{Lowest common denominator} = 5 \times 3 \times 4 = 60$$

Then, determine what value each denominator should be multiplied by in order to reach the common denominator, and multiply both the numerator and denominator by that value.

$$(\frac{4}{5} \times \frac{12}{12}) + (\frac{1}{3} \times \frac{20}{20}) - (\frac{3}{4} \times \frac{15}{15})$$

This yields:

$$\frac{48}{60} + \frac{20}{60} - \frac{45}{60}$$

Now, all we have to do is add the numerators together over the common denominator.

$$\frac{48 + 20 - 45}{60} = \frac{23}{60}$$

Multiplication

With fractions, multiplication is different from addition and subtraction. First, no common denominator needs to be in place for multiplication to work. For multiplication, you simply need to reduce both diagonally and vertically, and then multiply numerators together and denominators together.

$$\frac{5}{9} \times \frac{3}{4} \times \frac{8}{15}$$

This is reduced to:

$$\frac{1}{3} \times \frac{1}{1} \times \frac{2}{3}$$

Then, multiply it all together:

$$\frac{1 \times 1 \times 2}{3 \times 1 \times 3} = \frac{2}{9}$$

Division

Division works just like multiplication and, in fact, all you do is multiply the reciprocal of the divisor, the number going into the other number. To get the reciprocal, invert the fraction by changing the position of the numerator and denominator. Let's look at an example:

$$\frac{4}{3} \div \frac{4}{9}$$

We first have to find the reciprocal of $\frac{4}{9}$, which is $\frac{9}{4}$.

Now we multiply the reciprocal of the divisor:

$$\frac{4}{3} \times \frac{9}{4}$$

We then reduce this to:

$$\frac{1}{1} \times \frac{3}{1}$$

which equals 3.

Decimal Fractions

Decimal fractions are simply fractions in decimal form. To find the decimal form of a fraction, multiply to the power of ten in the denominator.

In addition, each digit in the decimal has a name. The GMAT will sometimes test you on this, so here is a quick guide. For example,

527.236

5 = the hundreds digit

2 = the tens digit

7 = the units digit

2 = the tenths digit

3 = the hundredths digit

6 = the thousandths digit

Now, let's look at examples of how to change decimal fractions into actual fractions using an example question from the GMAT.

Arrange in order from smallest to largest: 0.5, 0.55, 0.05, 0.505 and 0.055

$$.5 = .500 = \frac{500}{1000}$$

$$.55 = .550 = \frac{550}{1000}$$

$$.05 = .050 = \frac{50}{1000}$$

$$.505 = .505 = \frac{505}{1000}$$

$$.055 = .055 = \frac{55}{1000}$$

Therefore, the order should be: .05 < .055 < .5 < .505 < .55

When adding or subtracting these, make sure that all of the decimal points line up properly, one on top of the other. This will ensure that the tenths add with the tenths, the hundredths add with the hundredths, and so on.

Let's look at this example:

$$.9 + .09 + .009$$

In this case, you will convert it into vertical form:

$$
\begin{array}{r}
0.9 \\
+\,0.09 \\
+\,\underline{0.009} \\
0.999
\end{array}
$$

The same holds true when subtracting, so whenever using addition or subtraction, always remember to line up the decimal points to ensure that you get the proper answers.

In terms of multiplication, multiply as you would with any other integer. Then decide where the decimal point should be. The number of decimal places for the answer equals the sum of the number of decimal places from each of the two decimals you are multiplying together.

For example:

$$0.5 \times 0.3 = 5 \times 3 = 15 \text{ and two decimal spaces} = 0.15$$

$$1.2 \times 1.7 = 12 \times 17 = 204 \text{ and 2 decimal spaces} = 2.04$$

When dividing a decimal with another decimal, multiply each by the power of 10 so that the divisor becomes an integer. Then, simply carry out the division as you would with integers, placing the decimal point in the quotient directly above the decimal point in the dividend.

For example:

$$8 \div 0.4 =$$

$$(8 \times 10) \div (0.4 \times 10) =$$

$$80 \div 4 = 20$$

> **More Practice from the GMAT® Review 13th Edition:** Questions 27, 46, 76, 97, 226 (Fractions)
> **More Practice from the GMAT® Review 13th Edition:** Questions 20, 41, 42, 85, 156 (Decimals)

Number Properties

To do well on the GMAT, you need to learn many different concepts related to the properties of numbers. Some will be easier to master than others, but we will cover them all here for you in the simplest way possible so that you can use logic to more quickly and accurately answer the math questions.

Number Line and Absolute Value

What is a number line? Plainly put, it is a line of numbers.

A number line will extend infinitely in two directions, one continuously toward infinity and the other continuously toward negative infinity. In other words, as you move to the right on the number line, values become larger. The farther you move to the left on the number line, the smaller the numbers become.

Zero separates the positive numbers from the negative numbers. For example, there is 3 and there is –3, there is 12 and there is –12, there is 1,385,388,905 and there is –1,385,388,905.

What is an absolute value?

The absolute value of any number is the number without its negative sign. What it really represents is the distance from zero on the number line. It is written simply as a number between two vertical lines. An example of this is:

$$|-5| = |+5| = 5$$

Look at it this way: -5 is 5 units from zero, so its absolute value is 5.

Properties of -1, 0, 1 and Other Numbers

What are the properties of zero? Can zero have properties or is it simply the lack of everything, a void, and therefore without properties? Well, the good news is that it can have properties and we will cover them here, along with the properties of some other numbers.

Adding or subtracting zero from any number does not change the value of the number.

$$0 + 7 = 7$$

$$9 + 0 = 9$$

$$8 - 0 = 0$$

Now, the rules change when you multiply by zero. In this case, the result of any number multiplied by zero is zero. See the following examples:

$$25 \times 0 = 0$$

$$198 \times 0 = 0$$

Dividing by zero cannot be done. If you put that sort of equation into your calculator, you will get an error.

Now that we have looked into the properties of 0, what about 1 and -1?

Multiplying or dividing any number by 1 does not change that number.

$$7 \div 1 = 7$$

$$9 \times 1 = 9$$

$$-17 \times 1 = -17$$

Things change slightly when we begin to multiply by -1. In this case, doing so changes the sign of the number are multiplying. Let's look at some examples.

$$z \times (-1) = -z$$

$$9 \times (-1) = -9$$

$$-6 \div (-1) = 6$$

To get the reciprocal of a number, we simply write 1 divided by that number. For example, the reciprocal of 6 is $\frac{1}{6}$. With fractions, the reciprocal can also be found by interchanging the denominator and the numerator. Moreover, the reciprocal of a number between 0 and 1 is greater than the number itself. Here is an example:

The reciprocal of $\frac{3}{4}$ is: c $\frac{1}{3/4} = \frac{4}{3}$

As we can see, this figure is larger than the original number.

Conversely, the reciprocal of a number between 0 and -1 is less than the number:

The reciprocal of $-\frac{2}{3}$ is: $\frac{1}{-2/3} = -\frac{3}{2}$

For the square of a number, when it is a square of a number between 0 and 1, the reciprocal is much greater than that number.

$$(\frac{1}{3})^2 = \frac{1}{9} = \frac{1}{1/9} = 9$$

Multiplying any negative number by a fraction between 0 and 1 will result in a number greater than the original number.

$$-7 \times \frac{1}{5} = -\frac{7}{5}$$

Operations and Signed Numbers

We looked at operations in a previous section, and now it is time to review them again. This time, we are looking at operations with regards to signed numbers (numbers with a + or - sign).

For addition of numbers with the same signs, we simply add them and keep the sign:

$$-9 + -2 = -11$$

However, if we are dealing with numbers with different signs, then we take the difference of the absolute values and keep the sign of the larger absolute value.

$$(-9) + (+3) = -6$$

Subtracting a number is the same as adding its inverse.

$$(-4) - (-8) = (-4) + (+8) = +4$$

In multiplication and division, the product or the quotient of the two numbers with the same sign is positive. Here is an example:

$$(-3) \times (-4) = +12$$

$$-100 \div -50 = +2$$

The product or the quotient of two numbers with opposite signs is negative:

$$(-4) \times (+3) = -12$$

$$-100 \div 50 = -2$$

Odd and Even Numbers

Odd and even numbers only apply to integers. Even numbers are integers divisible by 2, while odd numbers are not divisible by 2.

Any number that ends in 0, 2, 4, 6, or 8 are even, while integers ending in 1, 3, 5, 7, or 9 are odd. Negative numbers can also be odd or even. Zero is considered an even number.

When dealing with operations for odd and even numbers, there are some simple rules to follow:

Odd + Odd = Even

Even + Even = Even

Odd + Even = Odd

Odd × Odd = Odd

Even × Even = Even

Odd × Even = Even

Factors and Divisibility of Primes - The Facts

- Any integer divisible by another integer is effectively a multiple of that integer:

    - 16 is a multiple of 4 because $16 \div 4 = 4$; $4 \times 4 = 16$

- In division, when you are dealing with a remainder, the remainder is always smaller than the number we are dividing by.

    - 17 divided by 3 is 5, and the remainder is 2

- A factor is a divisor of a number that can evenly divide into that integer.

    - 9 has 3 factors: 1, 3, 9

    - $1 \times 9 = 9$; $3 \times 3 = 9$

- The greatest common factor is the largest factor that can be shared by two numbers. For example, the common factors of 8 ad 12 are 1, 2, and 4. The greatest common factor is therefore 4.

- One great thing about factors is that you can do divisibility tests to see if the number is divisible by 2, 3, 4, 5, 6, and 9. Here are the rules:

  - Any number can be divided by 2 if the last digit is divisible by 2.

  - *224 is divisible by 2 because 4 is divisible by 2.*

  - If the sum of all of the digits of a number is divisible by 3, then the entire number is divisible by 3.

  - *135 is divisible by 3 because 1 + 3 + 5 = 9.*

  - A number is divisible by 4 if its last two digits are divisible by 4.

  - *1,240 is divisible by 4 because 40 is divisible by 4.*

  - A number is divisible by 5 if its last digit is a 0 or a 5.

  - *2,517,545 is divisible by 5.*

  - A number is divisible by 6 if it is divisible by BOTH 2 and 3.

  - *4,422 is divisible by 6 because the last digit is divisible by 2, and the sum of its digits (4+4+2+2) is 12, which is divisible by 3.*

- A number is divisible by 9 if the sum of the digits is divisible by 9, much like how the division rule for 3 works.

- *14,832 is divisible by 9 because sum of its digits (1+4+8+3+2) is 18, which is divisible by 9.*

You can use these rules of divisibility to figure out factors and multiples of larger numbers as well. For example, you know that 12 does not go into 270 because the factor pairs of 12 are 6 ×2 and 4 × 3. If 270 is divisible by 6, 2, 4, and 3, then it is divisible by 12. That may seem like a lot of work and the long division may appear easier. But you don't have to test 2, because any number divisible by 4 is divisible by 2. You don't have to test 6 because 6 is 2 × 3. So just use the rules of 3 and 4. Since 70 is not evenly divisible by 4, 270 is not a multiple of 12.

Now let's move on to prime numbers. **A prime number is any integer greater than 1 that can only be divided by 1 and itself.** The first prime number is 2, and is the only even prime number. Here is a quick list of the first ten prime numbers: 2, 3, 5, 7, 11, 13, 17, 19, 23, and 29.

Prime factorization is the breaking down of a number into just its prime, rather than all, divisors. No matter how you begin the process of factorization, a number's prime factors will always be the same. For example, if you want the prime factor of 36, you can start with the prime number 2 and write:

$$36$$
$$2 \times 18$$
$$2 \times 9$$
$$3 \times 3$$

So the prime factors of 36 are 2, 2, 3, and 3. If you start with the prime number 3, you still end up with the same result.

$$36$$
$$3 \times 12$$
$$3 \times 4$$
$$2 \times 2$$

Determining the prime factorization for a number can be difficult, but there is an easy way. Let's look at this example:

$$150 = 10 \times 15 = (2 \times 5) \times (5 \times 3) = 2 \times 5 \times 5 \times 3$$

First we break 150 into two numbers. There are multiple combinations, 10 × 15, 2 × 75, 3 × 50 ...etc. Any combination will do; let's pick 10 × 15

$$150 = 10 \times 15$$

Next we factorize the two components.

$$10 \times 15 = (2 \times 5) \times (5 \times 3)$$

Great! We only have prime numbers in the equation. Therefore the prime factorization of 150 is

$$2 \times 5 \times 5 \times 3.$$

However, if the question specified the distinct prime factors of 150, there are only three: 2, 3, and 5. Distinct means that you don't count duplicates.

Consecutive Numbers

If the numbers in a list are at a fixed interval, then they are consecutive numbers. They need to have a pattern to be considered consecutive numbers. Also, all the consecutive numbers that you encounter on the exam will be integers.

1, 2, 3, 4, 5... is consecutive in intervals of +1, adding up

2, 0, −2, −4, −6... is consecutive in intervals of −2, subtracting down

2, 4, 16, 256... is a consecutive in intervals of squaring

The concepts in this chapter can help you narrow down your answer choices and avoid careless mistakes. Before you start solving a question, pause and analyze the properties of the numbers in the question and the way each number relates to the others. You will find that sometimes you can quickly eliminate the odd or even numbers, the fractions, or certain other answer choices based on the way number properties affect each other.

> **More Practice from the GMAT® Review 13th Edition:** Questions 77, 80, 87, 90, 174

Statistics

Averages

If you love sports and watch them on a regular basis, then you know all about averages. A frequently used average is a pitcher's earned run average (E.R.A.), which is calculated by adding up all of the runs that a pitcher had in the innings he pitched, and then dividing that by the number of innings. For example, if a pitcher had 47 runs in 19 innings pitched, then his E.R.A is 2.47 (47 ÷ 19 = 2.47).

Averages are easy to calculate, as they are simply the sum of values divided by the number of values used.

Here is an example:

Craig is 180 pounds, Jim is 201 pounds, and Francis is 257 pounds. What is the average weight of the three men?

$$180 + 201 + 257 = 638$$

$$\frac{638}{3} = 212.67$$

The average weight is 212.67 pounds.

Finding the average is simple enough, but can you find the sum of the values with nothing but the average and the number of values? Well, this is also easy, since we have two of the variables we need to find the solution.

$$\text{Sum of Values = Average Value} \times \text{Number of Values}$$

$$212.67 \times 3 = 638$$

As long as you have the two variables – average value and number of values – to complete the equation, it is fairly easy to figure out.

When looking at a series of numbers, with only the average known, how do we solve that problem?

Here is an example:

The average of $3, 5, 6$, and x is 6. What is x? Since we know that the average is 6, we figured it out backwards. There are four numbers here: $3, 5, 6$, and x. The sum of these numbers divided by four is the average.

$$\frac{3 + 5 + 6 + x}{4} = 6$$

$$3 + 5 + 6 + x = 6 \times 4 = 24$$

$$x = 24 - 3 - 5 - 6$$

$$x = 10$$

We can then verify this by adding the values:

$$3 + 5 + 6 + 10 = 24$$

$$\frac{24}{4} = 6$$

Now that we have looked at these examples, what about the **average rate?** This is often seen in examples that are worded as: Average A per B. Here is an example to help you understand average rate:

Frank packaged 17 boxes in 3 hours and then 37 boxes in 4 hours. What is his average box per hour rate?

Well, average box per hour rate = total boxes / total hours

$$\frac{17 + 37}{3 + 4}$$

$$= \frac{54}{7}$$

= 7.714 boxes per hour is his average.

➢ **More Practice from the GMAT® Review 13th Edition:** Questions 12, 16, 30, 53, 208

Standard Deviation

Once again, if you pay attention to sports, then you already have a handle on statistics, and probably a bit of a handle on probability.

With statistics and probability, we will deal with various terms like mean, mode, median, range, and standard deviation.

Standard Deviation is the measure of a set of numbers (how much they deviate from the mean or average). The greater the spread, the higher the standard deviation.

Thankfully, you never have to calculate standard deviation on the GMAT, so we will move on. However, it does help to know what standard deviation means.

> **More Practice from the GMAT® Review 13ᵗʰ Edition:** Question 112

Probability

Probability, as any gambler knows, is determined for a finite number of outcomes. Obviously, the higher the probability, the greater the possibility that a desirable or undesirable outcome will occur.

We find probability by dividing the number of desired outcomes by the number of total possible outcomes:

$$P = \frac{D}{T}$$

(P = probability, D = desired outcome, T = total possible outcomes)

An example: *John is reaching into a prize bin with 321 names on it, including seven names of people whom he knows. Therefore, what is the chance that John pulls out the name of someone he knows?*

$$D = 7 \text{ and } T = 321$$

$$P = \frac{7}{321}$$

$$P = .022$$

Therefore, the probability of John selecting someone he knows is .022, or 2.2%

Calculating this form of probability is not so difficult. What is harder is calculating the probability of a certain outcome after multiple repetitions of the same or different experiment. Typically, you will find that these questions come in two different forms. One is where each event must occur in a set way, and another is where each event has different outcomes.

To determine the probability in multiple-event situations, there are two steps we should take:

- Find out the probability of each event;

- Multiply the probabilities together.

Here's an example to help understand this further:

There are 15 Canadians and 15 Russians in the NHL Entry Draft. What is the probability that the first two picks of the draft will both be Canadian?

Looking at the fractions of these two picks, we have $\frac{15}{30}$ and $\frac{15}{30}$, which can both be reduced to $\frac{1}{2}$.

Once one draft pick is made, there is a $\frac{14}{29}$ possibility that the next pick will be a Canadian player. Therefore, we multiply the two fractions:

$$(\frac{1}{2}) \times (\frac{14}{29})$$

$$= \frac{7}{29}$$

This then converts to .24 in decimal form.

As a result, the chance of two Canadian players being selected first and second in the draft is 24%.

The previous example calculated the probability that each individual event will occur a certain way. What about situations in which different outcomes may occur?

To calculate this, we must determine the total number of possible outcomes by figuring out the number of possible outcomes for each individual event and multiplying those together. For example:

Audy sees four doors. Behind some is money, behind others is nothing. What are the chances that Audy finds money behind at least three of the four doors?

Since each door has two possible outcomes, four tries have $(2 \times 2 \times 2 \times 2)$ = 16 possible outcomes. We list the possible outcomes where three of the four doors have money behind them.

($ = Money ; E = Nothing)

1. **E $ $ $**

2. **$ E $ $**

3. **$ $ E $**

4. **$ $ $ E**

5. **$ $ $ $**

Now we know that there are five outcomes where money is behind three of the four doors; therefore, the number of possible desired outcomes is 5 and the number of possible total outcomes is 16. Using what we learned a few pages back, we have the following:

$$\frac{5}{16}$$

$$= .3125$$

$$= 31.25\%$$

The chance of Audy finding money is 31.25%.

> ➢ **More Practice from the GMAT® Review 13th Edition:** Questions 68, 107, 193, 215

Ratios

Ratios are the comparison of two quantities by division.

So, on to the next section!

Actually, there is a bit more to know about ratios than just that.

Typically, ratios can be written in two ways: as a fraction $(\frac{y}{z})$ and with a colon (*y:z*). You can also say "the ratio of y to z" if you want.

Usually, ratios are expressed as $(\frac{y}{z})$.

Whenever you are dealing with ratios, it is always best to reduce them to their lowest terms.

Craig is 26, Layla is 22.

The ratio of Craig's age to Layla's age is $\frac{26}{22}$ (26 to 22).

Therefore the lowest terms are $\frac{13}{11}$.

Ratios, which are worded in the way we have seen, "y to z," should be turned into this format:

The ratio of 17 to 22 is $\frac{17}{22}$.

When working with ratios, we often hear the word "proportion," which is simply an equation in which two ratios are equal to one another.

Ratios are two pieces, parts, and wholes, where the whole is the entire set and the part is the portion we are taking out.

Describing a ratio is then worded as "what fraction of the whole is this part?"

Or, to more easily understand this, let's look at this example:

Out of 37 players on the British & Irish Lions team, 12 are from Ireland.

So, the whole is 37, and the part is 12.

Therefore, the question can now be worded as:

What fraction of the British & Irish Lions team is from Ireland?

$\frac{12}{37}$

$$= 32.4 \text{ percent}$$

Knowing what we do about ratios, let's move on to part ratios and whole ratios. A ratio can either compare a part to a part or a part to a whole.

The ratio of trucks to cars is 2:7. As a result, what fraction of the total cars and trucks is trucks?

By adding 2 and 7, we know that for every 9 vehicles, 2 are trucks, which means that the fraction or ratio of trucks to total cars and trucks is:

$$\frac{2}{2+7}$$

$$\frac{2}{9}$$

Ratios with more than two terms are usually ratios of various parts, and usually these parts equal the whole, which allows us to find the part : whole ratio.

The ratio of trucks to cars to SUVs is: 2:7:3

What ratios can be determined here?

$$\text{Ratio of trucks to whole} = \frac{2}{(2+7+3)}$$

$$\text{Ratio of trucks to whole} = \frac{2}{12} = \frac{1}{6}$$

$$\text{Ratio of cars to whole} = \frac{7}{12}$$

$$\text{Ratio of SUVs to whole} = \frac{3}{12} = \frac{1}{4}$$

Ratio of SUVs to cars and trucks = 3:9

Ratio of trucks to cars: 2:7

Ratio of cars to trucks and SUVs = 7:5

As we have seen above, ratios are always reduced to their simplest form, which can cause some confusion. Just because the ratio of trucks to total vehicles is 2:12, this does not mean that only two trucks were sold. The actual ratio may be much higher, like 20:120.

There is one more term you need to know: rates. **A rate is a ratio that compares two different types of quantities, often seen in the example of miles per hour:**

Henry drove 126 miles in four hours. His average rate is:

$$\frac{126}{4} = 31.5 \text{ miles per hour}$$

The exact formula is *distance = rate × time*.

That is all there is to rates. They are also more or less the same as averages, which use the formula *sum = number of items × average*.

> ➢ **More Practice from the GMAT® Review 13th Edition:** Questions 98, 105, 113, 125, 179

Percentages

Probably one of the most common forms of math relationships is percentages. We deal with percentages on a daily basis and as a result, it is highly likely that you will find percent questions on the GMAT.

Percentages are very easy to figure out from their decimal or fraction form:

$$\frac{23}{100} = .23 = 23\%$$

To turn a fraction into a decimal, all we do is divide the numerator by the denominator. To get our percentage, we simply multiply our decimal form by 100:

$$.23 \times 100 = 23\%$$

The same is true when we want to move backwards from a percentage to decimal form to fraction form:

$$16 \text{ divided by } 100 = .16 = \frac{16}{100} = 4/25$$

Let's move on to problems involving percents. Most of these problems will come in the form of, "What is (percent) of (variable)?" Or, put in a way similar to what we covered with ratios: percent x whole = part.

What is 32% of 183?

$$.32 \times 183 = 58.56$$

We can do the reverse when we want to figure out a question worded like this: "5 is 10 percent of what number?" To determine this, we use the format of whole = part / percent:

$$x = 5 / 10\% = 5 \times \left(\frac{1}{10\%}\right) = 5 \times (10)$$

$$x = 50$$

Of course, this can be avoided if there are certain percentages in the question. For example, "40 is 50 percent of what number?" This is easy to answer because we know that 50 percent is half, so $40 \times 2 = 80$, which is the number we are looking for. This primarily works for 10, 25, 50, and 75 percent.

Now, if we have the whole and the part, how do we figure out the percentage? Easy! We just reorganize the previous formula to read % = part / whole.

22 is what percent of 293?

$$\% = \frac{part}{whole} = \frac{22}{293}$$

$$= .075$$

$$\% = .075 \times 100$$

$$= 7.5\%$$

Moving on now, let's review percent increases and decreases, along with combining percentages.

First, when you increase or decrease a percentage, be careful about the amount of the increase or decrease of the original whole, not the new figure.

If the price of a $30,000 car increases by 13 percent, what is the new price?

All we do is take the original price of $30,000 and multiply it by the percentage:

$$30,000 \times .13 = 3900$$

This means that the increase was $3,900 and the new price is:

$$30,000 + 3,900 = 33,900$$

The new selling price is $33,900.

Combining percentages is simply taking one percent and applying it to another. Here is an example:

The price of a car is $20,000, but that was reduced recently by 17 percent, and then was reduced by another 5 percent. What is the final price?

So, if a price was reduced by 17 percent, then it is:

$$100\% - 17\% = 83\% \text{ of what it once was.}$$

The new price is then $20,000 \times .83 = 16,600$.

Now, we reduce that by 5%:

$$16,600 \times .05 = 830$$

$$16,600 - 830 = 15,770$$

The final price is $15,770.

An important point should be made here. You have to reduce the price two separate times; you cannot simply add the percentages together. We will use the same variables in this question to see the incorrect results that this creates:

$$17\% + 5\% = 22\%$$

$$20,000 \times .22 = 4,400$$

$$20,000 - 4,400 = 15,600$$

The value is close, but not correct.

> ➤ **More Practice from the GMAT® Review 13th Edition:** Questions 94, 114, 115, 136, 144

Word Problems with Percents, Ratios, and Rates

Most of the percentage problems on the test actually come in word form. Since we already know how percentages work, we will delve right into these word problems starting with a few examples.

Chris earns a commission of 17 percent of the selling price of each television and 23 of the selling price of each DVD player that he sells. In one day, he sold four televisions each worth $988, and two DVD players each worth $127. How much did he earn in commission on that day?

$$4 \times (988 \times .17) + 2 \times (127 \times .23)$$

$$= 4 \times 167.96 + 2 \times 29.21$$

$$= 730.26$$

Chris made $730.26

Shoji and Anna sell jeans on their Web site. One pair costs $29.99. If you buy ten pairs, then you get 10% off. If you buy 100 pairs, then you get 30% off. How much do Shoji and Anna make if they sell 10 pairs to one customer and 100 pairs to another customer?

$$\text{Difference} = ((29.99 \times 10) \text{ x } .10) + ((29.99 \times 100) \times .3))$$

We have to remember to use the Order of Operations here, which states that multiplication must be done before addition. The full order is PEMDAS (parenthesis, exponents, multiplication, division, addition, subtraction).

$$\text{Difference} = (299.90 \times .10) + (2999 \times .3)$$

$$\text{Difference} = 29.99 + 899.7 = 929.69$$

$$\text{Profit} = (299.90 + 2999) - 929.69$$

$$\text{Profit} = 3298.9 - 929.69 = 2369.21$$

Other common word problems use ratios and rates. We have already reviewed ratios and rates, so let's move on to some examples expressed as a word problem.

There are five oranges in a bag, along with three apples and two plums. What is the ratio of apples to oranges and plums to apples?

$$\text{Oranges} = 5$$

$$\text{Apples} = 3$$

$$\text{Plums} = 2$$

$$\text{Apples to Oranges: } 3:5$$

$$\text{Plums to Apples: } 2:3$$

Taking the above into consideration, what is the ratio of oranges to total fruit?

$$\text{Total fruit} = 5 + 3 + 2 = 10$$

$$\text{Oranges to Total Fruit: } 5:10 = 1:2$$

Rates. If Jim jogs 12 miles in five hours, what is his average speed?

$$\text{Speed} = \frac{12}{5}$$

$$\text{Speed} = 2.4 \text{ miles per hour}$$

Using the data from the above question, if Jim continues jogging at the same rate without stopping for another three and a half hours, how much distance will he cover?

Distance = rate × time

$$\text{Distance} = 2.4 \times 3.5$$

$$\text{Distance} = 8.4 \text{ miles}$$

That is about all there is for ratios, percentages, and rates in word problems. Having covered these topics in arithmetic form makes things much easier when you begin to tackle the word problems.

➢ **More Practice from the GMAT® Review 13th Edition:** Questions 57, 66, 79, 82, 84

Exponentiation

When we think of zy^x, z is the coefficient, y is the base and x is the exponent. The exponent is the number of times the base of something is multiplied by itself.

$$2^2 = 2 \times 2 = 4$$

$$2^4 = 2 \times 2 \times 2 \times 2 = 16$$

In terms of multiplying and dividing, these are generally done in the same way as we have seen over the course of this book. Here is an example:

$$2^3 \times 2^4 = (2 \times 2 \times 2) \times (2 \times 2 \times 2 \times 2)$$

$$= 8 \times 16$$

$$= 128$$

$$\frac{2^4}{2^3} = \frac{2 \times 2 \times 2 \times 2}{2 \times 2 \times 2}$$

$$= \frac{16}{8}$$

$$= 2$$

Additionally, $2^{3+4} = 2^7 = 2 \times 2 \times 2 \times 2 \times 2 \times 2 \times 2$

$$= (2 \times 2 \times 2) \times (2 \times 2 \times 2 \times 2) = 2^3 \times 2^4.$$

And $2^{4-3} = 2^1 = \dfrac{2 \times 2 \times 2 \times 2}{2 \times 2 \times 2} = \dfrac{2^4}{2^3}.$

So remember that:

$$A^{m+n} = A^m \times A^n$$

$$A^{m-n} = \frac{A^m}{A^n}$$

Sometimes, you may have to raise your exponent to another exponent, but this can easily be done as well:

$$(4^2)^3 = (4 \times 4)^3$$

$$16^3 = 16 \times 16 \times 16$$

$$= 4096$$

You might also see negative exponents on the test. To calculate a negative exponent, take the reciprocal of the base and then change the sign of the exponent.

$$2^{-4} = (\frac{1}{2})^4$$

This can then be further reduced to:

$$(\frac{1}{2})^4 = \frac{1}{2^4}$$

$$= \frac{1}{2 \times 2 \times 2 \times 2}$$

$$= \frac{1}{16}$$

That is about all there is to know about **calculating the power of something.** You won't find many questions like these on the GMAT, but you'll see a few so be sure you know how to do them.

> **More Practice from the GMAT® Review 13th Edition**: Questions 65, 106, 111, 117, 122

Combinations and Permutations

Combinations and permutations are ways of arranging items or people. If you remember working on these types of problems in middle school, you'll likely recall having to remember difficult formulas with an exclamation point in the middle of them. The good news is that even though these questions are on the GMAT, you don't need a formula to solve them. You just have to go through a series of questions to figure out the correct order. We will use the following example to talk through those questions:

There are 8 electives that a business school could offer its students in the upcoming semester. The schedule only allows room for 5 of them, one on each day of the week, Monday through Friday. How many different arrangements of these classes are possible?

The first question to ask is "How many spaces do I need to fill?" The answer for this question is 5, one for each day Monday through Friday. Draw the spaces out on your scratch paper.

____ ____ ____ ____ ____

The next question is "How many items from the pool are eligible for each space?" For example, if one of the electives is Business Ethics, is there any reason that Business Ethics cannot be held on a Monday? This question does not give us any restrictions, so any one of those 8 electives could be on Monday. After that, there are only 7 electives left to choose from, so fill in the spaces appropriately.

$$8\ 7\ 6\ 5\ 4$$

You should realize that sometimes you can repeat items (e.g. if you are making an ice cream sundae, you could have two helpings of whipped cream instead of one helping of whipped cream and one of chocolate sauce) and if you do repeat, you should reduce the number of eligible items. Just be sure to pay attention to the criteria give by the problem.

The final question to ask is "Does order matter?" This question is looking for *arrangements*, so offering Business Ethics on Monday is a very different thing than offering it on Thursday. Other words that indicate order matters include: **schedule, line, row, and order**. If order matters, you are almost finished. All you have to do is multiply straight across.

$$8 \times 7 \times 6 \times 5 \times 4 = 6{,}720$$

So, our answer in this case is 6,720. Remember, if this is problem solving, work smart and use estimation instead of spending time doing all of this multiplication. 6×5 is 30 and 4×7 is also about 30, so you have $30 \times 30 \times 8$, or 900×8, which is 7,200. You rounded up (since 4×7 is 28, not 30) so choose an answer that is a little lower than your estimate of 7,200.

What happens when the order doesn't matter? Teams are a good example of this. A team of ABC is not different from a team of CBA, so you wouldn't want to count those separately. Other words that indicate order does not matter are: committee, group, pair, and class. This is where the factorial (!) sign you remember from middle school comes in. When order doesn't matter, divide by the number of spaces! (factorial, that is.) Let's change our original question to see how this works.

There are 8 electives that a business school is offering this year. Daniel wants to take five of them. How many combinations of electives are possible?

In this case, the order does not matter. We just want to know what group of electives Daniel will take. Let's go through the questions.

How many spaces do I need to fill? 5

___ ___ ___ ___ ___

How many items from the pool are eligible for each space? 8, no repeats

$$8\ 7\ 6\ 5\ 4$$

Does order matter? No

$$\frac{8 \times 7 \times 6 \times 5 \times 4}{5 \times 4 \times 3 \times 2 \times 1} = 56$$

As you can see, we are working with the same numbers as before, but the answer is much smaller because we cut out the duplicates. Again, this looks like a huge calculation, but use the reducing techniques you learned in the fractions section and everything in the equation will disappear except 8 ×7.

So what happens when there are restrictions? This is easy – just fill in the restricted spaces first. Let's rework the question again.

There are 8 electives that a business school is offering this year. Daniel will take 3 his first semester and 2 his second semester. Two of the electives are only offered in the first semester. How many combinations of electives are possible for Daniel?

How many spaces do I need to fill? 5

_____   _____   _____   _____   _____

How many items from the pool are eligible for each space? Fill in the second semester first because only 6 of the 8 will be offered that semester. That leaves you with 4 for the first semester, but you have to go back and add in the two you eliminated from the second semester. So you are still at 6.

6 5 4 6 5

Does order matter? No

$$\frac{6 \text{ x } 5 \text{ x } 4 \text{ x } 6 \text{ x } 5}{5 \text{ x } 4 \text{ x } 3 \text{ x } 2 \text{ x } 1} = 30$$

> ➤ **More Practice from the GMAT® Review 13th Edition:** Questions 128, 148

Algebra

Remember this from high school? Not a popular one. I'm afraid we have to recap algebra for the test, **but** we'll try to keep it **short and sweet!**

Terminology

A *term* **is a number, a variable (e.g.** x, y, z**), or a combination of both**

(e.g.. 3z). Terms come in many different formats, such as: $7x$, $21y$, and $3\dfrac{x}{y}$.

Expressions, **are combinations of a variety of** *terms*, **separated by + or**
– signs, for example:

$$7x + 21y - 3\frac{x}{y}$$

Substitution is very important in algebra. It is a method used to evaluate the expression.

For example:

$$\text{Evaluate } 7x + 21y \text{ if } x = 2 \text{ and } y = 1$$

This means the numbers will be substituted into the expression as:

$$(7 \times 2) + (21 \times 1)$$

$$= 14 + 21$$

$$= 35$$

We previously discussed the various laws of operations, and those same laws apply to expressions in algebra including the commutative law, the associative law, and, at times, both laws. The distributive law is also found in algebraic expressions. (See the Arithmetic section for a recap of these laws)

Factoring Expressions

When you factor a polynomial expression, you are expressing it as the product of two or more simpler expressions.

The common monomial factor is common to every term in the polynomial and can be factored out using the distributive law.

The difference of two perfect squares can be factored into the product of:

$$b^2 - c^2 = (b - c)(b + c)$$

Polynomials using the expression $a^2 + 2ab + b^2$ are equivalent to the square of a binomial.

$$(a + b)^2 = a^2 + 2ab + b^2$$

Polynomials of the form $a^2 - 2ab + b^2$ are equivalent to the square of a binomial, where the binomial is the difference between the two terms:

$$(a - b)^2 = a^2 - 2ab + b^2$$

If a question isn't testing any one of the three common expressions above, you can always use the FOIL method. FOIL stands for First, Outer, Inner, Last. Multiply the first two terms of each factor, then multiply the two outer terms, the two inner terms, and finally the two last terms. This will yield:

$$(x + m)(x + n) = x^2 + xn + xm + mn$$

This may seem like a lot to take in, but don't worry, you will get the hang of it – and algebra is only a small portion of the test.

> ➤ **More Practice from the GMAT® Review 13th Edition:** Questions 37, 45, 209

Word Problems with Algebra

Word problems will test what you learned in algebra, arithmetic, and even geometry from your school years. All they do is ask the same questions in a different way. Look at this example to understand how:

In Algebra Form: $3x + 2 = y$

In Word Problem Form: *If the number of cars on the lot tripled, the car lot would have only 2 fewer than the lot next door.*

In this case, the number of cars on the lot is x, and the lot next door is y.

If $x = 23$ cars then: $3(23) + 2 = y$

The number of cars (y) on the other lot is 71.

The key to understanding word problems is to convert what they are saying in English into the universal language of mathematics. This is sometimes easier said than done.

Let's do some simple math to ease back into the concept of word problems. We will cover addition, multiplication, subtraction, and division in the next four examples.

If Jim bought eight apples for $.29 each and four pears for $.79 each, how much did he pay in total?

$$(8 \times .29) + (4 \times .79)$$

$$= 2.32 + 3.16$$

$$= 5.48$$

If there are 72 people in the room and 27 are men and 33 are children, how many women are there in the room?

$$72 - 27 - 33$$

$$= 45 - 33$$

$$= 12$$

If you buy one television for $3,300, then how many will 9 cost you?

$$3,300 \times 9$$

$$= \$29,700$$

If Jason bought eight apples for $3.72, how much is each apple?

$$\frac{3.72}{8}$$

$$= 47 \text{ cents}$$

Right there, we can see quickly and easily what we are dealing with – all based on the information in the word problems. Most simple mathematical word problems follow this method.

Since we just covered algebra, it's now time to put algebra into word problems. This may help you understand the problem much better. Let's look at an example to see how algebra fits into word problems.

Frank weighs the sum of Jim's weight multiplied by two, and Mary's weight multiplied by three. This can be shown as:

$$F = 2J + 3M$$

Of course, we need more information to answer this question. If we know that $J = 120$ and $M = 97$, then we can do more math:

$$F = 2(120) + 3(97)$$

$$F = 240 + 291$$

$$F = 531$$

So, Frank weights 531 pounds and should probably start looking into joining a gym ;)

That's it for the basics of word problems. Turn English into math, use the algebra we learned previously and you are all set! In the next section, we will move on to more complex problems.

> **More Practice from the GMAT® Review 13th Edition:** Questions 6, 64, 135, 153, 140

Geometry

Geometry on the GMAT is very basic and the questions relate just to lines, triangles, circles, and other relevant concepts. So you only need to know a few fundamental definitions and formulas.

Brandon's Tip

Diagrams are a big part of the geometry portion of the exam. Keep in mind when dealing with diagrams that:

- *All diagrams in the problem solving questions on the GMAT are to scale, unless otherwise noted by the question.*

- *This means that you can eliminate a lot of choices simply by looking at the diagram and estimating what you see in terms of length.*

Lines and Angles

We will begin by reviewing lines and angles.

As we know, a line is a one-dimensional object. It has no width, and is infinitely long. A line segment is part of a straight line, and has two end-points. Typically, a line is named for its end points: AB. The midpoint of the line is the point on the line segment that divides the line in two equal parts.

In the above example, A and B are the endpoints. M, the midpoint, is in the exact middle of line segment AB.

If we know that the distance between AM is 6, then the distance between MB is also 6. This means that the total distance of line AB is 12.

We know that an angle is formed whenever two lines, or line segments, intersect at a certain point. This point is the vertex of the angle, and the angle is measured in degrees.

There are four common types of angles.

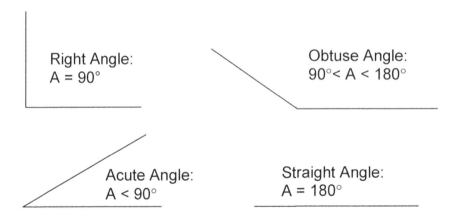

A right angle is exactly 90 degrees. An acute angle is anything less than 90 degrees, while an obtuse angle is greater than 90 degrees but less than 180 degrees. A straight angle is 180 degrees.

Lines are perpendicular if they are at 90-degree angles to each other.

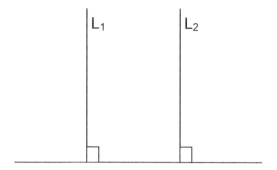

When two angles added together measure 180 degrees, then the lines that make up the angles are called **supplementary.** If the angles measure 90 degrees, the corresponding lines are **complementary.**

As can be seen from the examples above, when a line goes through an angle, it splits it into two smaller angles. If the split is equal, then the line is said to **bisect an angle.** A line that splits a 90-degree angle into two 45-degree angles is known as **bisecting that angle.**

Two intersecting lines create vertical angles, which are the opposite angles formed at the point of intersection. In the example below, w and y are vertical angles, as are x and z. This means x = z and w = y, and you already know that a straight line has 180°. Therefore:

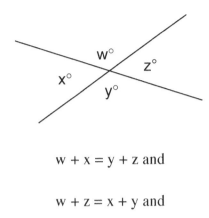

$w + x = y + z$ and

$w + z = x + y$ and

all of the equation equals 180 degrees

If two parallel lines are intersected by a third line, which is called a **transversal**, the two parallel lines will intersect that third line at the same angle, as can be seen below.

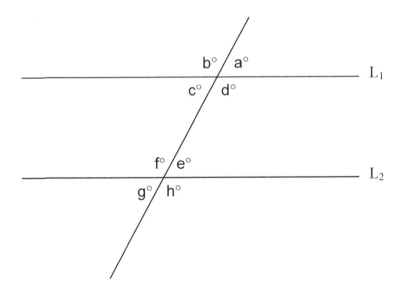

In the example above, we see that a and e are equal to each other. Also, since $a = c$ and $e = g$, then $a = c = e = g$ while $b = d = f = h$.

Coordinate Geometry

The next concept that we will look at here is slopes. When we talk about a slope, we are talking about how steeply a line goes up or down. If a line gets higher as you move to the right, then the slope is positive. Conversely, if a line gets lower as it goes to the right, then it has a negative slope.

We can find the slope of a line using the equation:

$$\text{Slope} = \frac{\text{rise}}{\text{run}}$$

The rise is the difference between the y-coordinate values of the two points on the line, while the run is the difference between the x-coordinates on the lines. Let's look at an example below.

What is the slope of a line with two end points at (2, 1) and (3, 6)?

$$\text{Slope} = \frac{\text{change in } y}{\text{change in } x}$$

$$\text{Slope} = \frac{6 - 1}{3 - 2}$$

$$\text{Slope} = \frac{5}{1}$$

Therefore, the slope is 5

Remember that a line that passes through the origin also gives you coordinates (0,0) that you can use to find slope. However, not all of the questions will give you the coordinates of a line, and you will have to figure out the slope using nothing but an equation.

All we have to do is turn the equation into $y = mx + b$, where m is the slope of the line and b is the y-intercept. The y-intercept is the point at which the line crosses the y axis. The value of the x coordinate at this point is always zero. For example, if you are given an equation of a line as follows:

$$2y - 8x - 10 = 0$$

We first convert the equation into the y = mx + b form by moving everything but the term y to the right side of the equation, and then divide all terms by 2.

$$2y = 8x + 10$$

$$y = 4x + 5$$

$$m = 4 \text{ and } b = 5$$

Then we know that the slope of the line is 4 and the y-intercept is 5, as shown on the graph below.

➢ **More Practice from the GMAT® Review 13th Edition:** Questions 7, 28, 61, 202, 206

Triangles

We all know what a triangle is and how it looks, but there are a few more things we need to learn about triangles for the GMAT.

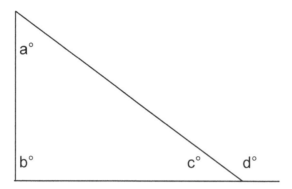

First, remember the rule that helps when figuring out the angles of a triangle: **The sum of the interior angles of any triangle is 180 degrees.**

Each interior angle in a triangle is supplementary to an adjacent exterior angle. The degrees of the exterior angle are then equal to the sum of the measures of the two non-adjacent, interior angles.

Confusing? Let's look at an example to help clarify this.

In this figure, the interior angles are a, b, and c, while d is the exterior angle. Looking at the three interior angles, a + b + c = 180 degrees, and since d is supplementary to c,

d + c = 180. Therefore, d + c = a + b + c and d = a + b. That means that d is equal to the sum of the two remote angles in the triangle: a and b.

Let's look at a brief equation for this:

If a = 45 and b = 90, then 45 + 90 = d, and

d = 135. Therefore the angle is 135°.

The altitude of a triangle is the distance between the vertex and the side opposite the vertex. This can be inside, or even outside, the triangle.

Let's look at two examples of the triangle vertex, inside and outside.

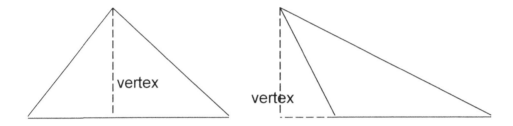

The sides of a triangle are very important. They allow us to figure out the area of the triangle when we do not have all of the information at our disposal. The length of each side of a triangle is less than the sum of the lengths of the other two sides, and greater than the positive difference of the lengths of the other two sides. This can be seen in the following equations:

$b + c > a > b - c$

$a + b > c > a - b$

$a + c > b > a - c$

Area

Knowing this, we can begin to figure out the area of a triangle.

The area of a triangle can be figured out with the following formula:

$$A = \frac{1}{2} (b \times h)$$

where A = area, b = base and h = height.

If a triangle has a base length of 6 and an altitude (vertex) height of 3, then we have an area as follows:

$$A = \frac{1}{2} (6 \times 3)$$

$$A = \frac{1}{2} \times 18$$

$$A = 9$$

If we are dealing with a right angle triangle, then we can use the following formula to calculate the area:

$$A = \frac{1}{2} L_1 \times L_2 \qquad$$

L_1 and L_2 are always the legs that come out from the right angle. If their value is 6 and 21, respectively, then we can figure out the area of the triangle.

$$A = \frac{1}{2} (6) \times 21$$

$$A = 3 \times 21$$

$$A = 63$$

Perimeter

When perimeter is talked about in terms of triangles, it means **the distance around the triangle.** This means that the perimeter is equal to the sum of the lengths of the sides.

Here is an example:

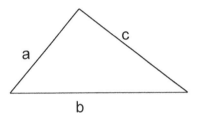

$a = 5, b = 12, c = 13$

Perimeter $= 5 + 12 + 13$

Perimeter $= 30$

Isoceles and Equilateral Triangles

An Isosceles Triangle is a triangle with two sides of equal length, called the legs, while the third side is the base. As a result of the legs being the same length, the two legs on opposite sides of each other have the same angle.

In this triangle, b = c.

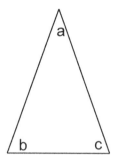

The other type of triangle is the **Equilateral Triangle**. These triangles have three sides of equal length, and three 60-degree angles.

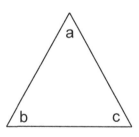

a = b = c = 60 degrees

Right-angle Triangles

Right angles are the most recognizable triangles in geometry. The longest side of the right angle triangle is called the hypotenuse (a), while the other two sides are the legs (b and c), as mentioned in the previous example.

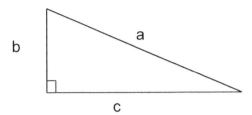

To calculate the area of a triangle, we can use one of the most famous mathematical equations in history: the Pythagorean Theorem.

This theorem dictates that the square of the hypotenuse is equal to the sum of the squares of the other two sides. Expressed as an equation, it reads:

$$a^2 = b^2 + c^2$$

Let's look at an example of this for a better understanding of how the equation is used.

What is the length of the hypotenuse if the legs are of lengths 11 and 12?

$$a^2 = 11^2 + 12^2$$

$$a^2 = 121 + 144$$

$$a^2 = 265$$

$$a = 16.27$$

You can see that sometimes the Pythagorean Theorem can be difficult to calculate. The good news is that the GMAT likes to test certain special right triangles repeatedly. If you can memorize the patterns and be on the lookout for them during the test, you won't have to do any calculations. These special right triangles are:

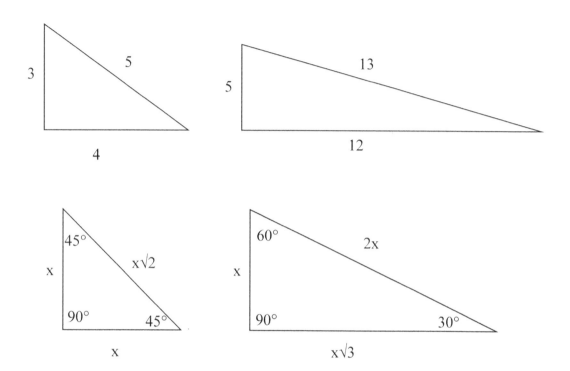

For that GMAT, that is about all we need to know about triangles. It is important to remember the differences between triangles, as well as how to find their areas and perimeters.

Only a few more sections and we will be done with geometry!

> **More Practice from the GMAT® Review 13ᵗʰ Edition:** Questions 75, 92, 206, 211, 228

Polygons

"Polygon" is a Greek word. Poly- means many, while -gon means angle. A polygon is a "closed" figure (all the lines connect) with straight-line segments for sides. This means that the perimeter of a polygon is the sum of the lengths of its sides.

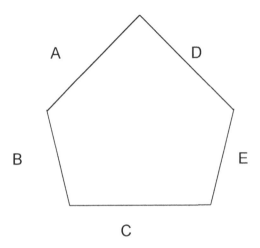

In the example above, we can calculate the perimeter as follows:

$$A + B + C + D + E$$

So, if B = E, A = D, and B = 2, A = 3 and C = 4, then the total perimeter is:

$$3 + 2 + 4 + 3 + 2 = 14$$

The diagonal of the polygon is a line segment connected to two nonadjacent vertices. The dotted lines in the image below are examples of diagonals in a polygon. If all the sides are of equal length and the interior angles are equal, then the polygon is regular. Otherwise it is irregular.

Polygons have different names, depending on the number of sides they have. If it has **three sides, it is called a triangle**. If it has **four sides, it is a quadrilateral.** If it has **five sides, it is a pentagon.** If it has **six sides, it is a hexagon**. Triangles and quadrilaterals appear most frequently on the GMAT.

The interior and exterior angles of a polygon can easily be found by simply dividing the polygon into triangles. See below for an example:

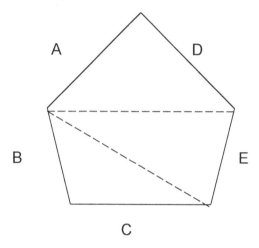

From the previous chapter, we already know that the sum of the interior angles of a triangle is 180 degrees. Since there are three triangles whose interior angles add up to 180 degrees, the sum of the interior angles in the polygon is 3 x 180 degrees, or 540 degrees.

Let's look at another example:

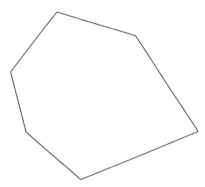

In the example above, what is the sum of the angles if the polygon is divided into sections with three interior lines?

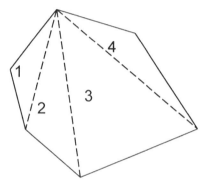

Dividing the polygon into sections with three interior lines creates four triangles. Therefore, the total sum of the angles is 180 x 4 = 720 degrees.

Quadrilaterals

Quadrilaterals are the most important aspect of geometry that appears on the GMAT, since they are by far the most frequently encountered concept on the test.

A quadrilateral, as we mentioned above, is **a four-sided polygon, where the sum of the interior angles equals 360 degrees in total.**

The two most common forms of quadrilaterals are squares and rectangles. A rectangle is a quadrilateral with four equal right angles, with the opposite sides of the rectangles equal in length. A square is a rectangle of four equal sides and angles.

Calculating the area of quadrilaterals, is easy. To find the area of a rectangle, simply multiply the length of the rectangle by the width (A = L x W), while the area of a square is its side squared, since all sides are of equal length ($A = s^2$). Let's look at a few examples:

What is the area of this rectangle?

$A = L \times W$

$A = 19 \times 14$

$A = 266$

What is the area of this square?

$A = s^2$

$A = 13^2$

$A = 169$

> ➢ **More Practice from the GMAT® Review 13th Edition:** Questions 62, 78, 104, 121, 147

Circles

Many of the questions that you will see related to geometry have to do with circles. Thankfully, circles are pretty easy to understand.

Defining a circle is a bit harder than simply looking at it. In layman's terms, if all points on a plane from a certain point are of the same distance, then you have a circle. This point is the center of the circle, and all circles are labeled for their center point. **The diameter** of a circle is a line that connects two points of a circle and passes through the center point. **The radius is a line segment from the center to the edge of the circle and is always one-half the length of the diameter.**

Central angles are formed by the radii coming out from the center of the circle.

A tangent of a circle is a line that touches only one point on the circle and runs perpendicular to it.

Now we get to one of the most important pieces of information related to a circle: Pi (or "π"). The circumference of a circle is the distance around a circle. Pi is the ratio of a circle's circumference to its diameter. The value of Pi is 3.1415926... and the decimal places never, ever end - Pi is the longest non-repeating number in the universe. Thankfully, just using 3 will be enough for your GMAT calculations, but keep in mind that it is actually a little more than 3. Since Pi is equal to the ratio of the circumference to the diameter, the formula to find the circumference is $C = \pi d$ or $C = 2\pi r$.

Before moving on to arcs and areas, let's just draw a circle and figure out some of the stuff we have just talked about here.

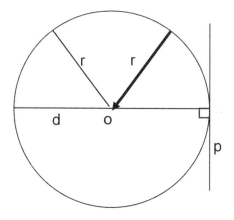

o = center of the circle

r = radius line

p = tangent

d = diameter line

Now, **the arc** of a circle is the portion of the circumference of a circle. **A major arc** is an arc of a circle having measure greater than or equal to 180 degrees, while **a minor arc** is an arc of a circle having measure less than or equal to 180 degrees. If the arc is exactly half the circumference, then it is a **semi-circle**. Let's look at three examples.

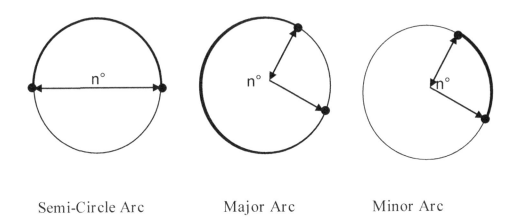

Semi-Circle Arc   Major Arc   Minor Arc

To find the length of the arc with a central point, we use the formula:

$$\text{Arc length} = \frac{n}{360} \times \text{circumference}$$

Let's look at an example.

What is the length of the arc XYZ?

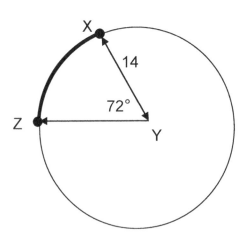

Since we know that the length of the radius is 14, we can figure out the circumference.

$$C = 2(\pi)r$$

$$C = 2(3) \times 14$$

$$C = 6 \times 14$$

$$C = 84 \text{ (plus a little bit more)}$$

We know the angle is 72 degrees, which means it is 72 out of 360 degrees or:

$$\frac{72}{360} = \frac{1}{5}$$

This means that the length of the arc is one-fifth the circumference or:

$$\frac{1}{5} \times 87.92$$

The equation for the area of a circle also uses Pi in the formula Area = (pi)r^2 . Let's find out the circumference and area of the circle below:

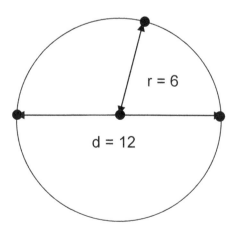

Since we know the diameter and the radius, it is easy to figure out the circumference and the area.

$$\text{Circumference} = \pi \times d$$

$$C = 3.14 \times 12$$

$$C = 37.68$$

$$\text{Area} = \pi \times r^2$$

$$A = 3.14 \times 6^2$$

$$A = 3.14 \times 36$$

$$A = 113.04$$

There we have it – the area and the circumference of the circle.

> ➤ **More Practice from the GMAT® Review 13ᵗʰ Edition:** Questions 36, 69, 175, 213

Multiple Figures

One aspect of geometry that you may not be familiar with is the concept of multiple figures. You will probably see multiple figures on your test, albeit not many of them.

Multiple figures are combinations of shapes. For example, you may find that the hypotenuse of a triangle is the side of a rectangle. Since you will be required to find the area of a particular shape, you need an eye for shapes.

Here's a sample question for a better understanding of this.

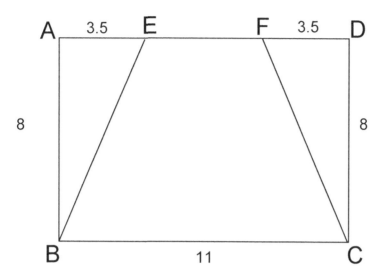

If ABCD is a rectangle, what is the perimeter of the polygon BEFC?

To figure this out, we have to look at the shapes inside the rectangle. We can clearly see a right angle triangle to the left.

Since we know that for right angled triangles, $a^2 = b^2 + c^2$, we can figure out one side of the polygon:

$$a^2 = 8^2 + 3.5^2$$

$$a^2 = 64 + 12.25$$

$$a^2 = 76.25$$

$$a = 8.73$$

Now we know that one side of the polygon is 8.73. Since the triangle on the other side is the same shape, this means that the three sides of the polygon are 8.73, 8.73, and 11. To figure out the top side of the polygon, we use simple math.

$$11 - 3.5 - 3.5 = 4$$

Now we have all sides of the polygon, so the perimeter is:

$$a + b + c + d = 4 + 8.5 + 8.5 + 11$$

$$= 32$$

Other types of multiple figures:

- A circle is inscribed in a polygon (an inscribed figure)

- A circle is circumscribed around a polygon (a circumscribed fig.)

Here are two examples of this:

Inscribed

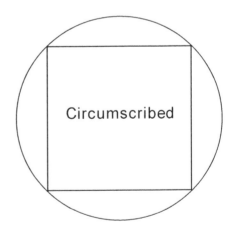

Circumscribed

How do we figure out the perimeter of the square if we only know the circumference or diameter of the circle? Well, it is actually pretty easy. Let's look at an example.

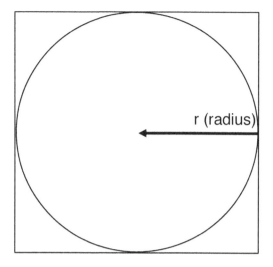

The area of the circle above is 36(π). What is the perimeter of the square?

We know that the area of a circle is $A = (\pi)r^2$. So if the area here is $36(\pi)$, then we need the square root of 36, which is 6.

Now that we know the radius, we can find the diameter, which is 6 × 2 = 12.

The diameter is 12, and since this is a square, all sides are equal. The diameter equals one side; therefore, the perimeter is:

$$12 + 12 + 12 + 12 = 48$$

We could also use the same information to find the area of the square:

$$\text{Diameter of the circle} = 12$$

$$\text{Area of Square} = 12^2$$

Therefore, the area of the square is 144.

Now, what about when we are dealing with a circumscribed figure? Let's try an example to figure it out.

If the circumference of the square is 8, what is the area of the circle?

First we find the length of each side of the square: $\frac{8}{4} = 2$

Notice that the diagonal of the square is also the diameter of the circle.

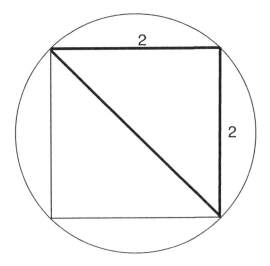

Our next step is to use the Pythagoras theorem to find the diagonal.

The diagonal is the square root of ($2^2 + 2^2$) which equals $\sqrt{8}$.

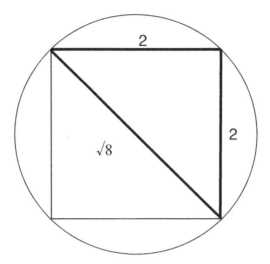

Therefore the circle has a diameter of $\sqrt{8}$ (or $2\sqrt{2}$ if you just used the memorized patterns from the special right triangle) and a radius of $\dfrac{\sqrt{8}}{2}$.

We get the area of the circle by using the equation:

Area of circle =

$$(\frac{\sqrt{8}}{2})^2\pi = \frac{8}{4}\ \pi = 2\pi$$

The important thing to remember when you are working with multiple figures is to get accustomed to viewing the object within the figure. This should help you to begin to figure out how everything goes together. The above is a perfect example of this.

These are the primary shapes that you will have to deal with, and knowing your areas and perimeter formulas from previous chapters will help greatly in figuring out the answers to these questions.

Data Sufficiency

Now we come to a very unique part of the GMAT Quantitative section, the data sufficiency portion. These types of questions are only found on the GMAT, and about a third of the points available on the math section come from these questions. The rest of the points in this section are from problem-solving questions, as we covered in previous sections.

With problem-solving questions, you are looking at the problem and finding the answer choice that best matches it. However, with data sufficiency, you don't actually have to solve problems; you only have to determine *whether* the question can be solved with the information provided.

As with the problem solving questions, these questions will only cover basic arithmetic, averages, fractions, decimals, algebra, factoring, and basic principles of geometry (triangles, circles, and areas/volumes of simple shapes). Okay, so it sounds like a lot when you list it out like that! But my point is that you shouldn't expect any surprises beyond these!

These types of questions will seem difficult at first, but as you move on, you will find that they get easier and easier. In this section, we are going to **take a look at the basic structure of Data Sufficiency question stems and answer choices** to make sure that you are familiar with the layout before moving into any of the techniques for handling these questions. **Next, we'll discuss the two main Data Sufficiency question types, the core topics tested, and other Data Sufficiency strategies. Finally, we'll try a bonus question that's a little more difficult** and shows how sneaky the GMAT writers try to be. Don't worry though, you'll learn how to out-smart them here! ;)

Basic Question Structure

All data sufficiency questions come in a similar format. You are given a question stem followed by two statements that, together or apart, may or may not answer the question in the passage. You have to choose one of the five options.

You will get a question followed by two statements that contain data. You then choose the correct answer based on the data in the statement, what you know, and common sense. Here is how the answers choices look:

A. **Statement (1) ALONE is sufficient, but statement (2) is not sufficient.**

B. **Statement (2) ALONE is sufficient, but statement (1) is not sufficient.**

C. **BOTH statements TOGETHER are sufficient, but NEITHER statement ALONE is sufficient.**

D. **EACH statement ALONE is sufficient.**

E. **Statements (1) and (2) TOGETHER are NOT sufficient.**

You can use this method to try to answer data sufficiency questions when you come to them. It is a step-by-step process that's quite easy once you get the hang of it.

1. **Look at the question thoroughly.** This may seem obvious, but the number of people who do not look at the questions when trying to answer them is surprising. You need to be able to decipher the question quickly, and then consider the information you may need

to answer it properly. Do not be afraid to ask yourself questions like:

    i.   What is the focus of the question?

    ii. Does it require a formula calculation?

    iii. What are the variables?

    iv. Do I have all of the values?

2. Next, as we have done with the reading part of the exam, we have to **split everything up and look at it separately**. Look at everything and try and determine again what you may need to answer it. You will want to go over the question twice before moving on.

3. **Look at the statements and make sure that you understand them.** Focus on them and think about what you just read in the passage. By this time, you should be able to focus on what answers can remain and what answers you can eliminate. You can then begin to answer the question.

4. **The last step is to answer the question to the best of your ability.** Remember, it is better to get it wrong than to skip it, so be sure to answer it.

That is about all there is to data sufficiency questions. For questions that make up a third of your math grade, they are pretty straightforward. Don't worry, we aren't going to throw you to the wolves yet; we'll look at a couple of questions here before moving on to the practice section.

A Couple of Sample Questions

As I mentioned, first, you are presented with a question stem:

What is the value of w if w and z are two distinct integers and w x z = 60?

Then, you are given the following statements:

  1. w is an odd integer

  2. w > z

  A. Statement (1) ALONE is sufficient, but statement (2) is not sufficient.

  B. Statement (2) ALONE is sufficient, but statement (1) is not sufficient.

  C. BOTH statements TOGETHER are sufficient, but NEITHER statement ALONE is sufficient.

  D. EACH statement ALONE is sufficient.

  E. Statements (1) and (2) TOGETHER are NOT sufficient.

The correct answer in this choice is E, **the value of *w* cannot be determined from the information provided**. Did you get it? Here's why it's the right answer:

We were given enough information to know that the two variables added together is 60. By looking at simple multiplication, we can determine that the following numbers conform to this:

$$1 \times 60$$

$$2 \times 30$$

$$4 \times 15$$

$$3 \times 20$$

$$5 \times 12$$

$$6 \times 10$$

Their negative values also conform (-1×-60, etc).

We know that w is odd because of the statement, and that means w can be 1, 3, or 5, along with -1, -3, or -5. As a result, we cannot determine which of these will answer the question. From that data alone, we know that the first statement is automatically eliminated. You can cross off answer A, but the cool thing is that you can also cross off answer D. Remember that D means both statements *independently* can answer the question, and you have just prove that A independently cannot answer the question.

Also, since w has more than one value, we cannot use statement 2, which will not allow us to find the value of w. When you look at statement 2, be sure to look at it independently. You don't want to apply any information you learned from statement 1 right away because then you might mistakenly choose answer B when you really mean answer C. Answer C means that you are using the two statements together to limit each other.

Since we cannot get the value of w, the next two statements are also eliminated because they do not provide sufficient data to answer any of the questions. **This is why the last statement is correct, because with statements 1 and 2 together, we are not able to answer the question and we need more information to do so.**

How was that? Let's try one more before moving onto the practice section.

How many people are members of both a certain town's softball team and bowling team?

   1. The softball team has 24 members and the bowling team has 9 members.

   2. 31 softball and bowling team members went to the town's annual picnic last year and no team members were absent.

   A. Statement (1) ALONE is sufficient, but statement (2) is not sufficient.

   B. Statement (2) ALONE is sufficient, but statement (1) is not sufficient.

   C. BOTH statements TOGETHER are sufficient, but NEITHER statement ALONE is sufficient.

   D. EACH statement ALONE is sufficient.

   E. Statements (1) and (2) TOGETHER are NOT sufficient.

Looking at the five answers, we can determine that answer C is the best choice for this question, which is ***Both statements are required to answer the given question***.

We know from statement 1 how many members each individual team has, but we don't know how many people play on both teams. This statement does not give us enough information, which eliminates answers A and D.

The second statement tells us that 31 members from both teams were at the picnic, and that 31 represents the total number of softball and bowling players. If there are only 31 players altogether, rather than 33 (24 + 9), 2 people must play on both the softball and bowling teams. **Therefore, an-**

swer C is correct because we have the information to answer the question, but we need both statements together to do so.

Two Main Data Sufficiency Question Types

Now that you've got the basic understanding of the structure of the Data Sufficiency section and a couple of general strategies for handling these types of questions, let's take a deeper look at the two main question types and some ways to tailor your approach to fit these questions.

The two question types that we'll be looking at are **concrete value** and **yes/no** questions. Although these questions may initially appear to be easier than other question types, the test makers usually add hidden wrinkles into the question stem that will need to be identified and handled in order to get the question right. Let's take a look at some ways of doing just that.

Question Type: Concrete Value

One common question type is called a **concrete value question**. This question type won't be new to you. It's asking for you to find the value of a particular variable that's provided in the question stem. When the GMAT test-makers ask for a variable's value in the Data Sufficiency section, it means the one and only value.

What is the value of x?

> *1. $x^2 - 9 = 16$*
> *2. $2x (x - 5) = 0$*

A. **Statement (1) ALONE is sufficient, but statement (2) is not sufficient.**

B. **Statement (2) ALONE is sufficient, but statement (1) is not sufficient.**

C. **BOTH statements TOGETHER are sufficient, but NEITHER statement ALONE is sufficient.**

D. **EACH statement ALONE is sufficient.**

E. **Statements (1) and (2) TOGETHER are NOT sufficient.**

Taking a look at the question stem in this example doesn't take long. No tricks to be found here – you're looking for the value of x. Taking a look at each statement that you're given in the question takes a little more time. Statement (1) looks simple but you have to remember that $x^2 = 25$ can mean that x is either +5 or -5. This is a good lesson because if you're able to solve the equation that simply, you're probably falling into a trap! Eliminate answers A and D.

For Statement (2), you could also have either 0 or +5 as possible values for x – so (2) is insufficient on its own as well.

Since neither of these statements were able to give us the value of x alone, we should try to look at them together and see what we can get.

Statement (1) tells us that the value of x is either +5 or -5; (2) says that x is either 0 or +5.

When they're combined, BOTH must be true and be satisfied by one value – in this case +5 works for both. The answer can't be 0 because that contradicts statement (1) and it can't be -5 because that contradicts statement (2). The bottom line is if the statements share just one value, they are sufficient (when combined) for answering the question.

Therefore C is the correct answer.

> ➤ **More Practice from the GMAT® Review 13ᵗʰ Edition:** Questions 1, 15, 46, 58, 147

Question Type: Yes/No

Yes/no questions generally represent about a third of the questions that you'll encounter in the Data Sufficiency section. That's both good news and bad news. The bad news is that questions generally appear to be fairly simple but you may have to brush up on some numbers properties or memorize a few basic mathematical rules in order to allow yourself to work through these problems in a reasonable amount of time. The good news is that if you can spend your time before the test figuring out these details, you'll have a much more organized approach to these problems during the actual test – and your score will show it.

While concrete value questions look for one value and one value only, yes/no questions look for one answer – yes or no – to the question posed.

Let's take a look at a basic **yes/no** question stem to clarify:

Is the product of x, y, and z equal to 6?

   1. x + y + z = 6
   2. *x, y, and z are each greater than 0*

The standard answer choices for data sufficiency apply to this problem:

   A. **Statement (1) ALONE is sufficient, but statement (2) is not sufficient.**

   B. **Statement (2) ALONE is sufficient, but statement (1) is not sufficient.**

C. BOTH statements TOGETHER are sufficient, but NEITHER statement ALONE is sufficient.

D. EACH statement ALONE is sufficient.

E. Statements (1) and (2) TOGETHER are NOT sufficient.

Looking closely at the question stem, it's pretty clear that what you'll need to determine is **the value of the product of** *xyz*. Keep in mind that when you're looking for a product, you'll either need to know the value of all of these variables or you can use a rule or property of multiplication to help you along. For example, if the product is 0, you know that at least one of these variables must be zero.

Taking a look at the question stem and using some of the techniques that we've discussed previously, it should be fairly obvious that statement (2) is not sufficient to provide the answer for us alone – the numbers that make up all of the values greater than 0 are just too broad to provide us with an answer.

This means that if the values are 1, 2, and 3, you will have an answer of 1, 2, and 3, you will have an answer of **yes** to the question stem. If the values are 4, 5, and 6, you will have an answer of **no** to the question stem. Since we only want one of those answers, you can eliminate B right away, and if you can eliminate B, you can eliminate D. You've already increased your chances of getting this answer correct by 40% - great!

Next, pick some numbers to satisfy statement 1. Again, choosing simple numbers like $x = 1, y = 2, z = 3$ is a good place to start. In this case, the product does equal 6. When you plug in some different numbers to test the properties of this equation (maybe $x = -5, y = 0, z = 12$) the product is 0 and the product is not equal to 6 – you've now eliminated answer A.

At this point, we're left with the possibility that the two statements combined will either be enough for us to get the yes/no answer that we're seeking or that they will still be insufficient. Going back to picking numbers is easy enough. This time, we'll just adjust our previous values so that they fit both rules – say $x = 1$, $y = 1$, $z = 4$. Even though the problem uses two different variables, x and y, you can assign them the same value if the problem doesn't say they must be distinct.

Remember, with these yes/no questions, it will only take one example that doesn't give you the desired output in order to show that the statement is not sufficient. In this case, the values that we substituted fit the rules of both statements and the resulting product is not 6 – C is not the answer. **We've eliminated all other possibilities so choice E is our answer.**

Although walking through the details of this process may seem somewhat lengthy, in reality these steps should take very little time for you to execute – especially if you are comfortable with this type of question stem and the way to methodically work through it for a solution. Always keep in mind that picking numbers to substitute for variables is a great technique but don't forget to pick strategically – include *positive* numbers, *negative* numbers, and *fractions* in order to get a better sense for where things stand.

Important Tip!

If you simply go for the obvious selections, you'll be playing right into the test maker's hands. Part of what the GMAT is trying to identify is which test takers are capable of complex thinking and problem solving. Even if this isn't your natural strength or if some of these approaches seem difficult initially, building good habits by practicing them now will pay off time and time again during the test.

Here's another **yes/no** question type that will take a slightly different approach to get to the solution:

Is $6 + \frac{x}{8}$ *an integer?*

> *1. x is between 80 and 90*
>
> *2. x has exactly one factor pair*

    A. Statement (1) ALONE is sufficient, but statement (2) is not sufficient.

    B. Statement (2) ALONE is sufficient, but statement (1) is not sufficient.

    C. BOTH statements TOGETHER are sufficient, but NEITHER statement ALONE is sufficient.

    D. EACH statement ALONE is sufficient.

    E. Statements (1) and (2) TOGETHER are NOT sufficient

The mathematical properties involved in this question stem are pretty straightforward. We need to know whether x is a multiple of 8 because if $\frac{x}{8}$ is an integer, it will remain an integer when we add it to 6. Let's take a look at the choices to see where things stand.

First, we know that A is insufficient because there are numbers between 80 and 90 that will give us a **yes** and **no** answer. 88 is a multiple of 8 and 85 is not. Eliminate answers A and D.

Now look at statement (2). This statement is telling us in a roundabout way that x is a prime number. If x is a prime number, it will never be divisible by 8 and therefore the answer to the question will always be **no.** This means that B is the correct answer.

You may be confused at this point because you have been conditioned your whole life to think that no is a bad answer. But on yes/no Data Sufficiency, no is a good answer! Remember that we want a definite **yes** or a definite **no.** Either one is fine because it provides an answer to the question.

This question is also a reminder that you won't always have to work through your entire problem-solving process in order to arrive at a solution. We don't actually care what the value of *x* is. We just needed a response of **yes** or **no.** In fact, once you are proficient in using all of these techniques, you should rarely have to work through an entire problem from start to finish. Shaving a few seconds off the easier and moderate problems may help give you the time you need to crack the really difficult "stumper" questions that you're bound to encounter.

> ➢ **More Practice from the GMAT® Review 13ᵗʰ Edition:** Questions 7, 13, 14, 27, 32

Core Topics

Let's look now at the most commonly tested concepts on Data Sufficiency. If you have already read through the whole Problem Solving section, you'll see that there aren't any new topics here. But what is different is the way you will apply the information you learned previously.

Core Topic 1: Linear Equations

While most of the techniques that we've discussed are solid and detailed approaches to certain types of problems, it's sometimes nice to have a quick tip that will allow you to get certain questions out of the way and move on to something more difficult – this is one such tip.

You will probably encounter at least one Data Sufficiency question that will provide you with a couple of linear equations. If you know enough about the nature of these equations, you might be able to recognize that a solution is possible without working to solve a part of it. Since that's all you need in a Data Sufficiency question, it's perfect.

Here's the tip: Solving for x variables requires x distinct, linear equations containing those variables. What this means is if you have two variables (say, x and y), you will need two distinct linear equations to solve both variables.

For example, given:

$x+y=4$

$x-y=2$

You can solve for both x and y. Although it's not difficult to solve for x and y in this example, you can imagine that things get considerably more difficult on the test. A good example is when the equations are disguised as sentences as in this example:

Peter took a trip from his parents' house to his grandmother's house. If he did not stop along the way, how long did it take Peter to finish his trip?

1. He traveled a total of 240 miles.
2. He traveled half the distance at 30 miles per hour, and half the distance at 60 miles per hour.

A. **Statement (1) ALONE is sufficient, but statement (2) is not sufficient.**

B. **Statement (2) ALONE is sufficient, but statement (1) is not sufficient.**

C. **BOTH statements TOGETHER are sufficient, but NEITHER statement ALONE is sufficient.**

D. **EACH statement ALONE is sufficient.**

E. **Statements (1) and (2) TOGETHER are NOT sufficient.**

Translate each sentence into an equation using *distance = rate × time*. Statement 1 will give you 240 = rate × time. Statement 2 will give you $\frac{distance}{2} = 30 \times time$ and $\frac{distance}{2} = 60 \times time$. Notice there you can substitute the distance given in statement 1 into the equations in statement 2, which will leave you with one variable. Once you have gotten to that point, you can quickly select the corresponding answer (C) and move on to the next question.

A couple of notes about this tip. First, you have to make sure that the equations can't be simplified to the same equation. If that's the case, there are actually fewer distinct equations than it might appear and your final answer might be totally different. Second, this tip will only work if no variables are raised to exponents (e.g. no x^2, y^3...etc). Overall, you should continue to practice all of the other techniques that have been provided but if knowing this tip helps you shave time off just one Data Sufficiency question, it will have been worth reviewing.

➤ **More Practice from the GMAT® Review 13ᵗʰ Edition:** Questions 9, 17, 34, 36, 60

Core Topic 2: Simple Geometry

It would probably be useful at this point to take a look at a totally different type of Data Sufficiency problem as a reminder of some of different issues that you might run into during your actual exam. This one is based on simple geometry:

What is the area of isosceles triangle XYZ?

> *1. The length of the side opposite the largest angle in the triangle is 6cm.*
>
> *2. The perimeter of triangle XYZ is 16cm.*

A. Statement (1) ALONE is sufficient, but statement (2) is not sufficient.

B. Statement (2) ALONE is sufficient, but statement (1) is not sufficient.

C. BOTH statements TOGETHER are sufficient, but NEITHER statement ALONE is sufficient.

D. EACH statement ALONE is sufficient.

E. Statements (1) and (2) TOGETHER are NOT sufficient.

This question does require some basic knowledge of geometry but you have likely done a little brushing-up on these basic rules by this point. **As a reminder, in a triangle the largest angle will be opposite the longest side. Similarly, the side opposite the smallest angle will be the shortest.** We also know from the question stem that this is an isosceles triangle. This tells us several things – most importantly for this question, we know that two of the sides and two of the angles are equivalent.

Since statement (1) refers to a "largest angle", we know that the side opposite this angle must be the longest in the triangle. The alternative in an isosceles triangle would be to have two equal angles that are equivalently large. Since we know that this largest side is 6, we know that the other two sides must be equivalent and that they measure no longer than 3 each (or they wouldn't be able to join to form the triangle. Take a look at the diagram below to get an idea of what you should be able to take from the question at this point:

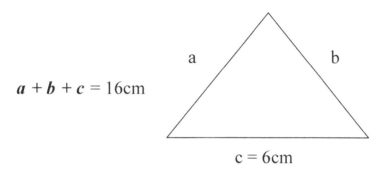

$a + b + c = 16$cm

$c = 6$cm

Although we know the measure of the base and have some idea about the other sides, we have no idea about the height at this point and can't calculate the area of a triangle without it – statement (1) is NOT sufficient. You can eliminate A and D.

Taking a look at statement (2) alone, we not have to forget everything that we learned while looking at statement (1). We know that calculating the perimeter is going to require us to sum the values of each side of this triangle. We can express this as $a + b + c$ = perimeter. From the question stem, however, we know that this triangle is an isosceles triangle and has two equivalent sides. This allows us to simplify our equation to calculate the perimeter into: $2a + b$ = perimeter.

Since we know the value of the perimeter, we can further simplify to:

$2a + b = 16$. At this point, we know that there's no way we'll be able to solve this equation without the help of another since we've discussed that two linear equations are necessary in order to solve for two variables. Statement (2) is NOT sufficient. This allows you to eliminate B. To get down to our final answer, it's time to evaluate the two statements together and see if C or E is the correct choice.

Since we've already essentially come up with an equation from looking at each statement individually, we'll just need to translate them into common variables to see if we'll be able to solve for each when they're combined. From statement (1), we know that:

The longest side = 6cm

From statement (2), we know that:

$2a + b = perimeter$

Since we know that the single longest side is also a distinct value from the other two sides (which are equivalent), we can substitute like this:

$2a + (longest\ side) = perimeter$

$2a + (6cm) = 16cm$

$2a + 6 = 16$

$2a = 10$

$a = 5$

This gives us the measure of the two equivalent sides of the triangle – so we know that the measures of all sides are 5cm, 5cm, and 6cm as in this diagram:

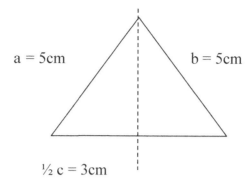

a = 5cm   b = 5cm

½ c = 3cm

Since we ultimately want to know if we can find the area of the triangle ($\frac{1}{2}$ bh), we must just calculate height knowing that the base is bisected by the height which intersects it at a right angle – giving a 3-4-5 special right triangle. Since we now know the height is 4, we know that statement (1) and (2), when taken together are SUFFICIENT to answer this question – answer C is correct.

Keep in mind that this question is one of those that is much easier to work through graphically. Remembering a couple of geometric ideas will have got you far with this one.

It is a good reminder that you'll see MANY different question types and there is potential for any of them to be more difficult . Using a consistent approach and not getting bogged down unnecessarily will keep you moving ahead regardless of the question type – you may even be hoping for some of the more difficult questions on this computer adaptive test (CAT) because it means that you're within striking distance of the higher scores that you're seeking. More difficult questions also mean that there's a better possibility that your fellow test takers will be tripped up – and your score will be higher as a result.

> ➤ **More Practice from the GMAT® Review 13th Edition:** Questions 11, 30, 35, 56, 73

Core Topic 3: Mean, Median, and Mode

Let's review a problem that requires some very basic knowledge about a common topic that comes up often in the Data Sufficiency section – mean/median/mode:

How many students scored more than the average (arithmetic mean) of the class on Monday's test?

1. The average (arithmetic mean) of the class was 78

2. Ten students scored below the arithmetic mean of the class

A. Statement (1) ALONE is sufficient, but statement (2) is not sufficient.

B. Statement (2) ALONE is sufficient, but statement (1) is not sufficient.

C. BOTH statements TOGETHER are sufficient, but NEITHER statement ALONE is sufficient.

D. EACH statement ALONE is sufficient.

E. Statements (1) and (2) TOGETHER are NOT sufficient.

In this case, it is VERY clear what this question is looking for – how many students scored higher than the average?

The first statement provides us with the average (as a reminder, that is the sum of all scores divided by the number of scores). This doesn't tell us anything about the individual scores. With an arithmetic mean (as opposed to a median or mode), there could be many students who are above average or only a few. Statement (1) is clearly insufficient to solve this problem.

Statement (2) still tells us nothing about the number of students that we're trying to determine. Statement (2) is insufficient to solve this problem.

Combining the two statements doesn't get us to the answer either. Even when combined, these statements fail to provide us with enough information to get the answer. The properties of an arithmetic mean inherently leave room for an outlier at the top or the bottom of the range that would pull the average score up or down. Since we are still unable to answer the question, our answer is E.

Keep in mind that although this question required you to do some reasoning through the question stem and statements, the only real outside information that you had to bring to the process was the knowledge of **how to calculate an average.** You probably learned and understood this years ago – the tough part is figuring out how to apply that 7th grade knowledge to a much more abstract concept. Keep this in mind. You've got the basics covered. Now use that noggin of yours to work out when and where to apply them!

> ➤ **More Practice from the GMAT® Review 13th Edition:** Questions 20, 37, 70, 84, 95

What Else do I Need to Know to Do Well?

By now, you undoubtedly can see why Data Sufficiency questions, though intimidating at first, are easier than problem solving. Let's talk about two more tips that will help you work through these questions efficiently and accurately.

Quick Tip 1: Diagrams Are Your Friend!

One part of the GMAT Data Sufficiency section that isn't unique is the diagrams that are provided with some of the questions. It's worth reviewing some key details about these diagrams and also a little bit about how these diagrams might be different from others that you may have encountered before.

First, there are some key things to keep in mind when working your way through a problem that includes a diagram.

It is important to realize that these diagrams are *not intended to be accurately drawn or scaled representations of the information in the problem*. Really, they are largely intended to help you with the relation between different points or figures. For instance, if there is an angle in a triangle that appears to be a right angle, you can't assume that that's the case unless you're told so by some other source in the question.

In fact, it's probably safe to assume that it's not a right angle if it's not marked as such. **If a diagram of a line segment with several points spaced equally along the segment, it's probably a mistake to assume that these points are actually evenly-spaced and so on.**

You'll always want to keep in mind that part of what the test makers are testing is your ability to move forward with a problem using only what you are given. **Sometimes it's helpful to purposely imagine (and draw) the diagram with skewed proportions on your scratch sheet in order to remind yourself that you're only dealing with the relationships that have been provided.**

Patience and flexibility in your approach to problems with diagrams will ensure that you don't fall for the distracting answer choices that are provided for the test takers who don't understand these ideas.

Quick Tip: Abstract Thinking

One of the higher-level skills that the GMAT is trying to measure is the test taker's ability to think about concepts in <u>an abstract way</u>. You should keep this in mind and use this fact to your benefit when working with all of the other techniques that we have discussed up to this point.

What does it mean to think about concepts in an abstract way? It means that, for instance, when you're choosing numbers to substitute in to an equation, you might want to recognize that there are certain boundaries that define groups of numbers. For instance, in the following question stem, think about how y changes when you substitute x for a positive number, negative number, or fraction:

$$y = (\frac{2}{x})^2$$

You can see that the resulting relative value of y is different in each case. A test taker looking at this problem for the first time with no preparation might choose numbers like 0, 1, 5 for x. That would certainly be a good starting point. Looking a little closer at this problem shows that choosing a larger, positive value for x means that the value of y actually gets smaller.

Choosing a negative value for x means that the sign of y will still be positive since the base fraction is multiplied by itself. Using a fractional value for x gives you still another result based on the type of fraction.

Becoming familiar with these number properties and being able to substitute strategically and determine what your likely answer choice will be is a great skill that only takes practice and close attention.

Thinking abstractly about the different groups of numbers that would affect the outcome is something that will allow you to reach those three results more quickly than blindly picking numbers. As a result, taking a little time up front to look at the question in a more abstract way will ultimately help you save time by getting to the correct answer more often and saving you time on the way there. Since this isn't the easiest approach to take initially, it may take a little work to get in the habit of taking a step back to consider the problem before diving in more deeply. **Pushing yourself this way can really be beneficial – even small improvements in abstract thinking and approach can gain extra points for you on the Quantitative section of the GMAT – and those are definitely extra points we are looking for!**

Bonus Question: The Stumper

Even if you're thoroughly prepared and as familiar as possible with each question type, you're likely to run into at least one question during the course of the Data Sufficiency section of the GMAT that throws you off balance.

Maybe it's the particular construction of the question. Maybe the question is based on a subject matter with which you're not familiar (this shouldn't matter). Regardless of how you arrive at a position of helplessness (!), there are things that you can do – when you don't know what to do, your "plan B".

In data sufficiency, all of the answer choices are based on the two statements that are provided in the question stem. That makes things difficult, but it also provides you with a great opportunity to narrow down the choices in many cases. If you've tried to attack the question with most of the tips that we've discussed to this point and haven't had any luck, take the statements individually. We'll discuss how you move forward with that approach.

Many times, the test makers will provide one statement that is fairly straightforward and another that is trickier. If you can evaluate the simpler statement using the tools that we've discussed in order to knock out some of the potential choices, it will increase your odds of choosing the correct answer – even if it's a complete guess – dramatically.

If you can get it down to two remaining answers, you've got a 50/50 shot at getting a "stumper" question right – that's a much better scenario than blindly guessing at a question with a 20% chance of success initially. It might be easier for us to look directly at a problem that will demonstrate this approach.

For the sake of this exercise, don't try to solve this problem traditionally until we've worked through the process as if you didn't know how to move forward.

What was the maximum temperature in swimming pool A on Sunday, July 23?

   1. The average (arithmetic mean) of the maximum daily temperatures in pool A from Sunday, July 23 to Saturday, July 29 was 72 degrees Fahrenheit, which was two degrees less than the average (arithmetic mean) of the maximum daily temperatures in pool A from Monday, July 24 to Friday, July 28.

2. The maximum temperature on Saturday, July 29 was 5 degrees Fahrenheit greater than the maximum temperature in pool A on Sunday, July 23.

A. Statement (1) ALONE is sufficient, but statement (2) is not sufficient.

B. Statement (2) ALONE is sufficient, but statement (1) is not sufficient.

C. BOTH statements TOGETHER are sufficient, but NEITHER statement ALONE is sufficient.

D. EACH statement ALONE is sufficient.

E. Statements (1) and (2) TOGETHER are NOT sufficient.

As we approach this problem, we want to remember the approach that we've successfully been practicing to this point – just because this one looks complicated, doesn't mean that an organized approach will not be beneficial here. Concentrating on the question stem gives us some good information. We're essentially looking for one number – the maximum temperature of the pool on a specific date. Reading carefully through the statements that follow the question stem gives us a great deal of information. Maybe these statements give us too much information. Statement (1) alone seems like a very detailed set of circumstances to work through – let's skip it for now and take a look at statement (2) to see if things can be narrowed down first.

This statement essentially gives us a comparison of the maximum temperature on two different dates but never gives us a concrete reference temperature to start with. We can tell that this statement will not be sufficient on its own. If not, that eliminates answer B and D. We've already increased or odds of selecting the correct answer from $\frac{1}{5}$ to $\frac{1}{3}$.

We'll work through how to actually solve this problem but even if you could get no farther, you've still improved your odds significantly by working through the easier of the two statements. There is no golden key that will unlock a higher GMAT Data Sufficiency score, but **by constantly chipping away at the questions, you will get better bit by bit. Before you know it, you're looking at a much higher score!**

Now let's take a look at the solution for this problem (in case you were wondering!) Starting with the first part of Statement 1, the average maximum temperature from July 23 to July 29 was 72. This means that the sum of the maximum temperatures for those days is 7 × 72=504. If the average maximum temperature from July 24 to July 28 was two degrees warmer than the average maximum of 72 for the other time period, we know that it is 72 + 2 or 74.

The sum of the average maximum temperatures for those days (5 × 74 = 370). Since we now have concrete values for each of these two sums, it would make sense to try to relate these two values in a way that would allow us to bring in what we know from statement (2) in order to make our way to a solution. Since statement (2) is essentially telling us that the temperature on Saturday was 5 degrees warmer that that on the earlier Sunday, we can express that as $y - x = 5$.

From our earlier strategies, we know that if we have two unknown variables, we can solve for those values if we have two corresponding linear equations. Using the variables that we extracted from statement (2), we know that we're looking for another equation that involves x and y. We can see from the values provided in statement (1) that adding together Sunday and Saturday will be the same as if we subtracted the five-day period from the seven-day period (also leaving us with Sunday and Saturday). Thus, we can translate these into an equation:

Saturday + Sunday = (seven-day period) – (five day period)

Substituting the concrete values that we know gives us:

Saturday + Sunday = 504 - 370

Next, we substitute in the variables that were established in our first equation:

y + x = 504 - 370

And perform the simple arithmetic:

y + x = 134

Thus, we've reduced all of that down to a linear equation with two variables that are common with the other equation. We know from our previous discussions that we will now be able to solve for both variables using these two equations. As such, the two statements TOGETHER allow us to solve the problem – C is the correct answer.

The good news is that we don't even have to solve both equations to know that C is the answer since the Data Sufficiency section isn't testing your ability to actually solve these equations but, rather, to know whether the equations CAN be solved using the statements provided. Sometimes, knowing when to stop before working through a problem on the GMAT can be as important as being able to actually work through the entire thing – this is definitely one of those cases.

As you're moving forward, keep in mind what each statement can tell you individually. In addition to a complete solution to the problem:

- If **statement (1) is sufficient**, *you can eliminate (B), (C), and (E). You've got a 50/50 shot at getting the answer right with a guess!*

- If **statement (1) is insufficient**, *you can eliminate (A) and (D). You've increased your odds from 1/5 to 1/3 already.*

- If **statement (2) is sufficient**, *you can eliminate (A), (C), and (E).*

- If **statement (2) is insufficient**, *you can eliminate (B) and (D).*

Things to Remember...

Know that you do NOT need to know the solutions to the questions; you just need to know whether you can answer the question with the given information. **Most data sufficiency questions do not require mathematical calculations and you can usually answer them faster than problem-solving questions.** You need some practice to become familiar with data sufficiency questions because they are quite different. But once you are familiar with them, you'll find them easier than a lot of the problem solving questions.

Here's an overview of how I answer data sufficiency questions and how you can run through them efficiently too:

1. Read the question quickly and decide what information is required to solve it. How many variables are in the equation? How many of them are unknown? Think before you look at the two statements, as this will help you quickly decide how relevant they are.

2. Read the two statements carefully and independently. Keep in mind that the information contained in each statement is unique and does not involve the other statement. Do not mix them up!

3. If both statements are insufficient individually to solve the question, look at them together and see if the information contained in both statements, taken together, is sufficient to solve the problem.

4. Finally, do NOT try to solve the question! As soon as you know whether the question can be solved, move on the next question and don't waste your time doing calculations.

5. For questions on number properties and algebra, you can come up with numbers and assign them to the variables and unknowns in the questions/ statements to help you understand them better.

Also remember some of the concepts that we've covered in this section:

Basic Question Types:
- **Concrete Value**
- **Yes/No**

Core Topics:

- **Linear Equations**
- **Simple Geometry**
- **Mean, Median, and Mode**

Quick Tips:

- **Diagrams are Your Friend**
- **The Stumper**

Bonus Question :

- **The Stumper**

Is this a lot of information?   Absolutely! If it were easy to ace the Data Sufficiency section of the GMAT, everyone would be able to do it. But you're already at a huge advantage - now that you know these basic techniques and question structure, the complexity of Data Sufficiency questions will work in your favor. Remember that these sections are always graded on a curve – the harder the questions, the better you will do in comparison to the others who are taking the test.

For each trick that you can avoid, many of the others will take the bait. (Sounds mean, but unfortunately with it being a standardized test, the GMAT is a little bit dog-eat-dog). For every question type that you recognize immediately from your practice, many other test takers will have no idea what to do. Start this section with the confidence that you've done your homework and that you can handle any surprises that come your way.

INTEGRATED REASONING

Integrated Reasoning

Welcome to the new section of the GMAT! If you are a repeat test-taker, you are probably wondering what this new section is all about, so I'll start off this section with a few questions and answers to set your mind at ease.

FAQ about Integrated Reasoning

The GMAT has changed?

Yes, but have no fear. You won't suddenly see sine waves and matrices on the Quantitative Section or analogies and foreign languages on the Verbal Section! The only change is the addition of the Integrated Reasoning section, a 30-minute section that comes after the Analytical Writing Assessment. In fact, the Integrated Reasoning section has taken the place of one of the essays, which means that the total length of the test remains the same.

Why was this change made?

The Integrated Reasoning section gives business schools another way to differentiate well-qualified applicants. The change is intended to measure your ability to analyze, evaluate, organize, and synthesize information from a variety of different source formats and then apply that information to problems that reflect the type of coursework typical for a business school student. Or maybe the change was made just because some people out there really enjoy writing test questions...

Is this new Integrated Reasoning section computer adaptive?

No.

What's this about a calculator?

The rumor is true! The Integrated Reasoning section has a basic calculator that you can access by clicking a button at the top left of the screen. This addition was made to make clear that the purpose of this section is not to test your ability to do simple calculations by hand. But remember, the calculator only understands what you tell it, so it is not a substitute for careful analysis of the information. The calculator is very basic, containing the 4 fundamental math operators (+, -, /, *) as well as the square root ($\sqrt{}$), percent (%), and reciprocal (1/x) functions.

Most of these you are probably familiar with and use quite frequently, but you may be wondering what the reciprocal function is. If you press this key after you enter a number, the result will be 1 divided by your number. For example, if you first press "9" and then "1/x," the result will be .11111. This function is useful for converting fractions into decimals and for calculating the value of a number raised to a negative exponent.

How does this change affect scoring?

The Integrated Reasoning section is not factored into the overall 800 score. The Quantitative and Verbal sections are still each given a score on the 0–60 scale and then mixed together with the secret GMAT algorithm to produce your total out of 800. Your Integrated Reasoning results are calculated by an equally mysterious algorithm to produce a score on a scale of 1–8, in single digit intervals. The percentile scale will be different from that of your main 800 score. The Integrated Reasoning percentiles are expected to be standardized by 2013.

How will I find out my Integrated Reasoning score?

Like the Essay score, the Integrated Reasoning score will not be immediately available when you complete the test. You will receive this score when your official score report arrives in the mail within 20 days of taking your test.

Do business schools care about my Integrated Reasoning score?

Well, the developers of the GMAT certainly hope so and they have conducted plenty of research among management faculty to support the inclusion of this section. Even so, exactly how much the admissions committees in the particular schools you are applying to care about this score is difficult to say. But with all the effort you are putting in to doing well on this test, why not do well on every section? The Integrated Reasoning score will be on your official report and gives you just one more chance to show what a rock star you are.

OK, great – so what exactly will I have to do on this new section?

The Integrated Reasoning section attempts to measure your skills related to the use of both quantitative and verbal information. The information in the questions is provided through text, tables, graphs, flowcharts, budgets, spreadsheets, and more. Some questions contain only one source of information and some contain multiple. And even though the test claims to only have 12 questions on the Integrated Reasoning section, many questions contain multiple parts, which means you really have to answer closer to 20 questions. The topics range from business applications to sociological studies to scientific research, and they may combine verbal and quantitative information within a single question. Although there may be subject matter with which you are unfamiliar, no external knowledge is needed to answer the questions. All questions can be answered with the information provided. Among the tasks you will have to complete are:

- Drawing conclusions, predicting trends, and making inferences

- Evaluating information for accuracy, consistency, and sufficient supporting evidence

- Calculating probabilities, rates, and basic statistics

- Identifying relationships and correlations among various sources of information

- Making strategic judgments and decisions about potential courses of action

Let's take a closer look...

Question Type 1

Graphics Interpretation

How is the information presented? You are most likely to see a scatter plot, line graph, bar graph or flow chart. You could also see some other visual representations of information, such as a Venn diagram (two or more interlocking circles used to show overlap among members of various groups) or a pie chart.

What is the format of the questions? Each visual is followed by 2 questions that have answers pre-populated in a drop-down menu. The number of options in the drop-down menus varies.

What concepts are tested? Frequently seen question types are about probability, slope, direct and indirect variation, averages, and percent change. Some questions also simply test your ability to interpret the graph or table correctly.

Example #1

$$y = 0.7937x + 0.7674$$
$$R^2 = 0.65498$$

Peer Rankings

Personality Test Rankings

The graph above is a scatter plot with 50 points. Each point represents a score that measures how well a first year MBA student works in a group. A score of 1 indicates that a student does not work well in a group and a score of 10 indicates that a student works very well in a group. To obtain these scores, the students were administered a personality test at the beginning of the semester and then ranked by their peers at the end of the semester. The solid line is the regression line and the dashed line is the line through points (0,0) and (10,10).

Use the drop-down menus to fill in the blanks for each of the following statements based on the information given in the graph.

The slope of the regression line is the slope of the dashed line.

Select...
less than
greater than
equal to

The scatter plot demonstrates that the personality test ranked most students ability to work in groups [Select... ▼] than their peers did.

Select... ▼
lower than
higher than
about the same as

Answer & Explanation

The slope of the regression line is less than the slope of the dashed line.

Remember that the slope formula is $\dfrac{y1 - y2}{x1 - x2}$. Coordinates are given to you for the dashed line, so you can put those into the formula to see that the slope of the dashed line is 1. The change in y is the rise on the graph and the change in x is the run. Because the regression line is rising more slowly than the dashed line, its slope is less.

The scatter plot demonstrates that the personality test ranked most students ability to work in groups higher than their peers did.

The dashed line with the slope of 1 is the line along which all points would lie if the personality test and the peer rankings yielded the same results. However, the majority of the points lie beneath that line. This means that the peer rankings were lower than what was expected, so the personality test rankings were higher. Another option is to select several points on the graph and look at their coordinates. By comparing the actual x values (personality test) with the y values (peer rankings), you can tell the x values are most often higher.

Example #2

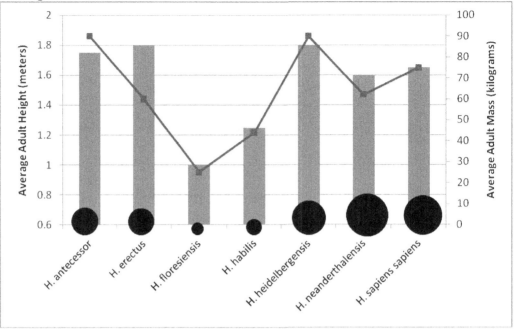

The graph above gives key developmental data, gathered from fossil records, about several species within the *Homo* genus. The bars indicate the average height (in meters) of an adult in the species, the points on the line indicate the average mass (in kilograms) of an adult in the species, and the bubbles offer a relative comparison of average adult cranial capacity (in cubic centimeters). *H. sapiens sapiens* is the only species still in existence.

The correlation between average cranial capacity and average adult mass for the species shown in the graph [Select... ▼] .

is positive
is negative
cannot be determined

The probability of a species having both a greater average adult height and greater average adult mass than does *H. sapiens sapiens* is [Select... ▼] .

1/3
3/7
1/2

Answer & Explanation

The correlation between average cranial capacity and average adult mass for the species shown in the graph cannot be determined.

You should select several species and compare the values of cranial capacity and mass. For example, *H. heidelbergensis* and *H. sapiens sapiens* both have a mass greater than that of *H. neanderthalensis*, but a smaller cranial capacity. Conversely, *H. antecessor* and *H. erectus* have both a mass and cranial capacity greater than those of *H. floresiensis* and *H. habilis*. There is no consistent pattern, so the correlation cannot be determined.

The probability of a species having both a greater average adult height and greater average adult mass than does H. sapiens sapiens is $\frac{1}{3}$.

Probability is calculated with the formula $\frac{\text{What I Want}}{\text{What I've Got}}$. In this case, there are six other species to compare to *H. sapiens sapiens*, so what you've got is six. Two of those fit the criteria of having both a greater average adult height and a greater average adult mass than does *H. sapiens sapiens*, so what you want is 2. Therefore, the answer is $\frac{2}{6}$, which reduces to $\frac{1}{3}$.

Remember!

- **Even if the graphic seems simple, take time to read all the information given before you begin.** This includes the text, which can offer information that will make the graphic easier to understand.

- **Pay attention to units.** This means comparing the units given in the chart or graph to the units in the question. If they are not the same, make a note on your scratch paper to remind yourself to convert the quantities. This also means knowing the numerical value of a symbol in a chart or a graph. A chart may contain a symbol that stands for a value in the hundreds or thousands. You may need to consider that actual value when calculating your answer.

- **If a graph has two vertical axes, make a note of which lines or bars correspond to which axes.** This information will be included in the text if the graphic does not have a legend.

- **If the graphic is a flow chart, pay attention to not only the direction of the arrows and lines,** but also any conditions that are stated in order to move from one step to the next. Flow charts may contain repeated loops if certain criteria are not met, so be sure to trace the path carefully. A rectangle indicates an action and a diamond indicates a decision.

- **Use the answer choices in the drop-down menu to help yourself understand the question better.** You may be able to answer the question many ways just based on the graphic, but the answer choices will make the question more specific.

Question Type 2

Two-Part Analysis

How is the information presented? These questions usually contain a lot of text in paragraph form but can also include supplemental information, such as formulas or bulleted lists.

What is the format of the questions? Each problem contains two questions given in a table with three columns. The first two columns each contain a question and the final column contains the answer choices to select from. You will select one answer choice for each question. The answer choices may be numbers, formulas, or text and the number of answer choices available will vary. The two questions may or may not be dependent on each other. If the questions are not mutually exclusive, there may be one answer choice that is correct for both questions.

What concepts are tested? Frequently seen question types are about direct and indirect variation, percent change, rate formula, and logical inference.

Example #1

The manufacturing facilities of Factory ABC operate 50 hours per week over a span of 5 days. Under normal operating conditions, Factory ABC can produce x widgets per hour. These widgets are sold wholesale for $8.00 each. The cost of production of the widgets is y dollars per widget, plus a fixed cost of z dollars per business day. The CEO of Factory ABC

335

is considering implementing lean manufacturing measures to lower the cost of production. These measures will not change the cost or selling price per widget, but the CEO estimates that they will reduce the fixed costs by 20 percent.

In terms of the variables x, y, and z, select the expression that represents Factory ABC's profit if it sells all the widgets, without a discount, that it manufactures in one week under normal operating conditions. Then, select the expression that represents Factory ABC's potential profit if it implements lean manufacturing measures and then sells all the widgets, without a discount, that it manufactures in one week. Make only two selections, one in each column.

Profit Under Normal Operating Conditions	Profit Under Lean Manufacturing Measures	
○	○	$40x - (50y + z)$
○	○	$400x - 5(10xy + z)$
○	○	$50(10x - xyz)$
○	○	$\dfrac{40x - (50y + z)}{1.2z}$
○	○	$320x - 4(10xy + .8z)$
○	○	$2(200x - 25xy - 2z)$

Answer & Explanation

Profit under Normal Operating Conditions: **$400x - 5(10xy + z)$**

This question contains a lot of variables and some very complicated formulas. Rather than running the risk of making a mistake with all those letters, a good option is to assign numbers to the variables, which will turn this algebra problem into simple arithmetic.

Let's say that the factory produces 3 widgets per hour, each widget costs 2 dollars to make, and the fixed costs are $20 per day. In other words, $x = 3$, $y = 2$, and $z = 20$. Profit equals revenue minus cost, so let's calculate each of those.

The revenue is the number of widgets per hour, times the total number of hours, times the wholesale price per widget. With our numbers, this is $3 \times 50 \times 8$, or 1,200. The cost equals the number of widgets per hour, times the total number of hours, times the cost per widget. This is $3 \times 50 \times 2$, or 300. In addition, you need the fixed cost per day times the number of days. This is 5×20, or 100. Therefore, revenue minus cost equals $1,200 - 400$, which makes the profit 800.

When we put those numbers into the correct answer, we see that we get the same result: $(400 \times 3) - 5((10 \times 3 \times 2) + 20)$. $1,200 - 5(80) = 800$. No other answer will yield that result with those values for x, y, and z.

*Profit under Lean Manufacturing Measures:***2(200x – 25xy – 2z)**

You already know that the answer to the second question cannot be the same as the answer to the first. The profit must be higher because there was a decrease in cost. So you have already eliminated one answer choice. Next, just use the same numbers you assigned in the first question to answer this one, but remember that z should be reduced by 20 percent to 16.

Let's use the equation from question one to avoid unnecessary rework, remembering to substitute 16 for 20 to get the new result. $(400 \times 3) - 5((10 \times 3 \times 2) + 16)$. $1,200 - 5(76) = 820$. Now enter the values for the variables (z reverts back to 20) into the remaining choices to see which matches 820. In our correct answer choice, this looks like: $2((200 \times 3) - (25 \times 3 \times 2) - (2 \times 20))$, or $2(600 - 150 - 40) = 820$.

On a side note, if you really were not sure how to answer these questions, or you were down to your last few seconds and just had to take a guess, you could guess the correct answers just by understanding the principle that profit is revenue minus cost. Since the revenue does not change under lean manufacturing, you could select the correct answers because they are the only two with the same value for profit ($400x$ and $2(200x)$). But that's just guesswork. Be sure to solve it out if you have the time!

Example #2

The following excerpt discusses the necessary conditions for successfully growing *Apium graveolens*, (better known as celery!)

Apium graveolens is a finicky crop that rarely yields a reward proportionate to the effort required to grow it. The ideal combination of soil quality, climate, and weather patterns is nearly impossible to achieve in most standard home gardens. The seeds have a germination period of two weeks, during which time they must be kept at a temperature of 70°F. After germination, seedlings can be transplanted outdoors, but only if the outdoor temperature will not go lower than 55°F. The growing period for *Apium graveolens* is five months, but few climate zones will maintain that minimum temperature for such an extended period of time. Compounding the difficulty of finding an appropriate climate zone is that *Apium graveolens* will not grow well in areas that are hot and arid yet requires six hours of direct sunlight per day. The shallow root system of this plant necessitates human intervention, primarily through constant weeding and the use of mulch, to retain moisture, and the soil should have a pH of 6.0–6.5, which is to say it has a slight acidity level.

Based on the explanation above of the difficulty of growing *Apium graveolens*, which of the following must occur for successful growth, and which of the following must not occur for successful growth? Make only two selections, one in each column.

Must Occur for Successful Growth	Must Not Occur for Successful Growth	
○	○	Transplanted seedlings are kept indoors to protect them from frost
○	○	Climate control in the plant's environment for almost half year
○	○	A professional farm or garden designed just for growing *Apium graveolens*
○	○	Wind transportation of the seeds to a neighbor's garden without his awareness
○	○	*Apium graveolens* reproduces asexually in the wild

Answer & Explanation

Must Occur for Successful Growth: **Climate control in the plant's environment for almost half a year** is correct because germination requires 2 weeks and the subsequent growing season is 5 months. In both phases, the plant will not grow well if the temperature dips below a certain level and if adequate sun and moisture are not provided. A professional farm or garden designed just for growing *Apium graveolens* may be ideal, but is not necessary. The passage only states that it *is nearly impossible*, but not completely impossible, to grow *Apium graveolens* in a standard home garden.

Must Not Occur for Successful Growth: **Wind transportation of the seeds to a neighbor's garden without his awareness** is the correct answer because the passage emphasizes the amount of human intervention required to grow *Apium graveolens* in a home garden. Keeping transplanted seedlings indoors to protect them from frost does not necessarily prevent successful growth because it is possible to provide 6 hours of direct sunlight from an indoor location. Asexual reproduction of *Apium graveolens* in the wild is incorrect because the passage only discusses *Apium graveolens* grown in a garden. No inferences about wild *Apium graveolens* can be made. In addition, one might logically assume that since the parent *Apium graveolens* was already growing successfully in the wild, in order to reproduce there, its offspring will grow successfully as well.

Remember!

- **Read the full question carefully.** The headings in the columns are often just abbreviated explanations of the questions and you may misunderstand the task if you do not read all of the information.

- **Decide whether the two questions are dependent on each other or influence each other in some way.** If they are dependent, find the answer to the easier question first and then use that knowledge to eliminate answer choices for the second question. Often times, you can use the relationship between questions to determine which will yield a larger answer. Then you can eliminate answer choices that are too big or too small.

- **If the questions are independent, remember that one answer can satisfy both questions.** You can still answer the easier question first, but don't let your answer to the easier one influence your answer to the remaining question.

- **If the answer choices contain equations with variables, considering assigning numbers to the variables.** Working with real numbers can be easier than working with unknowns.

- **If the answer choices contain numbers instead of variables, use properties of numbers and the criteria in the problem to eliminate answer choices.** For example, if a problem discusses a group of MBA students who need to be split into three equally-sized groups to work on a project, you know that the total number of students must be divisible by three because you cannot have a partial student. Eliminating answers before you start calculating can help you make a good guess if you are running out of time and can help you avoid careless errors.

Question Type 3

Multi-Source Reasoning

How is the information presented? The information is presented across three separate documents, which are accessed via tabs at the top of the screen. The tabs have a brief title that describes what the documents contain. You can only see one document at a time. The documents can take a variety of formats, such as emails, budgets, standard paragraphs, or tables. When a source is primarily text, it will generally be limited to fewer than 300 words.

What is the format of the questions? Some of these questions have three statements with Yes and No options. You will have to determine whether the statement can be proven true by the information given. The three statements might also contain algebraic expressions or numerical values and you will have to determine whether those expressions or values will solve a given question. You might also see multiple-choice questions with 5 options. Unlike the other Integrated Reasoning problems, Multi-Source Reasoning can have several independent questions that appear on different screens. You have to answer each question in order to move on to the next, and you cannot move back and forth among the questions.

What concepts are tested? Frequently seen questions types are about logical inference.

Example #1

Email

*Email from **Marketing Director** at Company Q to **Project Manager** at Company Q*

April 8, 9:53 a.m.

As you know, the marketing proposal is due in two weeks and even though this is a relatively low budget client, winning this account is important to our company. The information you have already gathered on the client's history, market positioning, and target audience is substantial and well researched. I have also put together a few documents that will help you write the proposal. Attached is the budget that we have created for this project. Also attached is a fact sheet on our competitors who will also be submitting tenders for this job. This sheet will help you compose our value proposition in a way that shows the client how we are unique to ensure the success of our bid. Please review the documents and contact me as soon as possible with any questions you may have.

Budget

Contractors	**$75,000**
Materials	**$250,000**
Internal Resources	**$45,000**
Media	**$200,000**
Contingency Fund	**$50,000**
Total	**$620,000**

Competition

Company X: This company is the most widely known in the field of marketing. Many of its proposals are accepted simply because of the company's name. However, surveys published in trade journals reveal that clients of this company often do not feel that they received value commensurate with the price the company charges.

Company Y: This company is the cost leader in the marketing industry. It outsources much of its design work to foreign partners, which allows it to undercut its competitors. However, the company has made several, well-publicized errors in its recent work, which have really damaged its reputation. Still, clients who have a low marketing budget are more likely to use this company in order to keep expenses low.

Company Z: This company, which is new to the field, is already earning a good reputation for itself in the field as a highly innovative, cutting-edge marketing company. In addition, the CEO has many powerful connections and is well-liked. However, because of its dedication to innovation, the company tends to be inflexible. The employees view themselves as artists and are very protective of their work. They prefer to create a product that pleases themselves, rather than the client.

Which of the following statements about the company's market proposal is best supported by the information in the three documents?

○	Company Q could lower some of its Contractor and Internal Resources costs if it outsourced work to foreign partners.
○	Company Q's proposal is likely to win because its competitors have serious flaws that the client will not ignore.
○	Company Q's is damaging its chances of winning because its budget is too high.
○	Company Q's proposal should focus on factors other than reputation, cost, and innovation in order to win.
○	Company Q's Project Manager was lacking important information about the client before receiving the email.

Answer & Explanation

Company Q's proposal should focus on factors other than reputation, cost, and innovation in order to win.

The first answer choice is not supported because the documents offer no information about who Company Q's contractors are currently. Maybe

Company Q is already using foreign partners. The documents also offer no information about the wages Company Q pays its contractors, if in fact they are domestic, in comparison to wages for foreign partners.

The second answer choice is not supported because the documents offer no information about the desires and priorities of the client. It is possible that some of the flaws in the competition will not present a problem for the client.

The third answer choice is not supported because although the email indicates that the client has a low budget, no figures are offered. Company Q plans to charge $620,000 for the project, but none of the documents indicate whether this is a high or low figure for the client.

The fifth answer choice is not supported because the Project Manager received information from Marketing Director about the budget and the competition, not about the client.

So why is the fourth answer choice correct? The Marketing Director's email says that the project manager should incorporate the information from the competitor fact sheet in order to *compose our value proposition in a way that shows the client how we are unique to ensure the success of our bid*. Reputation, cost, and innovation are all ways in which the competitors differentiate themselves. Emphasis on those factors would not make Company Q look unique.

Example #2

Etymology

The modern American English lexicon is an amalgamation of many other languages, though the primary roots are West Germanic. American colonists borrowed many words from the Native Americans to describe the variety of plants, animals, and natural phenomena that were unknown in England at the time. The language of the nation of immigrants was also naturally populated by loanwords from foreign tongues as the nation expanded. And over time, societal changes, such as the American and Industrial Revolutions, generated a host of neologisms to describe new inventions and unprecedented cultural events.

But these words have not been static. They have morphed through the generations, claiming new meanings that may seem only distantly related to their origins and finding new life by transforming from nouns into verbs, or adjectives into nouns. They have joined with their comrades to create an army of compound words, in that great Germanic tradition. Some have even altered themselves so drastically as to move from a positive to a negative connotation.

Perhaps no word exemplifies the transitory nature of proper word usage in America as much as "OK" does. The origins of this word, which now has international renown, are imprecise, though one well-known explanation is that it was an abbreviation for *oll korrekt*, a comical misspelling of *all correct* that was popular in the 1830s in America. Regardless of the origin, the journey of this little word across the American lexicon has been nothing less than astounding. What other word has a rightful place in so many parts of speech and can betray its own significance in a single breath by denoting both an encouraging and a critical tone?

Parts of Speech

The following table identifies the ways in which the word "OK" is used in modern American English.

Part of Speech	Connotation
Adjective	positive
Adjective	mediocre
Adverb	positive
Adverb	mediocre
Exclamation	disbelief
Exclamation	frustration
Function Word	agreement
Noun	approval
Stand-alone Question	comprehension
Verb	approval

Hypotheses

The following table identifies some of the hypothesized origins of the word "OK."

Spelling	Year	Source
kay	1784	travelogue written by a European visiting America
okeh	1825	translations of the Bible written by domestic American missionaries who were working with the Choctaw Indians
Oll Korrect or O.K.	1839	newspapers in Boston and New York
OK	1840	an abbreviation for presidential candidate Martin Van Buren's nickname, Old Kinder-hook

ola kala	1942	scholarly article on the possible origins of the word from a Greek phrase meaning "all good"
och aye	1964	scholarly article on the possible origins of the word from a Scottish phrase meaning "oh yes"
o ke	1969	scholarly article on the possible origins of the word from a West African phrase meaning "yes, indeed"

For each of the following statements, select *Yes* if the statement can be inferred based on the information provided. Otherwise, select *No*.

Yes	No	
○	○	Considering the numerous parts of speech that the word "OK" has adopted and the fact that it can be positive or negative, it is unusual that "OK" is not also found in a compound word.
○	○	The modern word "OK" is known to be derived from a word that existed in print prior to the appearance of "O.K." in a Boston newspaper.
○	○	The linguistic influence of immigrants on American English and a predominance of hypotheses that indicate OK has origins in a foreign language discredit the idea that OK is an abbreviation for *oll korrekt*.

Answers & Explanation

Considering the numerous parts of speech that the word "OK" has adopted and the fact that it can be positive or negative, it is unusual that "OK" is not also found in a compound word. **No**

This answer choice is not supported because of the word *unusual*. The "Etymology" document indicates that adopting new parts of speech, changing tone, and becoming parts of compound words are all ways in which words in the modern American English lexicon have changed. What the document doesn't indicate is that a word that changes in one of those ways necessarily changes in the other two as well. There is no reason given to support the idea that "OK" should appear in compound words merely because it changed in two other ways.

The modern word "OK" is known to be derived from a word that existed in print prior to the appearance of O.K. in a Boston newspaper.   **No**

This answer choice is not supported because all of the possible origins given for "OK" are just hypotheses. The printed appearances of *kay* and *okeh,* in 1784 and 1825 respectively, may not be related to the modern "OK." The "Etymology" documents explicitly states that the origins of "OK"*are imprecise.* Therefore, this answer choice is too definitive to be supported by the documents.

The linguistic influence of immigrants on American English and a predominance of hypotheses that indicate OK has origins in a native language discredit the idea that OK is an abbreviation for oll korrekt. **No**

This answer choice is not supported because the of the word *discredit*. The documents offer no comparison or reason to believe any one hypothesis is superior to another. The "Etymology" document says that the *oll korrekt* hypothesis is well-known, but does not make any judgments regarding its credibility or lack thereof.

Remember!

- **Read through all the sources before you begin.** Don't read for a lot of detail, but try to get a general understanding of the main idea.

- **Make notes on how the different sources relate to each other.** Some possible relationships include:

    - **A series of correspondences.** In this case, take notes on who is communicating with whom in each case. Make sure that you don't confuse one person with another.

    - **A general theory or set of conditions or rules, and then a specific example of that information in action.** Make sure that you understand whether the specific example has followed all criteria laid out in the general tab.

    - **Data presented over different periods of time.** Make sure you know the time frame and the units of measure for all data presented.

- **After you read the first question, go back to the sources to read for more detail.** All information needed to answer the question will come directly from the sources, but the correct answer choice could be written in a confusing way. Take the time to find evidence for the correct answer choice instead of trying to answer a question from memory.

- **Think carefully about which source can answer a particular question.** Sometimes, one source may seem to be obvious, but you may have overlooked relevant information a second or third source.

- **If a source contains numerical data, take time to do the calculations required by a question.**

Question Type 4
Table Analysis

How is the information presented? The information is given in a spreadsheet that can be sorted by selecting the column you want to sort by from a drop-down menu above the spreadsheet. The number of rows and columns in each spreadsheet varies. The spreadsheet may also be accompanied by text that explains what the table is about or gives additional information.

What is the format of the questions? Each table is followed by three statements with two mutually exclusive options (for example, Yes and No). For some statements, you will have to determine whether the statement can be proven true by the information given or whether the statement is consistent with the information given. For others, you will have to decide whether the table even gives enough information to support the statement.

What concepts are tested? Frequently seen question types are about percent change, direct and indirect variation, median, average, and comparative rankings.

Example #1

Sort By:

Information on the Departments in Discount Grocery Store X

Grocery Store Department	% of Total Store Revenue	Average Markup Level	Customer Satisfaction Level
Bakery	7	High	Very
Dairy	11	Low	Very
Deli	4	High	Very
Dry Goods	21	Low	Very
Frozen Food	14	Low	Somewhat
Household Products	10	Moderate	Somewhat
Meat and Seafood	14	Low	Very
Pharmacy	7	Moderate	Not at All
Produce	12	Low	Somewhat

For each of the following statements, select *Yes* if it can be inferred from the information in the table. Otherwise, select *No*.

Yes	No	
○	○	Grocery Store X most likely sells a greater quantity of Dry Goods than Bakery items.
○	○	The level of customer satisfaction has a direct relationship to the revenue earned by a department.
○	○	Compared to other discount grocery stores, Grocery Store X offers customers a good value on non-food items.

Answer & Explanation

Grocery Store X most likely sells a greater quantity of Dry Goods than Bakery items. **Yes**

Sort the table by "% of Total Store Revenue." This sort order makes it easy to see that Dry Goods bring in much more revenue than Bakery does, but the Average Markup Level on Bakery items is higher. If Grocery Store X has a much higher markup on Bakery items, yet earns almost its lowest percentage of revenue from the Bakery, while Dry Goods bring in 3 times the revenue, the store must be selling a greater quantity of Dry Goods.

Note that the answer choice uses the words "most likely."Although there may be some other remotely possible explanation, this one is the most likely because the chart title states that Grocery Store X is a discount store, and therefore unlikely to have any high priced, gourmet Dry Foods that would influence the revenue.

Grocery Store Department	% of Total Store Revenue	Average Markup Level	Customer Satisfaction Level
Deli	4	High	Very
Bakery	7	High	Very
Pharmacy	7	Moderate	Not at All
Household Products	10	Moderate	Somewhat
Dairy	11	Low	Very
Produce	12	Low	Somewhat
Frozen Food	14	Low	Somewhat
Meat and Seafood	14	Low	Very
Dry Goods	21	Low	Very

The level of customer satisfaction has a direct relationship to the revenue earned by a department. **No**

Sort the table by "Customer Satisfaction Level." This sort order makes it easy to see that % of Total Store Revenue varies widely within any given Customer Satisfaction level.

Grocery Store Department	% of Total Store Revenue	Average Markup Level	Customer Satisfaction Level
Pharmacy	7	Moderate	Not at All
Frozen Food	14	Low	Somewhat
Household Products	10	Moderate	Somewhat
Produce	12	Low	Somewhat
Bakery	7	High	Very
Dairy	11	Low	Very
Deli	4	High	Very
Dry Goods	21	Low	Very
Meat and Seafood	14	Low	Very

Compared to other discount grocery stores, Grocery Store X offers customers a good value on non-food items. **No**

There is no need to sort the table to see that this answer choice is not supported. Although non-food items, Pharmacy and Household Products, are described as having a *moderate* markup, the table does not explain what *moderate* means. *Moderate* could in fact be relative to other stores' markups, but it could just be relative to the other items in Grocery Store X.

Example #2

Sort By

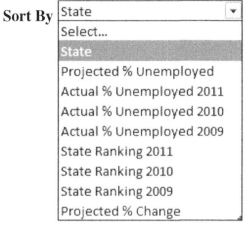

State	Projected % of Population Unemployed	Actual % of Population Unemployed			State Ranking Compared to All 50 States and the District of Columbia (1 indicates highest unemployment rate)			Projected % Change from 2011 to 2012
	2012	2011	2010	2009	2011	2010	2009	
Alabama	7.3	9.2	10.5	11.2	18	11	7	20.65%
Arizona	8.6	9.5	10.4	10	13	13	13	9.47%
California	11	12	12.2	11.3	2	3	5	8.33%
Colorado	7.8	9.2	8.7	7.4	17	27	37	15.22%
Connecticut	7.7	9.1	9.2	8.1	20	23	28	15.38%
Florida	9	11.1	11.1	10.4	3	5	10	18.92%
Georgia	9	10	10.7	9.8	8	9	16	10.00%
Idaho	7.9	9.7	9	8.5	12	24	23	18.56%
Kentucky	8.6	10.2	10.3	10.6	6	14	9	15.69%
Michigan	8.5	10.3	12.2	13.3	5	2	1	17.48%
Mississippi	9	10.2	10.9	9.2	7	8	20	11.76%
Missouri	7.4	9.1	9.5	9.4	19	19	19	18.68%
Nevada	12	13.2	14.4	11.3	1	1	4	9.09%
New Jersey	9	9.3	9.3	9.1	15	21	21	3.23%
North Carolina	9.7	9.7	10.4	10.4	11	12	11	0.00%
Oregon	8.6	10	11	11.5	9	7	3	14.00%
Rhode Island	11.1	11	11.3	11.2	4	4	6	-0.91%
South Carolina	8.9	9.9	11	11.8	10	6	2	10.10%
Tennessee	7.9	9.5	9.4	10.8	14	20	8	16.84%
Washington	8.3	9.2	10.2	9	16	16	22	9.78%

Each column of the table can be sorted in ascending order by clicking on the word "Select" above the table and choosing, from the drop-down menu, the heading of the column on which you want the table to be sorted. The table above gives information about seasonally adjusted unemployment rates in 20 states across a three year period. Seasonally adjusted rates take into account the normal fluctuations in unemployment caused by holidays, summer vacations, and weather patterns. The table also gives predictions for seasonally adjusted unemployment rates in 2012. The average percentage of unemployed people in the whole United States across the same period was 8.8% in 2011, 9.6% in 2010, and 9.3% in 2009. Those percentages are also seasonally adjusted.

Consider each of the following statements about the unemployment statistics of the 20 states in the table. For each statement, indicate whether the statement is true or false, based on the information provided in the table.

True	False	
○	○	The average percent of population unemployed for all states within the top ten ranked in 2010 was greater than the average percent of population unemployed for all states within the top ten ranked in 2009.
○	○	The state with the greatest projected percent change in population unemployed from 2011 to 2012 also had a higher percentage of population unemployed in both 2010 and 2009 than did at least half the other states shown.

s

Answers & Explanation

The average percent of population unemployed for all states within the top ten ranked in 2010 was greater than the average percent of population unemployed for all states within the top ten ranked in 2009. **True**

Sort the table first by State Ranking in 2010 and then by State Ranking in 2009. Then, use the calculator to obtain the average percent of population unemployed from the Actual % of Population Unemployed column for each year. The trick to this question is that in 2010, only 9 states listed in the table were in the top ten ranked. Alabama was number 11, so it shouldn't be included. In 2010, the average was 11.64 and in 2009, the average was 11.34, so the statement is true.

State	% 2010	Rank 2010		State	% 2009	Rank 2009
Nevada	14.4	1		Michigan	13.3	1
Michigan	12.2	2		South Carolina	11.8	2
California	12.2	3		Oregon	11.5	3
Rhode Island	11.3	4		Nevada	11.3	4
Florida	11.1	5		California	11.3	5
South Carolina	11	6		Rhode Island	11.2	6
Oregon	11	7		Alabama	11.2	7
Mississippi	10.9	8		Tennessee	10.8	8
Georgia	10.7	9		Kentucky	10.6	9
Alabama	10.5	11		Florida	10.4	10
North Carolina	10.4	12		North Carolina	10.4	11
Arizona	10.4	13		Arizona	10	13
Kentucky	10.3	14		Georgia	9.8	16
Washington	10.2	16		Missouri	9.4	19
Missouri	9.5	19		Mississippi	9.2	20
Tennessee	9.4	20		New Jersey	9.1	21

New Jersey	9.3	21
Connecticut	9.2	23
Idaho	9	24
Colorado	8.7	27

Washington	9	22
Idaho	8.5	23
Connecticut	8.1	28
Colorado	7.4	37

The state with the greatest projected percent change in population unemployed from 2011 to 2012 also had a higher percentage of population unemployed in both 2010 and 2009 than did at least half the other states shown. **True**

Sort the table first by Projected % Change from 2011 to 2012 to see that Alabama has the greatest projected percent change. Then, sort the table by Actual % of Population Unemployed in 2010 and 2009 to see where Alabama ranks in comparison to the *other states shown*, not in the rankings of all 50 states and D.C. In 2010, Alabama had the 10th highest % of population unemployed out of the 20 states shown and in 2009, Alabama had the 6th highest. Therefore, this statement is supported.

State	Projected % Change from 2011 to 2012
Rhode Island	-0.91%
North Carolina	0.00%
New Jersey	3.23%
California	8.33%
Nevada	9.09%
Arizona	9.47%
Washington	9.78%
Georgia	10.00%
South Carolina	10.10%
Mississippi	11.76%
Oregon	14.00%
Colorado	15.22%
Connecticut	15.38%
Kentucky	15.69%
Tennessee	16.84%
Michigan	17.48%
Idaho	18.56%
Missouri	18.68%
Florida	18.92%
Alabama	20.65%

State	% 2010
Colorado	8.7
Idaho	9
Connecticut	9.2
New Jersey	9.3
Tennessee	9.4
Missouri	9.5
Washington	10.2
Kentucky	10.3
Arizona	10.4
North Carolina	10.4
Alabama	10.5
Georgia	10.7
Mississippi	10.9
South Carolina	11
Oregon	11
Florida	11.1
Rhode Island	11.3
Michigan	12.2
California	12.2
Nevada	14.4

State	% 2009
Colorado	7.4
Connecticut	8.1
Idaho	8.5
Washington	9
New Jersey	9.1
Mississippi	9.2
Missouri	9.4
Georgia	9.8
Arizona	10
Florida	10.4
North Carolina	10.4
Kentucky	10.6
Tennessee	10.8
Rhode Island	11.2
Alabama	11.2
Nevada	11.3
California	11.3
Oregon	11.5
South Carolina	11.8
Michigan	13.3

The median actual percent of population unemployed was greater than 10 percent for 2009, 2010, and 2011. **False**

Sort the table by each of the three years in the question under the Actual % of Population Unemployed header. Remember that to calculate a median from an even list of items, you take the average of the middle two. Also, the numbers must be in order, so you have to sort all three times. But if you get lucky and happen to sort by 2011 first, your task is finished because the median in 2011 was only 9.8! In 2010 the median was 10.45 and in 2009 the median was 10.4.

State	% 2011
Connecticut	9.1
Missouri	9.1
Washington	9.2
Colorado	9.2
Alabama	9.2
New Jersey	9.3
Arizona	9.5
Tennessee	9.5
North Carolina	9.7
Idaho	9.7
South Carolina	9.9
Georgia	10
Oregon	10
Mississippi	10.2
Kentucky	10.2
Michigan	10.3
Rhode Island	11
Florida	11.1
California	12
Nevada	13.2

State	% 2010
Colorado	8.7
Idaho	9
Connecticut	9.2
New Jersey	9.3
Tennessee	9.4
Missouri	9.5
Washington	10.2
Kentucky	10.3
Arizona	10.4
North Carolina	10.4
Alabama	10.5
Georgia	10.7
Mississippi	10.9
South Carolina	11
Oregon	11
Florida	11.1
Rhode Island	11.3
Michigan	12.2
California	12.2
Nevada	14.4

State	% 2009
Colorado	7.4
Connecticut	8.1
Idaho	8.5
Washington	9
New Jersey	9.1
Mississippi	9.2
Missouri	9.4
Georgia	9.8
Arizona	10
Florida	10.4
North Carolina	10.4
Kentucky	10.6
Tennessee	10.8
Rhode Island	11.2
Alabama	11.2
Nevada	11.3
California	11.3
Oregon	11.5
South Carolina	11.8
Michigan	13.3

Remember!

- **Read all the information given before you begin.** This includes the text, which can offer information that will make the table easier to understand.

- **Compare the units given in the table to the units in the question.** If they are not the same, make a note on your scratch paper to remind yourself to convert the quantities. Also, if a table contains a combination of percents and values, you need to be careful not to mix them up. The percent sign is likely to be only in the table headers, not in the data itself.

- **The answer choice labels are important.** True/False and Yes/No labels require a definitive answer, whereas Would Likely/Would Likely Not labels are more flexible. If you have the second type, don't panic if you don't have an exact answer match. You will have to trust your estimation abilities.

- **Take advantage of the ability to sort the table.** Figure out what the subject of each statement is and then sort by that column in order to better see relationships among the variables. Questions that ask about variation, correlation, and ranking can often be answered simply by looking at properly sorted data.

- **If the relationship among variables is not readily apparent by sight, take the time to write out the necessary equations and do the math.** Questions that ask about averages, median, and percent change often require you to do the calculations.

Integrated Reasoning Strategy Recap

1. **Use the calculator wisely.** Graphs and charts are powerful visuals that you can use for estimation and logical inferences. Don't be tempted to waste time calculating what you can learn from sight. If you do use the calculator, remember that nerves and time pressure can make you enter numbers incorrectly without realizing you are

doing so. Since the calculator saves you a lot of time, you can avoid simple errors by doing the calculations twice.

2. **Read carefully and re-read the question before you confirm your answer.** You might find yourself getting so caught up in the calculations that you lose track of the actual question. You can spend 2 minutes solving for x, select the answer choice that matches, and then get the question wrong because it was really asking for the square root of x, not just x. Taking a few seconds to double check the task can save you a point or two.

3. **Remember that some questions only ask for the answer that is** *most supported, best supported, closest to,* **or** *nearest*. It can be unnerving to do a bunch of calculations and then find that the answer you came up with is not among the choices. But some questions are not asking for an exact answer. If the question is verbal, it can be easy to get hung up on two answer choices that both seem correct. In that case, pick the one that is more closely related to the main idea of the text.

4. **Check measurements and labels carefully.** A classic GMAT trap is to offer information in one measurement (minutes, for example) and ask a question about a different one (hours, for example). Taking the time to check labels can help you avoid making a careless error on a question you would otherwise have answered correctly.

5. **Don't skip over text that accompanies tables and graphs.** There is always a reason that the text is there. The text might offer important information about the data in the graphs or it may explain certain assumptions that were made. If you think that there isn't

enough information to answer a particular question, you may want to check the text more carefully.

6. **Review all of the answer choices and use them for guidance.** When the answers are numerical values, you may be able to use them to ballpark. When the answers are equations, they may give you an idea how to start interpreting the math. And when the answers are text, they may help you better define the question and narrow down the location of the source material where the answer can be found.

7. **Skip around.** Even though you can't move back and forth between questions, if you have a question with multiple parts, you should answer the easiest part first. Don't allow yourself to freeze up and waste time. If you are stuck, move to the next part of the question.

8. **Watch the clock.** Just as with the Quantitative and Verbal sections, it is important that you finish every question.

ANALYTICAL WRITING ASSESSMENT

Analytical Writing

"Let's face it, writing is hell". - William Styron.

It's easy to see why this section presents a problem for many test-takers. The first thing that you have to do on the GMAT is sit down and spend 30 minutes writing an essay on a topic that you may know nothing about!

The first bit of good news is that you don't have to know anything about the essay topic. The essay on the GMAT will ask you to break apart the reasoning of an argument, which is a task you have already mastered by practicing Critical Reasoning questions. The second bit of good news is that you can see the current list of topics the essays might be based on beforehand.

(See www.mba.com/mba/thegmat/teststructureandoverview/analyticalwritingassessmentsection for the complete list.)

Many people wonder why applicants to business school need to be tested on their essay-writing skills since a person's success in business is often dependent on his or her verbal skills, rather than written. Plus, a lot of the people who take the GMAT are from overseas and their language, sentence structure, and grammar are very different from those of English, putting them at a disadvantage on this part of the exam.

We mentioned before that many schools don't pay attention to the analytical portion of your test. However, some do and it is better that you do well on it than poorly. You don't want to be rejected by the school of your choice simply because you slacked on the analytical writing portion of the

GMAT. Let's go over the requirements of the essay and what you need to remember.

How is the Essay Graded?

Besides a GMAT essay grader, an "E-rater" or computer "bot" grading program that can scan essays also evaluates your essay. If the score from both the GMAT essay grader and the E-rater are in agreement, then that's the grade your essay will receive. If they disagree, then a second GMAT grader will grade your essay. The people who grade your essay vary, but initially they are part-time employees from the testing company, and are usually from graduate school programs.

One common question is how much time graders spend on your essay. The truth is that they spend about two minutes each on one essay. They have to grade a lot of essays and can't spend too much time on each one. The best that you can hope for here is a quick skim by the graders. The computer grader takes even less time to grade your essay. All it does is compare your essay to other essays on the same topic. This means that if you are original in your methods and points, the computer won't be able to pick this out and you may actually be penalized.

The Best Piece of Advice

What do the graders look at the most when grading your essay? Is it your grammar? Your vocabulary? Your ideas?

Nope. It's the length of your essay!

If you want to do well on the essay portion of the exam, make sure that you write as much as you possibly can. Your essay should contain at least four paragraphs.

There. You just aced the essay portion of the GMAT.☺

Actually, it's not that easy but you would be surprised by how much length-of-essay factors into your grade. If you haven't written a lot, it is unlikely that you have addressed all the points required by the task, and it is unlikely that you have written a convincing essay.

The Principles

Preparing for an essay test when you don't know the topic can be difficult. However, I have a few hints to help you prepare so that when you are given the topic, you can dive right in and begin writing your masterpiece.

The Analysis of an Argument essay must be approached like an argument in the critical reasoning section. As a result, you should follow these steps to ensure that you do well here.

1. Read the entire argument.

2. Identify assumptions in the essay and think of other assumptions that you can use.

3. Identify the premise or premises of the argument and think about how the conclusion might be flawed if it is based off those premises.

4. Identify how the assumptions can be used to make a better argument.

5. Edit your essay when you have completed it.

When grading this essay, your graders will determine whether you identified and analyzed the important aspects of the argument, and whether you supported your main points and demonstrated a superior grasp of language, including the direction of your argument. Note that the graders aren't interested in your opinion on the issue being discussed. Stick to writing about the way that argument is structured.

When building anything, whether a house, a sculpture, or essay, the person creating should have a plan in mind. This plan is his template and helps create what he envisions. Your template is your key to doing well on the analytical portion of the GMAT, and it should follow a specific format. Your essay should typically conform to a single form, as follows.

- **Summarize the conclusion of the argument in the first paragraph.**

- **In the second to fourth paragraphs, attack the argument and the evidence it uses to support itself.**

- **In the last paragraph, simply summarize what you have said and offer ways that the argument could be strengthened.**

Tips and Tricks

Now that we have gone over how you should write the essay and attack the argument, what about the meat – the words that make up the essay?

You want to include certain words that will catch the eye of the reader and allow him or her to quickly skim through your essay. Remember, readers only spend two minutes on each essay, so that is all the time you have to impress them.

1. If you are making points in your essay, be sure to separate them and identify them using the words "First", "Second", "Third", etc...

2. Whenever you support an argument with an example, which is important if you are trying to prove something, then you should use words like "for example", "to illustrate", "for instance", and "because".

3. If you are adding onto that example with additional support in the same paragraph, then use words like "in addition", "also", "moreover", and "furthermore".

4. If you want to emphasize the importance of something, then use the words like "surely", "truly", "clearly", "certainly", "in fact", and "most importantly".

5. When you reach your conclusion, use words such as "therefore", "hence", "in conclusion", and "in summary".

Final Word

We have come to the end! Well done for getting through it all and staying on track. It's not easy studying for any standardized test, and the GMAT makes you use parts of your brain that may not have been exercised in years! But if you have covered and understood all of the concepts presented in this book and taken several practice tests over the last 30 days, you should be good to go. Better than that - great to go. You should feel confident in your abilities and positive about getting that high score you are drooling over.

You're going to love business school. It truly was an amazing period of my life and I came away with so many great memories, experiences and friendships. Make the most of your time there and take every opportunity that is thrown your way. You never know where it might lead you!

Lastly, let me know how your 30 Day GMAT experience and test-taking experience was! I encourage you to check out the website that accompanies the book - www.30dayGMATsuccess.com. There you can find the latest GMAT resources, check out the blog, or drop me an email. If you've found the book useful for your GMAT preparation, I would sincerely appreciate a review for the book if you bought the book online - on Amazon, Barnes & Noble.com or GoodReads. Your feedback and support is what helps me to improve the book with each edition, and helps other test-takers make informed decisions in their choice of preparation.

Best of luck!

Brandon

Brandon@30daybooks.com | www.30DayGMATSuccess.com (Book site),
www.Pepwuper.com (Game studio), www.Plinan.com (Personal blog)

Are you sure today is your test day? No cheating! What's written on the next page should be read on your test day only.

Hi there,

Congratulations on the completion of your GMAT study!

You are now equipped with the necessary skill set, study habits and motivational mind-set to tackle what is considered to be the gold standard of graduate business program admission tests.

By now you are so familiar with the GMAT that it is no longer simply someone else's exam used to rate your knowledge and skills. This is your test. You own it and no one knows your abilities better than you do.

You are now closer to your goal than ever before. What you have learned in the past 30 days will help you more than you can imagine. This was the most difficult part of your journey towards achieving your goal and you did it! Remember – the end goal is not to get a perfect score on the GMAT. The goal is to do YOUR best and to use your abilities to their fullest.

On your test day, remind yourself how far you have come. If you become distracted, concentrate harder. Keep in mind that if you encounter a difficult question, it's not a bad thing; you will do even better on the rest of the test. By coming to your exam well-rested, fresh and physically prepared (with water and a snack) you are making sure your brain functions at full capacity.

Regardless of your test results, you have already improved your study and management skills. These will be of use to you in the future for taking other tests, in your career, and in many other areas of your life. You are already a winner and a more complete person compared to when you started!

Now – relax and clear your mind by engaging in something that you enjoy. This will help refresh your mind for what lies ahead. You will return to your GMAT mind-set with renewed energy and you will surprise yourself with your knowledge, skills and motivation.

Best wishes for your continued success and don't forget to celebrate after taking the test!

The GMAT: need to know logistics

Congratulations! You have decided to take the time to learn how to master one of the most important tests that you will ever face in your life. The GMAT is designed to measure how successful one will be in business school. Business schools use the results of the GMAT, along with recommendation letters, essays, and other application materials, when making decisions on admitting applicants to their MBA programs. The test is administered on a computer in North America. In some areas of the world outside of North America, it is a paper-based test given at test centers.

The fee to take the test is $250 regardless of where you are taking it. You can schedule a GMAT online at http://www.mba.com/the-gmat/schedule-a-gmat-appointment.aspx. The GMAT evaluates the verbal, math, and writing skills that you have developed through your educational and professional experiences. The GMAT does not measure your business knowledge or professional skills, nor does it measure other skills such as creativity, motivation, and interpersonal skills.

The GMAT is designed to allow a person who does not have English as his or her first language to still perform well. That said, it may not always reflect accurately the abilities of a person whose first language is not English.

Registration

You can register online at MBA.com and pay your registration fee by credit card, or you may call one of the following numbers to schedule an appointment at a test center: (correct at time of going to press)

North America

Telephone (toll-free within the U.S. & Canada only):

1-800-717-GMAT(4628)

Telephone: 1-952-681-3680 (not toll-free)

Victoria, British Columbia

Telephone: 1-866-442-GMAT(4628)

South America

Telephone: +1 410 843 8160

Asia Pacific

Telephone: +91 120-439-7830

Southeast Asia

Telephone: +60 3 467 8610

India

Telephone: +91 (0) 120 439 7830

China

Telephone: +86-10-82345675

Taiwan

Telephone: +886 2 369 1154

Europe/Middle East/Africa

Telephone: +44 (0) 161 855 7219

Australia

Telephone: +61 2 9478 5430

New Zealand

Telephone: +61-2-9323-5555

GMAT scores are valid at most institutions for up to five years from the date that you took the exam.

Made in the USA
Middletown, DE
02 November 2019